Surprise! You're Wealthy

Surprise! You're Wealthy

A Woman's Guide to Protecting Her Wealth

Patricia Lovett-Reid
with Donna Green

KEY PORTER BOOKS

National Library of Canada Cataloguing in Publication Data

Lovett-Reid, Patricia
Surprise! you're wealthy : a woman's guide to protecting her wealth / Patricia Lovett-
Reid; with Donna Green.

Includes index.
ISBN 1-55263-467-1

1. Women—Canada—Finance, Personal. I. Green, Donna M. II. Title.

HG179.L685 2002   332.024'042   C2002-904078-7

The publisher gratefully acknowledges the support of the Canada Council for the Arts
and the Ontario Arts Council for its publishing program.

We acknowledge the financial support of the Government of Canada through the Book
Publishing Industry Development Program (BPIDP) for our publishing activities.

The author, Patricia Lovett-Reid, is Vice President and Managing Director with
TD Wealth Management. While every effort was made to ensure the accuracy of
the material in this book, investors' situations are different and rules change.
TD Asset Management Inc., a member of TD Bank Financial Group and part of
TD's Wealth Management group of companies, assumes no responsibility or liability
arising from the use of the material in this book. The material is for information purposes only, and you should consult your own professional advisors.

Key Porter Books Limited
70 The Esplanade
Toronto, Ontario
Canada M5E 1R2

www.keyporter.com

Cover design: Tina Clark
Electronic formatting: Jean Peters

Printed and bound in Canada

02 03 04 05 06 07 6 5 4 3 2 1

Contents

Acknowledgements

This book was very much a team effort. I'd like to thank Anita Bruinsma, Justin Flowerday, Anna Petrole and Laura Sadak for their dedicated efforts researching, editing and coordinating this book from beginning to end. Their tireless work shaped the book in every way and I could not be more grateful for their support.

Many thanks, too, go to those at TD Bank Financial Group who saw the merit of this project and made it possible: Rob MacLellan, Chris Armstrong, Steve Geist, Peter Lee, Barbara Palk, John See and Rob Strickland.

Throughout the course of this initiative I had the benefit of being able to draw on the knowledge of a number of experts within TD who enthusiastically made time for this project. My gratitude goes to Robert Aggio, Jody Beaupre, Geoffrey Belisle, Jeanne Beverly, Jennifer Burk, Sandy Cimoroni, Bob Gorman, Adriana Groskopf, Kelly Hechler, Anna Iacobelli, Brenda Lee-Kennedy, Corey McCusker, Robert Murray, Juanita Soutar, Alan Walker and Christopher Wicks. Without their help this book would have been a far more modest undertaking.

Tina Clark designed a cover that delighted me, and Clare McKeon and Anna Porter at Key Porter Books were a pleasure to work with. Stephen Hewitt, Lisa Hodgins and David Lakoff at NATIONAL Public Relations have my thanks for their support and excellent promotional activities.

A number of other professionals also gave generously of their time and knowledge for which I am very appreciative: Michael Cochrane, Andrew J. Freedman, Malcolm Hamilton, Andrew D. Kirkpatrick, Helen Mallovy Hicks and Robert Micheli.

Special thanks go to the women who shared their stories for this book, Karen Fraser, Janice Wadge, and the many others who asked to go unnamed. Their personal contributions added a wisdom and immediacy that would have been impossible without them.

Thank you, Donna, for pulling it all together with outstanding professionalism.

PATRICIA LOVETT-REID

Author's Foreword

An astute observer once remarked that nothing is more surprising than growing old. It takes a long time to get there, but once you do, it seems to happen overnight. Becoming wealthy seems to me to have many parallels. In some cases, lucky and not so lucky, it does happen overnight, but for most of us wealth comes after long years of hard work, conscientious saving and smart investing. At one point, perhaps suddenly, you realize you've made it: Surprise! You're wealthy. Protecting and preserving that wealth will let you turn that surprise into enjoyment.

The idea for this book—my third on women's financial issues—arose from the disquieting results of a women's investing poll conducted by TD Wealth Management in 2001. The survey found that almost half the women interviewed did not consider themselves knowledgeable investors. Close to 40% of them lacked confidence in their ability to manage their own investments, and approximately 50% of the women considered themselves low-risk investors. The good news was that the poll also found that approximately two-thirds of the women report being more interested in investing than they were five years ago.

The poll results were disappointing to me because I've committed a good part of my professional life to educating investors. Recently, I have been travelling across the country with a presentation called "Wise & Wealthy Women," and before that I led the "Women in the Know" seminar program. These initiatives have allowed me to speak to women all over Canada about strategies for creating and preserving wealth. I also host a weekly personal finance television show on Report on Business Television, *MoneyTalk*, where viewers can ask the experts questions about their money, investment strategies and financial planning matters.

Women are better educated, experiencing greater professional advancement, making more money and investing more than ever before. So why are we still investing in low-risk vehicles and not making our money work harder? Because many of us still lack an understanding of financial risk, investment products and how to construct a portfolio.

I've done two things a little differently in this book. Where possible, I've tried to weave the real-life stories and wisdom of successful women into the chapters, and I've structured these chapters to address issues that arise from different sources of wealth. There are separate chapters for those who have well-paying jobs, those who have their own businesses, separated or divorced women, and those who have come by their money suddenly through inheritance, legal settlements, insurance or the lottery. You'll also find chapters on investing and estate planning, because everyone, no matter how they've come by their wealth, can use this information. The investing chapter brings into clear focus the ever-expanding universe of financial products. It should also help you with what I think may be one of the hardest investment decisions of all, what kind of financial services relationship suits you best—a conventional broker or financial planner, an on-line trading account or a full-service, discretionary money manager. There's plenty of information in each chapter that is useful no matter what your circumstances.

Tucked into the appendices you'll discover some helpful worksheets and checklists. There's a checklist for choosing an advisor and points to look for when hiring other professionals. A worksheet for calculating your net worth is included, along with a guide for determining your risk tolerance and suggested corresponding asset allocations. We've also included a budget worksheet, an estate planning checklist and another checklist for the duties of an executor.

Now that you've made it, you need to protect and grow your money. I'd feel very gratified if this book brought you closer to that very important objective.

I hope, too, that this book will make a difference in another way. All royalties will be donated to The Children's Miracle Network, a network of children's hospitals and foundations serving over two million Canadian children each year.

PATRICIA LOVETT-REID
July 2002

1 Women and Money

"Yesterday is a cancelled cheque; tomorrow is a promissory note; today is the only cash you have—so spend it wisely."
KAY LYONS

Megan Kerr owns a $500,000 condo in Toronto and has a tidy investment account. At 55, she has a lot of options, but she chooses to work because she runs her own business and feels the need, as she says, to make a difference. And make a difference she does. For years, she has been involved in very significant and high-profile fundraising events for charities in Ontario.

She wasn't always paid for her fundraising savvy, nor have her circumstances always been this comfortable. Megan has gone through a lot of transitions, and her life story touches upon almost every topic covered in this book: job, marriage, a family business, divorce, a common-law marriage, widowhood and self-employment. Along the way, she's acquired a lot of wisdom and learned a few financial lessons she agreed to share, though I've changed her name to protect her privacy.

A woman's life: Megan's story

Born into modest circumstances, Megan studied nursing and married at the age of 19. She subsequently attended teachers' college, became a special education teacher and taught for three years, until her first child was born. While their first child was still an infant, Megan and her husband started a children's summer camp on land they rented. With their excellent credentials as teachers—and their good management and public relations—the camp did well. After a few years, and now with two young children and a house, they were approached to buy one of the oldest children's camps in Canada. "The owner wasn't so much interested in making a lot of money as seeing the camp in good hands," she says, "so they made it very manageable for us." Megan was uneasy about having to use their house as collateral to finance the purchase. Fortunately, the business went well and their house was never in peril.

From then on, both she and her husband worked full-time building the business. "In a very short period, we tripled the business," says Megan. They flew to Mexico often to meet families who wanted their children to have a Canadian experience. The business prospered and the family moved into a larger house in a sought-after neighbourhood in Toronto. And through it all, Megan still found time to do volunteer work.

Then, after 19 years of marriage, Megan made a well-thought-out but heart-wrenching decision to separate. It was an amicable separation and Megan used her own judgement in following her lawyer's advice. She did not ask for spousal support and only for reasonable child support. "My lawyer thought I was crazy, but I wanted to be fair. If I made it too hard for him financially, he wouldn't be able to carry on with his life," she says. "But having really only ever worked for my husband, I had no idea of my earning capacity. That uncertainty was a big fear, almost an immobilizing fear, and it keeps a lot of women where they are even when they're unhappy."

Megan got half the value of the house and the business. She had to apply for credit cards in her own name, and at first the credit limit was much, much lower than she was accustomed to. She made up a new will to reflect her changed marital status. With some of the settlement money, she paid cash for a much smaller house in the same upscale neighborhood. "Five years later, I doubled my money on that house," she recalls. "I've always made good calls with real estate."

Meanwhile, Megan had been in charge of a high-profile public fundraising event in a volunteer capacity. That event was so successful, and the project had such a large scope and potential, she eventually became a contract employee with the institution. She was permitted to join the pension plan and made the maximum contributions. For 13 years, she worked tirelessly to restore some valuable historic properties and her vision contributed to turning those properties into money-making businesses that were delivering $5 million a year to the institution when she left.

She also met the love of her life. They bought a condo together, and when they got word of his cancer, they hung on in the hope that it would go into remission. Sadly, her common-law spouse succumbed to his illness five years later. Megan was 46 at the time. Her own money was tied up in the home they had shared, Registered Retirement Savings Plans (RRSPs) and her pension. She did not have an investment portfolio, nor was she interested in managing one, so when she received money from her spouse's estate, she contacted a trust company to manage it for her. "I'm all for specialists. I wouldn't work on my own teeth. I would never leave my portfolio to anyone but a professional."

Recently, Megan learned that she'd been entitled to spousal Canada Pension Plan (CPP) benefits when her partner died. "Nobody ever said anything about it," she says. "It was a costly lesson for me." Megan estimates she lost $40,000 in CPP benefits simply because she didn't know that she was entitled to benefits as a common-law spouse. She filed for back payments but discovered that CPP survivor benefits will go back only 11 months from the date of application.

After a period of introspection, Megan decided to get back to those things about her work she loved most. She incorporated a fundraising company with a partner who she believed would boost her confidence and bring other contacts and another skill set, including computer know-how, to the mix. Incorporation expenses, stationery and business cards altogether came to less than $2,500, which they split. And that was the only major amount of cash they ever had to put into the business. It quickly became apparent that Megan was driving the company's revenue and, when it came time to split the bonus, the 50:50 share they had initially agreed to no longer seemed fair. The partnership withered and Megan was left running her own flourishing business.

Despite a personality that exudes enthusiasm and self-confidence, Megan almost kicks herself for undervaluing her services for so long. Only a few years ago, a friend, a vice president with a blue-chip company, told Megan her fees were too low. "I changed my fee structure and nobody ever questioned it," she reports. "As a consultant, I'm saving them 30% on benefits." Now, if a client can't afford her fees for full-time work, she will scale back her time to give them what they can afford, but she admits this takes discipline because she drives herself hard to deliver results and is more goal-oriented than money-motivated. There is a skill to delivering only as much as your client pays for, and the self-employed especially are torn between doing excellent work and delivering a product commensurate with the fee charged.

Megan knows only too well another pitfall of the self-employed. She works from home and finds it a temptation to work evenings and weekends. "I clear it all away on Friday afternoons," she says. "Otherwise, it's too easy to work all the time."

The friend who told Megan her consulting rates were too low also suggested Megan read *Peak Evolution*, by Lauren Holmes. Megan credits her friend and that book for changing her outlook on life. "Holmes says when you're living your art, work is like play. I firmly believe that. When work is like play, doors keep opening." Megan has gone through many doors and it's hard to see how she could ever stop making a difference. She's busy living her art.

Megan built her financial security through years of work, successful real estate and financial investments, and a good business. Although she is loath to call herself wealthy, there's no doubt that she has achieved a level of financial success that puts her in charge of her options.

We each have our own definition of wealth, of what makes us say finally, "I've made it." Financial success offers opportunity, but it also demands responsibility. For most people, the sense of well-being we get from financial success, to be lasting and meaningful, has to be accompanied by family, health and a commitment to community. Nothing can replace a good balance of these things, though we can spend nearly a lifetime discovering just what that personal balance should be. The next few hundred pages will focus on the financial part of that balance.

The trends

More and more women are achieving financial independence, and becoming wealthy. Entrepreneurship among women is soaring and corporate offices are ever more populated by women in high-paying leadership roles. Women's personal incomes will continue to grow as their entrepreneurial initiatives take hold and as their educational backgrounds translate into well-paying jobs and senior management positions. In addition, by dint of sheer longevity, women are poised to receive a huge transfer of wealth amassed by the baby boom generation.

> **Wealthy Women on the Rise:** " 'Women already make up 43% of the North American affluent segment (above US$500,000 in financial wealth) and that percentage looks destined to rise.' ... [T]he number of wealthy women investors in the U.S. also is growing at a faster rate than that of men. From 1996 through 1998, the number of wealthy women in the U.S. grew 68%, while the number of men grew only 36%, according to data from The Spectrem Group. (That study defined wealth as having investible assets of more than US$500,000 or earning more than US$100,000 a year.)"[1]

Yet it seems we're ill-equipped to preserve and grow this wealth. A U.S. survey commissioned by OppenheimerFunds Inc. found that 49% of the women they polled weren't sure how a mutual fund works, even though 79% said they consider themselves more knowledgeable about investing than their parents were at the same age.[2]

Women have unique financial needs. We live longer than men, and family responsibilities often stop us from working as much or as long as men. These two simple facts commonly conspire to make our pensions and RRSPs inadequate. Women are different from men in our attitude toward money, too. While many men view money as a stream that can be replenished, women tend to see it as a pool that can be depleted. Perhaps this explains why women are so often risk-averse in their investment decisions—and why we so often fall short of our financial objectives.

Canadian women as a whole

In cooperation with Environics Research, TD Wealth Management polled 900 women of all ages and backgrounds across Canada to learn more about their attitude toward financial planning and investing.[3] Here's what we found.

WOMEN'S INVESTING POLL

Women have come a long way in planning for their future, and a significant portion of the results were encouraging, including:

- Of the women polled, 87% were "very or somewhat interested" in managing or playing a role in their household's finances and investments
- Almost two-thirds of the women said they had become more interested in financial planning and investing over the last five years
- Approximately one-fifth of the women had taken investment-related courses

Some of the findings were disappointing, including:

- Close to 40% of the women polled lacked confidence in their ability to manage their own investments
- Almost half of the women did not consider themselves knowledgeable investors
- Approximately 50% of the women considered themselves to be low-risk investors
- Of the women who had investments and answered the question, 80% between the ages of 36 and 55 had less than $100,000 in their personal investment portfolios

This lack of confidence and the desire to avoid risk can be quite damaging in the long term. Without taking on some risk, you probably won't be able to meet your financial goals. Ironically, being risk-averse brings with it its own risks. It frequently results in underperforming portfolios too heavily weighted in "safe," interest-bearing investments that may not keep up with inflation. Ultimately, too many "safe" investments will undermine your long-term prosperity.

Positive trends

Women have made great strides in education, employment and personal income. In Canada, more women than men graduate from university, and in the U.S., more women than men are enrolled in law schools.[4]

According to the U.S.-based National Foundation for Women Business Owners, women are starting new businesses at twice the rate of men. In Canada, half of new businesses are started by women. Women's earning power is increasing, too. In 1967, women earned 58.4% of what men earned. In 2001, that number was 81%.[5]

On the investment front, women are investing more than ever. In 1999, according to Statistics Canada, 46% of women tax-filers saved through an RRSP or Registered Pension Plan, which compares with 56% of men tax-filers. Men saved about 40% more in retirement accounts than women, with average contributions in 1999 of $6,546 compared to the female average of $4,690. However, for those earning between $20,000 and $79,999, women's average savings were greater than men's.

Income Sources, Senior Women and Men, 1997

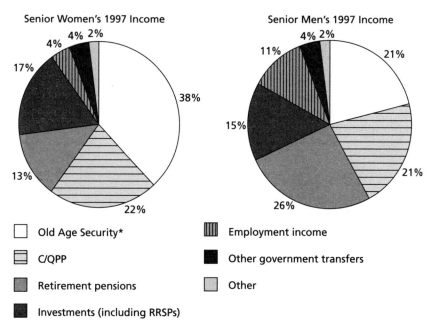

Source: Statistics Canada, prepared for Health Canada
*Including guaranteed income supplements

Senior women's main source of income is Old Age Security. For men, it's their company's private pension.

The spectre of the past

So many of these trends are positive, but the legacy of the past still remains. Take a look at sources of income for senior men and women.

An alarming 64% of senior women's income comes from public sources, compared to 46% of men's. Company pensions account for 26% of a male senior's income but only 13% of a woman's. Women seem to have saved proportionally more than men, but not nearly enough to offset their smaller company pension payments.

I very much hope that those ratios will change as the current workforce reaches its senior years, and part of my job is to reach out to women through educational initiatives to stress the importance of diligent financial planning, ideally from the very first paycheque.

Is our definition of financial success too low?

One of our poll's findings in particular surprised me. *A majority (67%) of those interviewed considered themselves financially successful.* With so few women with personal financial assets over $100,000, this seemed incongruous. We probed deeper in the poll to find out what financial success might mean to women.

Definitions of financial success included:
- Being able to live comfortably within their means (24%)
- Being able to retire in comfort (22%)
- Being on track to meet their financial goals (20%)
- Having some savings (12%)
- Having little or no debt (10%)

Women say they measure their investment success by how well they are meeting their goals rather than by how well their portfolio is doing relative to a market index. If the goals are objectively quantifiable, that's not necessarily a bad measure. When those goals are more nebulous, like "saving for a house" or "growing my retirement savings," this lack of bottom-line objectivity is unproductive. And not only is our definition of success too low in many cases, but we undermine ourselves by measuring our investment success against standards that are too hard to quantify. Maybe wanting to outperform the market by 5% in three years out of five is too ambitious, but some explicit and quantifiable financial goals should be established.

On average, women outlive men by seven years, and because they tend to marry older men, it's estimated that seven out of 10 women will outlive their partners by 15 years. Add to this the fact that, on average, women are out of the workforce 11 more years than men, and you can see how easily women can be at a disadvantage in retirement resources. Doing something is better than doing nothing, but a strategy pegged to desired goals and returns is a whole lot better than just investing your money and hoping for the best.

Sometimes, to achieve this kind of direct, results-oriented approach, you may have to change your investment arrangements. You must evaluate your current situation and decide what kind of arrangement is best for you. You might want to move from an on-line, "do-it-yourself" option to working with a financial advisor or discretionary money manager, or you might favour doing it yourself for a while.

In any event, don't delay laying out quantifiable investment goals, because procrastination is one of the biggest obstacles to financial well-being.

Common financial planning mistakes

This isn't to say that poor goal-setting and procrastination are the only mistakes we can make. Far from it. The Financial Planners Standards Council (FPSC), a not-for-profit organization that establishes standards for financial planners in Canada, says financial consumers share many more. In the opinion of many of the country's financial planners, here are the most common mistakes, in order of prevalence:

- Neglecting to evaluate their financial plan periodically
- Confusing financial planning with investing
- Failing to set measurable financial goals
- Being afraid of planning or not planning in general
- Thinking financial planning is the same as retirement planning
- Expecting unrealistic returns on investments
- Not understanding that good professional advice largely depends on getting good information from the client

- Failing to understand how advisors are compensated
- Having no idea what a financial planner does
- Looking for a quick fix instead of a long-term strategy [6]

It's a long list, and in the investing chapter, I offer up some of my own observations about the common obstructions to wealth-building, but one thing I want to caution against is discouragement. Financial planning is not rocket science. With a modest investment of time, you can take charge of your finances, whether you decide to do it yourself or with the help of an advisor or discretionary money manager. In my experience, it isn't limited knowledge so much as neglect that leads people astray.

MONEY HAS AN EMOTIONAL COMPONENT

A divorce lawyer once told me about a client who despised her husband because he had squandered the money her father had left her. It wasn't a huge sum, but it was money that had profound emotional significance for this woman. Many women come into money through a crisis, the death of a family member or a divorce—and this only adds to the feeling that money is an irreplaceable pool that needs to be as far removed from risk as possible.

Fortunately, the perception of risk changes with knowledge. Academic research has shown that adding a variety of investments to a portfolio can increase returns and decrease overall risk. Finding your balance between risk and returns—your place on the "efficient frontier," as it's called in Modern Portfolio Theory—is a critical step in overcoming the aversion to risk that so many of us harbour.

The stages of a well-defined wealth management strategy

Things that seemed attractive and right for us at 20 don't necessarily strike us that way at 40. Sports cars can't carry home the family groceries, and youth hostels in Europe have lost their allure. Our investment needs change with our life stages, too. Not all that long ago, almost all investing was done through a stockbroker. Then came the advent of mutual funds and a whole new way to invest became popular. The financial landscape has continued to change to reflect the greater diversity of our investment needs and now offers a broad continuum of options, from do-it-yourself on-line right up to discretionary money management.

We'll discuss this financial services continuum and where you might feel comfortable on it in the chapter on investing. Before we get there, though, I'd like to talk about the three basic stages of wealth management. Whether you choose to invest on-line, with the help of an advisor or through a discretionary money manager who does it all, you will pass through these three stages. Your goal is to manage the progression in the best way possible. Much of this is self-evident, but I'd be remiss if I didn't mention it.

Wealth determination: What do you have to build on?

Clearly, you need to know where you are today so you can plan for tomorrow. An annual net worth calculation is your biggest aid not only in determining where you are, but also in judging your progress. I often suggest setting aside the same day every year for a net worth exercise, perhaps a day that has had some financial significance for you, such as when you bought your first house or got your first big job. List your assets, subtract your debts, and you've got your net worth. (There's a net worth worksheet in the appendix for a more thorough guide.) Calculating your net worth every year also readily reveals the trend in your debt. Is it going up or down relative to your net worth? As we all know, a robust investment account can quickly be cancelled out by runaway debt.

Wealth accumulation: Building what you have

You accumulate wealth by saving more, getting better investment returns and retaining more of those returns with effective tax planning. Saving, investing and tax planning are the cornerstones of wealth accumulation, and each of those three are within your control to a large extent. Many investors save diligently but then fall down putting their money to work or protecting it from unnecessary taxes. Money is optimally employed in a well-planned portfolio. Some investors have too much fixed income for their stage in life, while others try to hit the ball out of the park with a big stock play—though as we'll see, one study has found that women are less likely to act on a "hot stock tip." In turbulent markets, a well-diversified portfolio will almost certainly be a lot less volatile than a collection of speculative bets. And not only is prudent portfolio construction a good defence against uncooperative markets, it is the best long-term strategy for managing your money effectively. We all know this, but somehow this knowledge isn't always put into action.

Many investors also focus only on their pre-tax returns and overlook their after-tax returns. What counts is what you get to keep, not how much you make before taxes. Tax planning is more than trying to mini-mize your year-to-year tax bill. It should be a long-term strategy that carries right into your estate planning. The benefits can be striking but are not all that well known, so please spend some time with the estate planning chapter.

I believe the key to implementing a good investment plan is disci-pline—the discipline to resolve to institute a good plan and stick to it. That resolve will stir you to seek out the professionals who can formu-late a plan for you if you lack the time or the skills to do it yourself. But another big part of that discipline is keeping emotions out of the invest-ment equation. Greed and fear, it's often said, are the predominant emotions affecting the stock market. In some cases, though, far more subtle emotions can be at work. Related to that is a reticence to establish objective and measurable financial goals for yourself and your advisor.

Wealth preservation: Keeping what you've got

Taxes, inflation and market turbulence can all prey on your wealth. Once you've got it, you want to keep it, and protecting your money from these predators is critical. Inflation's effects on your money can be anticipated and addressed with investments that keep up with inflation. Market upheavals can be managed to some extent by an intelligent mix of investments that respond differently to various market conditions. Taxes can be managed by knowledgeable tax planning strategies and insur-ance. We'll talk about these preservation strategies and more in the following chapters. There's no need to learn about money the hard way.

"What I know about money, I learned the hard way—by having had it."
Margaret Halsey, U.S. author

No matter what your age, putting your money to work and protecting it as much as possible from the ravages of inflation, market turbulence and taxes are the keys to making and protecting your wealth. With that aspect of your life in order, you will be free to pursue the other things that give your life balance and make a difference. Can there be a more gratifying feeling than that?

Notes

1. From James Langton **InvestmentExecutive.com**, "Women millionaires growing faster than men," 25 June 2002. The study refers to the *World Wealth Report 2002*, published by Merrill Lynch and Cap Gemini Ernst & Young.

2. As reported by James Langton in **InvestmentExecutive.com**, "Women investors smarter, more confident," 14 May 2002. Also see **www.oppenheimerfunds.com** for more details on the "Women & Investing—Ten Years Later" survey.

3. TD Wealth Management's women's investing poll surveyed 900 women across Canada between November 12 and November 23, 2001. Results are accurate plus or minus 3.3%, 19 times out of 20.

4. U.S. female legal enrollment from a report prepared by Deborah L. Rhode for the American Bar Association Commission on Women in the Legal Profession, "The Unfinished Agenda: Women and the Legal Profession," 2001, 9. See **www.abanet.org/women/**.

5. British Columbia Teachers' Federation research report, "Women's Earnings Relative to Men's," Anne C. Schafer, March, 2000, 1. See **www.bctf.bc.ca**, which cites the 1967 figure. Peter Smith, *The Toronto Star*. "Wage Variations," 31 March 2002, C3 reports the 2001 statistics.

6. From a press release by the Financial Planners Standards Council, 27 March 2002, "Consumers more confused than ever about financial planning." Based on a survey of 685 certified financial planners across Canada.

2 Running Your Own Show: The Self-Employed

"Whenever you see a successful business, someone once made a courageous decision."

PETER DRUCKER, MANAGEMENT AUTHORITY

There's a tenacity to the self-employed—a fierce independence and a passionate belief in their idea—that I respect tremendously. They take risks. They don't know if they'll have a paycheque but they're certain they'll always have a job. One entrepreneur we profile here actually ran her business by candlelight for six months. As she says, "Being an entrepreneur is like having a disease." Fortunately, it's a disease that often has a favourable prognosis.

If you're one of these driven people, you've probably spent so much time building your business or practice that you may have neglected your own financial needs—specifically, insurance, and retirement and succession planning. We'll take a look at how to make the most of your success by protecting yourself, your business and your future with sound planning. But before we dive into the details, I'd like to share with you a story about a very dynamic entrepreneur with some profound insights into women entrepreneurs.

I *Am* Mr. Fraser!

Karen Fraser peered over her book from behind a pyramid of cosmetics in a deserted mall and saw another bored cosmetic salesperson. It was 1972, and the two decided to join forces in a company that trained secretaries. When her partner had to leave the business three years later

22

because of family pressures, Karen's whole world tottered. Within a week of her partner's departure, the partner's husband initiated a suit against Karen for ruining their marriage, her live-in boyfriend moved out with all the furniture, and her landlord gave her four days' notice to vacate her office because he'd sold the building. "My mother said, 'Well, maybe now you'll get a real job,'" she recalls.

Instead, Karen went to a Halloween party over the weekend and told everybody there she needed a new office. The next week, someone from the party told her about a space for rent that happened to be owned by someone Karen knew. He agreed to give Karen a month to make the first payment. "In 29½ days, I paid him two months' rent." Unfortunately, she didn't have the $200 required as a down payment on a commercial hydro account.

Karen's business is called Women Like Me and offers training to help women and companies adapt to workplace and lifestyle change. At the beginning, the training was done in her office—by candlelight, which none of her students knew was by necessity rather than a heightened aesthetic sensitivity.

"Bell would not give me a business line in my own name because I was a woman. There had to be a man signing. I explained I wasn't married and finally talked them into it, but the bill came at the end of the month addressed to Mr. K. Fraser."

Her office was furnished with cushions from her apartment, a roll-top desk her grandfather had given her and some wicker furniture she had salvaged. "I sharpened my pencils on the sidewalk," she recalls, laughing.

Those pencils must have been sharp, because her business prospered, in part, she says, because she was always media savvy. For the benefit of the press, she filled her first seminar, called "Moving Ahead," with friends and relatives. In fact, there were only two paying students there. "I got my picture in the paper with my class and my mother called me and said, 'Isn't that woman beside you in the picture your neighbour?' The next course had 50 real live paying people."

For a while, Karen was paying her lecturers more than she was taking home and cash flow was a problem. In late December of 1975 she had to conduct a seminar at a company location.

"I didn't have the money for bus fare," she recalls. "So, in my one business suit, I was crushing my grandmother's plum pudding between my hands to find all the coins. That was the absolute bottom."

"People say to me, 'I don't think I'd have the discipline to get up and run a business every day.' And I say to them, 'Oh, yes, you will. Five a.m. your eyes open. It's called sheer terror. You don't need an alarm clock. Trust me.'"

Karen, now 56, has a cottage, a mortgage-free house in Toronto and a thriving business from which she has no plans to retire. She's president of Women Entrepreneurs of Canada, an association for established women entrepreneurs, and she initiated the Canadian Woman Entrepreneur of the Year Award. She's also produced 11 editions of *Women Like Me: The Entrepreneur's Networking Directory*. When the first edition came out, Karen hosted a party for the women listed in the directory. "Seven hundred women showed up, and the publisher had sent over only 40 books," she remembers with disappointment. The evening was upbeat despite the lost sales opportunity, until the waiter turned to Karen to ask when Mr. Fraser would finally be arriving to pay the bill, to which she responded, "I *AM* Mr. Fraser!"

The world has changed quite a bit since 1975. An Industry Canada study for the years 1991 to 1996 showed that the number of self-employed women grew by 44.3% in that time, compared with a rise of only 20% in the ranks of self-employed men. The study also found that almost four out of five businesses started by individuals under 30 are started by women.[1]

Women Entrepreneurs and the Glass Box?

- The number of self-employed women grew by 44.3% between 1991 and 1996, while the number of self-employed men grew by only 20%. The actual numbers show 430,305 women entrepreneurs in 1991 and 621,085 in 1996. Their male counterparts numbered 1,057,630 in 1991 and 1,268,895 in 1996.

- Women are now starting half of all new businesses.

- The number of unincorporated businesses owned by women has grown faster in Canada than in the U.S. since 1989, and this growth rate is the highest of all the OECD countries.

- Of working-age women in Canada, 8.7% are self-employed, compared to 7.6% in the United States.

- The number of single self-employed women rose 62.6%, compared with a 33.7% rise for men.

- Almost four out of five businesses started by those under 30 years old are started by women.

- Self-employed women make, on average, less than self-employed men.

- Self-employed women typically work fewer hours than self-employed men. In 1997, self-employed women worked one-third fewer hours than their male counterparts.

- About 42% of self-employed women said they had concerns about their access to financing.

All information drawn from Industry Canada, "Shattering the Glass Box: Women Entrepreneurs in the Knowledge-Based Economy," a study based on information from 1991 to 1996.

Women entrepreneurs are growing ever more numerous, so they are far from the anomaly Ms. Fraser represented in 1975. She laughs at how small the numbers that ran her life 27 years ago look now, but the stress of the obstacles is still vivid.

As an established entrepreneur or professional, you have already conquered the challenges of financing your business and have no doubt surrounded yourself with an established team of professionals for accounting, banking and investment advice and service. Nothing in this book is meant to replace the professionals you work with and who know your personal situation in detail—though I'd like to stress how important it is to work with professionals who are experienced in small-business issues, especially your accountant. A good team is invaluable in helping you build and maintain your business. In this chapter, I'd like to focus on protecting what you've already built so you can make the most of your team as you plan for the future.

For you, that future might mean transitioning your business into a corporate structure for tax and estate planning benefits. It should probably mean a review of your assets and liabilities and a look at the wide array of insurance coverage for a broad assortment of contingencies. And, finally, you'll want to start thinking, if you haven't already, about what is going to happen to your business when you want to retire or should you become unable to work. How are you going to finance a retirement as good as your current lifestyle? Will your business continue to thrive without you? Like retirement savings, succession planning isn't something to put off until you're within hailing distance of the event. It needs to be planned and worked toward for a long time to give comfort to your creditors, your employees, yourself and your family.

Is it time to incorporate?

Karen incorporated her business because she was hiring other people to teach and was liable for their actions. Others incorporate because their clients want or are required to deal with an incorporated entity. Sometimes the business reasons for incorporating precede the tax planning benefits.

Limited liability

Of the three types of business structures—proprietorships, partnerships and incorporations—only incorporation provides a separation between business and personal liabilities. The legal wall between the two is not impervious (and does not extend to incorporated professional practices, such as those of doctors, lawyers and accountants), but incorporation does usually limit a business's liabilities to the assets of the corporation.

This means that your personal assets are generally safe from your business creditors. That in itself provides a common reason for incorporating a business, and as long as you comply with certain restrictions, there are generally no tax consequences in transferring business assets into a corporation.

In practice, however, you will find that lending institutions commonly require personal guarantees for commercial loans. Even though you may be incorporated, your personal assets can still be on the line in the form of loan guarantees or personally secured lines of credit.

Tax advantages

Incorporating can also have numerous tax and estate planning advantages for those currently operating as proprietors or partners. For one thing, incorporated businesses can retain earnings and issue bonuses and dividends. These corporate characteristics allow a margin of tax deferral on your personal income taxes, and sometimes an out-and-out tax savings. By keeping income in your corporation, you defer paying personal income tax on it until you take that money into your personal income. Being able to issue bonuses and dividends means you can push your personal receipt of declared bonuses or dividends into another calendar year and thereby defer income tax on that money for a whole year.

In addition to these advantages, the first $200,000 to $300,000 of active business income earned through what Canada Customs and Revenue Agency (CCRA) deems a "Canadian-controlled private corporation" is taxed at very favourable rates. The federal corporate tax rate on the first $300,000 is 13%, compared with the regular federal corporate tax rate in 2002 of 26%. Provincial rates vary but are also considerably reduced, though they may not apply to a full $300,000. Generally, your combined federal and provincial tax rate will be around 20% on the first $200,000 and 26% to 38% on income from $200,000 to $300,000 or thereabouts, depending on your province's cutoff.[2]

What you need to earn for the maximum RRSP contribution: Here's the minimum earned income you need to make the maximum RRSP contribution in the following year:

In 2002, you need $75,000 for a $13,500 contribution in 2003.
In 2003, you need $80,556 for a $14,500 contribution in 2004.
In 2004, you need $86,111 for a $15,500 contribution in 2005.
After 2005, contribution limits are indexed to inflation.

Consider overcontributing to your RRSP for a lifetime maximum of $2,000. The overcontribution is not tax deductible, but the tax-free compounding will be beneficial if the overcontribution remains in the account long enough to more than offset the tax upon withdrawal.

Normally, you want to pay yourself at least enough salary to allow you to make the maximum RRSP contribution each year. Once your salary is established, then you have to figure out the optimal mix of dividends and bonuses to take from your company, if you want any at all.

Bonuses are taxed as personal income just like a salary. However, you can get a whole year of tax deferral by declaring the bonus toward the end of the calendar year and not paying it out until the following calendar year, as long as the bonus is paid out within 180 days of the company's year-end.

Dividends received from your company have the advantage of the dividend tax credit, but unless your underlying corporate tax rate is significantly below 23%, you will be getting nearly the same after-tax dollars whether you get that money from a dividend or a salary. Taking it as a dividend, however, allows that money to stay in the corporation tax sheltered until it is declared, whereas a salary is paid out regularly and usually at shorter intervals. You could actually save tax dollars on dividends if your first $300,000 or so of business income attracts an especially low rate of tax.

Yes, Virginia, the capital gains exemption does exist

The biggest tax advantage of incorporation is the alluring $500,000 capital gains exemption allowed on the sale of a "qualified small business corporation."[3]

The definition of a qualified small business corporation is complicated because the government wants to make sure it is giving this exemption to real businesses and not just to corporate entities. The definition sets restrictions on share ownership and the use of assets within the corporation. It also makes conditions on the use of assets and the ownership of the shares for two years prior to the sale of the corporation. Essentially, to qualify for the tax exemption, the rules require that 90% of the assets within the company have to be involved with the active business at the time of the sale, and more than 50% of the assets have to have been involved in the active business in Canada throughout the two years before the sale. Also, the shares must have been owned exclusively by you or persons "related" to you for the two years prior to sale.[4]

If you think your business could meet those rules, you might want to consider incorporating it, providing you take a few other things into account.

First of all, you have to have enough excess income to leave in the corporation or the tax sheltering will have no value to you. A rough estimate would suggest somewhere around $50,000 a year would make the tax sheltering worth the added expense of incorporating and filing a corporate tax return every year. As a sole proprietor or member of a partnership, you can deduct business losses from other sources of income, but once you incorporate, your losses stay within the corporation. So you want to be profitable before taking the step to incorporate, all other things being equal.

Also be aware that the full $500,000 will not be available to you if you have a cumulative net investment loss account, a "CNIL account" for short. Broadly speaking, investment costs such as investment loan interest, rental property losses and tax shelter write-offs that exceed your investment income can be deducted from your income. These net expenses must be paid back before you can access your capital gains exemption. Specifically, the CNIL account keeps track of your investment expenses less all your investment income since January 1, 1988.

Here's how the CNIL account works:

Sarah had an investment loan on which she deducted $10,000 more in expenses than in income. She had never before used a capital gains exemption (when such a thing was available). Sarah sold her qualified small business corporation for $600,000, for a capital gain of $500,000. Since half of all capital gains must be included in income, Sarah must include $250,000, but she expects the $500,000 capital gains exemption on the sale of her company to offset this. It would do so if Sarah had no CNIL account, but because of that $10,000 CNIL, she in effect has to pay back the $10,000 before being able to claim the capital gains exemption. Sarah can exempt only $240,000 of her capital gain and must pay tax on $10,000.

Personal services businesses

Suppose you decide to become an independent contractor, resign from your job and then continue working for your former employer in your former capacity. It's done every day, but if you incorporate, CCRA will consider your corporation a "personal services business" and disallow many deductions normally permitted a small business corporation. You might even be hit with double taxation in certain cases. If you incorporate, be careful to avoid being considered an employee under the cloak of a corporation.

Disadvantages of incorporation

Incorporating does cost money. Although it is possible to do it yourself for a few hundred dollars, most business owners would prefer the advice and services of a lawyer. A straight incorporation with a name search can cost in the neighbourhood of $1,500, more or less, depending on the firm that does it. A shareholders agreement can cost more if you need advice on just what should be in the agreement.

A shareholders agreement spells out what is to happen with the company's shares in certain situations, such as a shareholder's death, illness, disability or retirement. It should also address methods for resolving disputes, set out a formula for buying back shares when a shareholder wants to leave the business and stipulate what should happen if a shareholder's spouse gains control of a significant share position through separation or divorce.

A shareholders agreement is a crucial document that is often neglected because it takes time, money and some hard decisions that have to be agreed to by all the shareholders. It's not unusual for companies to do without a shareholders agreement, but when more than one person owns shares of the company, being without one is courting trouble.

In addition to the legal fees to establish a corporation, there are ongoing annual costs to maintain it. You must file minutes of an annual meeting through your lawyer and complete a corporate tax return every year.

Managing your risks

Small-business owners have to shoulder a variety of risks that can range from product and service liability to personal injury suits from employees and customers. Those who rent property could even be held responsible to a landlord for damage from fire, water and vandalism. Then there's the lurking risk that you, your partners or a key person in your business could suddenly drop out of the picture through accident, illness or death. When you think of all the untoward things that could cost you serious money, you've got to admire the resolute entrepreneurial spirit and the resourcefulness of the insurance industry.

Even if you've had commercial insurance for a while, it's a good idea to talk with a commercial insurance broker every few years to make sure your coverage has kept up with your risks and your assets. Personal health and life insurance requires regular review, too, because insurance needs change as your financial responsibilities change. Here's a look at the kinds of insurance a small-business owner might want to consider. Not all of them will be appropriate for you, but it's good to know your options.

Insurance for You and Your Business

- General liability
- Professional liability
- Owners, landlords and tenants liability
- Product or service liability
- Directors and officers
- Business property
- Company vehicle
- Crime
- Business overhead protection
- Key person
- Buy/sell life and disability
- Equipment breakdown
- Life*
- Critical illness*
- Personal disability*

*For detailed information on these types of personal insurance, please see "The High-Powered Job."

Commercial insurance

Commercial insurance covers property, personal injury, non-performance of a product or service, some types of crime, and income protection. One policy will not include all these risks, and even among similar policies, there are many variations on exactly what is covered.

LIABILITY

General liability insurance: A commercial general liability policy would typically cover you and your employees for bodily injury or damaging a client's property when involved in the company's activities. Policies, of course, differ in what they cover, how much they pay and what they cost. In addition to covering the cost of damages to personal property or bodily injury, will the policy, for instance, pay for emergency medical expenses and legal, investigative or defence costs?

Liability resulting from the practice of a profession requires separate coverage, as does coverage for accidents with vehicles. General liability also does not typically cover suits arising from the non-performance of a contract or product and the liability associated with that non-performance.

Professional liability insurance: In some professions, this is also known as "errors and omission insurance" because it covers professional practitioners for liability arising from errors or omissions in the conduct of their work. Doctors, dentists, lawyers, accountants—even many financial advisors—carry this kind of insurance.

Owners, landlords and tenants liability insurance: Office-based businesses can use this kind of coverage to protect them from liability arising from someone getting hurt on their premises. Commonly, the policy will allow tenants to add the landlord to their policy at no extra cost for an extra level of protection.

Product or service liability insurance: This protects you should you be sued for the non-performance of a contract or product. A professional practice needs more specific professional liability insurance.

Directors and officers insurance: Becoming an officer or director of a company could expose you to civil suits, so a specific kind of professional liability insurance is designed to cover officers and directors who might be sued for making an error in the operation of a company. Companies often provide this type of insurance to attract quality candidates to their boards.

PROPERTY

Business property insurance: This typically insures property, equipment and inventory for damage, loss and theft. If you work from home, be aware that your basic homeowner's insurance will probably not cover your business equipment and may even be voided if you operate a business on the premises. You should also inform your homeowner's insurance carrier when you establish a home office.

Company vehicle insurance: If you use your personal car for business, it is important to have a policy that includes and covers business use so your vehicle will be covered, as will damages to third parties, in the event of an accident during such use.

Ever have an employee use your car to pop out to the store for stamps?

You should consider an extension to your policy that will cover non-owner accidents. The employee will not be covered for her injuries, but your car and the property damage and injury to others will be covered.

Company vehicles, of course, require commercial insurance.

CRIME

One Canadian insurance company sells what it calls "comprehensive dishonesty, disappearance and destruction" insurance. Among other things, this policy protects against employee dishonesty, counterfeit paper, depositor forgery, credit card forgery and safe burglary. Sometimes this type of insurance is called more generally "fidelity" insurance. You must compare the exact crimes being insured against in different policies, since it should be obvious by now that little is standard in the insurance industry.

INCOME PROTECTION

Personal disability insurance: This insurance is designed to replace a large portion of your after-tax income with a maximum ceiling on monthly benefit payments, and it's quite costly because you are far more likely to need it at some point in your working years than you are to collect on your life insurance policy. There are two basic types of disability insurance. "Own occupation" insurance will pay when you can't work at your own job. This is a more expensive type of policy than "any occupation" disability, which pays when you can't perform any job for which you are reasonably suited by education and experience.

When you're buying this insurance, you have to carefully study terms and conditions. How long do you have to be unable to work before your payments will begin? The longer you must wait, (the "elimination period") the less expensive the coverage. Can your policy be cancelled? Are your premiums fixed? Will you be penalized for going back to work part-time? Are rehabilitation costs covered? Disability insurance is as complex as it is important. Be sure to deal only with a disability insurance specialist to guide you through the maze of conditions and help you select the most useful features for your situation. (Personal insurance is discussed in greater detail in the benefits section of "The High-Powered Job.")

Many entrepreneurs feel disability insurance is not worth the expense and caps out at too low an income level to be useful. If their personal net worth is large enough to sustain them and the ones they love through a prolonged disability, they may have a point. For those who haven't established that level of financial security, disability insurance is a critical part of managing your risks.

Business overhead protection insurance: This insurance reimburses your share of overhead expenses if you become disabled. You must watch for what qualifies as a reimbursable overhead expense and on what grounds the money will be paid and how long a period will be covered. For example, one company that offers this coverage as a rider to a disability policy requires your business to suffer a net loss due to your disability before it will pay out expenses, and the benefit period is just 24 months. Other insurance carriers offer partnership and corporation income replacement insurance as a stand-alone policy. Business overhead insurance is relatively cheap and can be used quite effectively to supplement disability insurance with a long elimination period.

Key person insurance: This insures the life of a key person in your business. Should a key person die, this will give your company the financial resources to sustain the hardship and time to find or train a replacement. You can also buy key person disability insurance so your company will have the resources to weather the absence of an important employee.

Buy/sell life and disability insurance: When a partner or shareholder dies, the other partners and shareholders may need cash to buy back the deceased's partnership interest or shares. This is easily done by having the company or the business owners themselves take out life insurance on each other. Should one of the owners die, the proceeds of the life insurance will fund the purchase of their interest or shares in the business. Similarly, should a partner or shareholder become disabled, a disability buy/sell plan pays a lump sum to the company or the other principals to buy the business interests back from the one disabled.

These kinds of arrangements are very important and quite common. Without them, your business could lose a vital member, with all the losses associated with that, and be burdened with finding the cash to buy out the member's share of the business. That's a hard blow for any small business to withstand.

Equipment breakdown insurance: What's commonly known as "all risk" general commercial insurance policies will generally have what the insurance industry so colourfully calls "perils" that are specifically excluded from coverage. These excluded perils—perhaps as ordinary as an electricity surge, for example—could incapacitate a major piece of machinery and cause a loss of business and/or perishable inventory. Equipment breakdown insurance specifically insures against this peril.

Critical illness insurance: This insurance fills the gaps between disability and life insurance because it is quite possible you could get a serious illness without becoming disabled long enough to activate your disability insurance. (Personal insurance is discussed in greater detail in the benefits section of "The High-Powered Job.")

A good commercial insurance broker is invaluable in helping you navigate through this abundance of offerings. Don't put off doing it, because so much rests on your ability to cope when a risk becomes a reality.

As Karen says, "I don't believe in luck. I had myself well-insured." She has general business liability insurance and disability insurance, but not life insurance. "*Someone* will bury me," she jokes, but her approach is clear. Since she has no dependants or children, she has protected herself from risks while she is alive. Her estate can cover the rest. That non-traditional attitude doesn't appeal to everybody, especially those who have a strong desire to leave an estate to someone—which leads us into succession planning.

What will happen to your business when you're no longer there?

In her mid-50s, an age when most people are working their calculators overtime to figure out if they can afford to retire, Karen is still going strong and has no plans to retire. "Why should I suddenly stop doing what I love just because I turn 65?" she asks pointedly. You might very well agree with her.

Unless they've established a mandatory retirement age with their business associates, professionals and entrepreneurs have the option of working until they can work no longer. For the driven and independent, it's an enviable sort of freedom knowing you'll be able to continue with your career and receive an income for a long time, while for others the new beginnings that a well-financed retirement can bring is a tantalizing lifelong goal.

No matter what your attitude toward retirement, every business owner should consider what will become of her enterprise once she's no longer around. Broadly, there are three options: sell the business, dissolve the business or pass it on to a family member. Because Karen doesn't want to retire, she has no plans to sell her business and she has no children to pass her company on to. Some entrepreneurs like her might believe their one-person operation has little value without them and expect their executor to dissolve the business when they die.

Karen knows that kind of succession plan could be discarding an asset that still has value. Helen Mallovy Hicks, a partner with PricewaterhouseCoopers Valuation and Strategy Advisory Group, says even small businesses whose main value is the personal goodwill of the owner or professional can extract value from the company, with some planning.

Don't ignore personal goodwill

Mallovy Hicks says the first thing to do in evaluating the worth of a business is to identify the "value drivers" in the company. "Value is dependent on the future income you can glean from a business," she notes, but to determine what that future income is likely to be you have to discover what exactly generates the business's income. In a manufacturing business, machinery, equipment, inventory and skilled employees will be the assets of value. In small service-oriented businesses like a professional practice or Karen's enterprise, personal relationships can be the biggest asset. Mallovy Hicks calls this "personal goodwill," as opposed to "commercial goodwill," which is the value associated with a business's brand, name, customer lists, business reputation, etc.

To get value from a company with a lot of personal goodwill, you somehow have to transfer that goodwill to your successor. This is commonly done by finding a person who is willing to buy the business and introducing them to clients or business contacts, with a hearty endorsement to help manage the transfer of personal relationships.

The buyer can further tie your personal goodwill to the business by having you sign a non-compete agreement whereby you promise to forgo opening a competing business nearby. An employment agreement is also useful in establishing a smooth transition if you are willing to agree to work in the business for a set time. This gives the new owner the comfort of your expertise and your clients a sense of orderly and amicable transition.

One more way a buyer might want to secure your personal goodwill is by tying the purchase price to the future performance of the business. A new dentist, for instance, might pay the retiring dentist for the office equipment and furniture, along with a portion of anticipated revenues, but hold back on paying the full price they've agreed on. Payment of the full price would be contingent on the new dentist realizing the expected revenue from the practice's established patients. That way, if many of the patients leave, the new dentist hasn't paid for their lost income stream. In this arrangement, the retiring dentist also has an incentive to induce her patients to stay with the new dentist, since she'll eventually get more money from the sale of her practice if the patients stay.

These arrangements are designed to capture the value of a business with intangible assets. You shouldn't assume that because your business is closely associated with you, your skills and your personal contacts, it has no value without you. Of course, you have to find someone willing to pay for your business, but once you do, there are many ways to work out a fair deal.

How much is your business really worth?

After you determine where the value of your business lies, you have to figure out exactly how much it is worth. There are many reasons to get a valuation apart from wanting to sell your business. You may be getting a divorce in a province that considers business assets a part of family assets; you could be trying to do some estate planning that involves transferring company shares that need to be valued for tax purposes; or you may merely need to judge how much life insurance to buy for a sharcholders buy/sell agreement.

Professional business valuations can be expensive and very small businesses might dismiss them on that account. Andrew Freedman, an accountant and chartered business valuator with Cole and Partners in Toronto, says the best way to judge whether a professional valuation is worthwhile for your situation is to ask your accountant and/or lawyer. He says there is no general rule.

Valuations can look at a multitude of things, including the replacement cost of fixed assets, future earnings, and what comparable businesses have sold for recently. The services of someone like Freedman or Mallovy Hicks are targeted to mid-market businesses. Very small businesses often fall off the radar screen of large accounting firms and specialized boutiques, but smaller accounting firms and private business valuators can do the job. A business broker should also be able to recommend a professional valuator.

If your goal is to sell your business, the sales skills of a professional business broker or merger and acquisitions specialist will give you a better chance of maximizing the value of your business, says Mallovy Hicks. "Normally, if you hire somebody to sell your business, they will have access to potentially interested parties and will know how to negotiate the deal and how to bring a number of parties to the table, or at least create the illusion that there are a number of parties at the table," she says. "Also, hiring a professional is seen as a more serious process in the eyes of potential purchasers."

But she has a warning for those thinking of getting their personal accountant to sell their business. "A lot of smaller businesses get their accountant to help them with the sale of the business, and that can be a mistake. It's just like getting your general practitioner doctor to do open-heart surgery on you. They are not experts in the area; they don't have the contacts or the experience to get you the best value," she says.

Mallovy Hicks tells an arresting story involving a colleague of hers and an entrepreneur with an enticing offer to buy his business. The client thought $8 million was a pretty good deal and intended to accept the offer, but he wanted some advice on the transaction. On learning more about the business, Mallovy Hicks's colleague thought there was more value in the company and convinced the owner to let the accounting firm act as advisor to sell the business for him.

"The moment he told the potential purchaser that he had hired PricewaterhouseCoopers, the purchaser raised his price to $12 million."

But it didn't end there. Other parties were approached and, recounts Mallovy Hicks, "The ultimate sale price was $18 million—but not from the original offeree."

She says it is well known that purchasers would rather work directly with the seller than with a professional because an inexperienced seller is very often leaving money on the table.

Perhaps you need a successor

An out-and-out sale to a third party might not be one of your objectives. A sole proprietor may hope to eventually pass the business on to a family member or sell it to a key employee. A member of a partnership may plan to sell to the other partners, and a principal in an incorporated business may will the company's shares to a spouse or sell them back to the company or other shareholders. But what if the other shareholders don't want to buy back the shares because they would have to go into debt to do so? Working out your options, figuring out the most tax-effective way of achieving your objectives, arranging financing for your plan, and making sure that others on whom the plan depends are able to see your plan through are all part of the succession planning process.

Deciding what is to happen to your business after you are gone is like making up a will. It is an irksome housekeeping matter that doesn't make money, takes time and emotional energy, and sometimes isn't all that easy to do. That's why many, many entrepreneurs put it off until it is staring them in the face and it's too late to make use of more advantageous options. Mallovy Hicks shares another true story, this one chilling, about the sad consequences of one successful business without a succession plan.

Two good friends were 50% owners of a prosperous service business. They had worked many years together and had a very good relationship. They had thought about writing a shareholders agreement, but they didn't feel motivated to go through with the physical exam to get life insurance on each other or to pay the legal fees to work out the agreement. Tragically, one partner—we'll call him Sam—was subsequently diagnosed with cancer and given three months to live. Naturally, Sam wanted his partner to buy his share of the business from him so Sam's wife and children would be provided for. His partner didn't want to assume that much debt and explored his options. He could buy the other 50% of the shares and immediately flip it to another buyer who would become his new partner, or he could refuse to buy the shares altogether, walk away from the company and start up on his own with his former employees and the contacts he had built up over the years. This option would leave Sam's family empty-handed, with nothing but a corporate shell.

We don't know what the partner decided in the end, but at the very least it's likely Sam's wife was left with a struggle to get fair value for a company whose value started declining the moment her husband became ill. At worst, Sam's family got nothing for his years of commitment to his business and his partner.

People can do strange and fearful things when money is on the line. Even if the character of those you work with is beyond reproach, planning before a crisis arises will prevent unwelcome burdens being imposed on your business partners. Had the company, or the two shareholders themselves, bought life insurance on the other, with an agreement to use the proceeds to buy out the other's shares, the difficult situation would have been avoided entirely. Unfortunately, when someone becomes terminally ill, it is too late to buy insurance. Nor is it a good time to negotiate the terms of departure when someone is already determined to leave. That puts a strain on everyone, and the departing partner is not guaranteed to feel the beneficiary of a fair deal.

So how do you work out a succession plan? The best time to do it is when you go into business with someone else. Agree on how you are to get your money out if and when you or your associates want to leave the business. Anticipate, too, that a business associate might want to leave because of a dispute. You might want to work out some kind of dispute resolution mechanism beforehand. What's known as a "shotgun clause" in shareholders agreements is popular when two shareholders want to part ways but they both want to retain the business. Under the clause, you would offer your associate a fixed price, say $1 million, for the business. If she won't sell her share to you for $1 million, she has the right to buy your share from you for $1 million. This means you are compelled to make an offer that you would be happy to accept yourself.

Buy/sell agreements of other varieties should specify how the value of the company is going to be determined for the purposes of the agreement itself. Simply stipulating "fair market value" will likely involve a pricey professional business valuation when the time comes. Indicating some multiple of cash flow might be unfair if the company is mired in debt. You can see that there are a number of sticky points to work out, and it is best done early on. These considerations will help you protect the value you have worked to establish in the company.

For those who have complete control of their own company, passing it on to family could take a lot more time than you might think. Your child, for instance, might need some formal business education in addition to hands-on experience. Employees have to get comfortable with the change, and your child has to feel it's the right decision, too. Very few small businesses pass to the next generation. Don't look at it as a failure should your business ultimately go to someone outside the family. Look at it rather as something of a small miracle if it does.

Freedman says to start succession planning early, at least ten years before you plan to step down, and certainly by the age of 50. The first step is to discover your options. Talk to an accountant who has experience in estate and succession planning. Banks and accounting firms also have a trained team to help you explore these issues. You'll probably want to have your business valued and get a clear picture of the tax consequences of the strategies you are considering. After you've narrowed down your choices, talk to those who already have an interest in your company. Ultimately, the best-laid plans will go awry if you don't gain the cooperation of all those affected by your decisions.

What's an estate freeze?

Tax planning and succession planning should go hand in hand, and an estate freeze can advance the aims of both. A freeze is a process of crystallizing, or "freezing," the gain in the value of your company and transferring future increases in value to your business successors. This can be accomplished in a number of ways, but the outcome is to limit your estate's future tax liability and to pass the future growth and its associated tax liability to someone else. Freezes do not necessarily trigger capital gains tax, but electing to trigger all or some of your gains will let you take advantage of the $500,000 capital gains exemption for qualified small business corporations.

An incorporated company can execute an estate freeze just by changing the company's share structure. You could, for instance, exchange your common shares for preferred shares (with or without voting rights) while your successor gets common shares. Any appreciation in the value of the company after this would be reflected in the common shares, but the original owner will still retain control over the company, if desired, and may receive dividend income.

This technique does not trigger capital gains tax because your common shares are exchanged at their full value for preferred shares. If you owned 100 common shares now worth $1 million, you could exchange them for 1,000 preferred shares each worth $1,000. The common shares, now of only nominal value, can be passed on to your successor whose work in growing the company will be reflected in the appreciation of the common shares while your preferred shares will remain at $1,000 each.

A similar outcome can be arranged by transferring the company's common shares to a holding company in exchange for preferred shares in the holding company and then selling the holding company's common shares to the successors.

Your successor will benefit from a freeze, too, because the $500,000 exemption will subsequently be available to the holding company's common shares.

Succession Planning for Small-Business Owners

If you transfer your business during your lifetime, you will be able to be a mentor and advisor to your successor and you can influence any future changes in the management and direction of your (former) business. The best succession plans evolve over time. Your plan should reflect your successor's current role in your business and be modified as this role develops.

If, however, you transfer your business through your will, there are four key issues to address:

1. Whom will you leave your business to? Some of your children may not want to participate in the business, so you may want to arrange that they receive assets of equal value, with or without a non-participating equity interest in the business.

2. Is your will valid and clear? You must be explicit and unambiguous in your directions concerning your business. General clauses regarding the business can create delays for the estate trustees and may affect the business's stability.

3. Has your will been kept up to date? Business names may have changed, proprietorships may have incorporated, and amalgamations or partnership changes may have occurred since your last will. Whenever changes happen that involve the status of your business, you should see your estate advisor to determine how these will affect your succession plans. Your will may need to be updated to stay accurate.

4. Who will be your executor? Your executor must be free of any conflicts of interests and have a thorough understanding of estate administration with a good dose of business savvy. This is especially important when the executor might have to retain some control over the business for a time.[5]

Getting retirement income from your business

Many creative arrangements can be designed for those who don't want to take a lump-sum payment for their business. Maybe you don't want to burden your children with the debt that buying you out would involve. Or perhaps you don't want the tax hit that would come from a sizable sale. In any event, many business owners look for ways of deferring income from the sale of their business.

You can gradually sell your company shares to the new owner, or you can have a contractual arrangement to stay on for pay in an undemanding capacity. Payments to you may be spread over years and depend on the performance of the business in the future. You may even finance a vendor take-back loan where you are financing the purchase of your own business in exchange for regular payment of principal and interest.

The only trouble with these deferred arrangements, of course, is the uncertainty of future payments. Cash deferrals may never materialize, and you must ensure that the arrangements you have made with the new owner will be paid out in full should she subsequently sell the business. I suspect some entrepreneurs choose a deferred arrangement because they don't want the headache of managing the cash—and paying the tax—when the cash option would really be the better financial arrangement.

Many people aren't aware that insurance products can also be useful in actually managing your wealth in a tax-advantaged way. Two products in particular, annuities and universal life insurance, can be used to generate secure income with the benefit of a tax break.

An annuity is a contract in which an insurance company promises to make certain regular payments for either a fixed period or until your death in exchange for a lump sum up front. It is a little like buying a bond, only an annuity pays out principal and interest. Because you are not taxed when the principal is returned to you, annuity payments are tax-advantaged to the extent that they give you your own money back. There are many varieties of annuities. Many guarantee a fixed rate of return, whereas others are variable and depend on the nature of the underlying investments.

Annuity rates are linked to interest rates, and when rates are low, annuities are not all that popular. Universal life insurance is perhaps a more interesting option. This kind of insurance has a term life insurance component and a tax-sheltered investment component. Although life insurance is usually bought with monthly premiums, you can also buy a universal policy with an up front cash investment, and you can decide what kind of investments you want within your policy. Your money grows tax-free and your beneficiaries get the insurance portion of your policy as a tax-free death benefit. The investment portion is also paid out tax-free upon your death.[6]

Something clever can be done with a universal life policy that will generate retirement income for you and a tax benefit, too. Financial institutions will allow you to borrow against a universal life policy, up to as much as 90% of the investment value of the policy, depending on the nature of the underlying investments. This borrowed money can finance your retirement. The advantage? You do have to pay interest on the borrowed money, but you don't have to pay tax on it. When you die, the bank gets the proceeds of the policy to discharge your loan, and you have received a retirement income for the cost of interest, not the cost of your marginal tax rate.

Selling a business is a sort of cash windfall, and you can in effect create your own but more secure sort of deferred arrangement with some investment planning.

> *"In business, you get what you want by giving other people what they want."*
> Alice Foote MacDougall (1867–1945), U.S. businesswoman[7]

Naturally, much of your retirement income planning is going to depend on your tax situation and how much money you need as retirement income. Since so many more tax planning opportunities are available to corporations, at some point every successful entrepreneur should look at the advantages of incorporating. Day to day, you could save taxes and limit liability with an incorporated business, but, when you eventually sell or transfer your business, the capital gains exemption available to qualified small business corporations will almost certainly make the minor inconveniences of maintaining a corporation seem trivial. Whether or not you are incorporated, all business owners without exception should keep up to date on their insurance coverage, personal and commercial. Protecting your wealth means planning for catastrophic developments beyond your control and, with the help of insurance, being able to offset the worst of them.

You need to protect your business now and in the future so you can enjoy the wealth your success brings. Whether that means working until you can't work any longer, living in a tropical paradise or helping to save the rainforests, sound financial planning makes it possible.

Notes

1. Industry Canada, "Shattering the Glass Box: Women Entrepreneurs in the Knowledge-Based Economy." June 2002. **www.strategis.ic. gc.ca/pics/ra/438%5Fe.pdf.**
2. The tax break on active business income below $200,000 is eroded in companies with more than $10 million in capital. For more detailed information on Canadian-controlled small business corporation taxation, see KMPG's *Tax Planning for You and Your Family 2002*, 199–200.
3. This capital gains exemption also applies to qualifying farm property.
4. Under certain conditions, the *Income Tax Act* does allow a sole proprietorship to be rolled into a corporation that can then be immediately sold with the benefit of the $500,000 capital gains exemption. Consulting a tax specialist is required.
5. This information follows closely a paper prepared by TD Private Client Group, Estates and Trusts, "Business Succession: Information Summary; Succession Planning for Small Business Owners." October 2001.
6. The most common type of universal life policy is called an exempt policy, and the investment proceeds are paid out tax-free. If the policy is not exempt, the investment proceeds can be subject to tax.
7. Robert Andrews, Mary Biggs, Michael Seidel, editors. *The Columbia World of Quotations* (New York: Columbia University Press, 1996), entry number 37150.

For Further Reading

Collins, James C. *Beyond Entrepreneurship: Turning Your Business into an Enduring Great Company* (Toronto: Prentice-Hall, 1995).

Collins, James C., and Jerry I. Porras. *Built to Last: Successful Habits of Visionary Companies* (Toronto: HarperCollins, 1996).

Profit magazine.

3 The High-Powered Job: Enjoying the Rewards

"Work hard to get your dream job...you'll reap the rewards for the rest of your life."

AKELA PEOPLES, FOUNDER AND CEO OF WOMEN IN MOTION AND WINNER OF THE 2002 YWCA ENTREPRENEURSHIP AWARD

Janice Wadge was tending bar in New Zealand when she got her parents' call: She'd been accepted to the MBA program at the University of Western Ontario. She returned home from 10 months of backpacking around the world to turn her undergraduate history degree into something more marketable. Now in her late 40s, and with a number of very senior positions behind her, she is President and CEO of Regal Greetings and Gifts Corporation, one of Canada's largest direct-selling distributors of general merchandise.

Less than 20% of her 1981 MBA graduating class was female. "I'm of the first wave of women who systematically started up the management ranks," says Janice. She landed her first job at Canada Packers as an assistant brand manager, marketing trainee, "the lowest-level managerial position," she recalls, but even at that she was told she was the third-highest ranking female and she reported to the most senior female executive. "The home economist was the second-most-senior executive," says Janice, still struck by the dearth of women in senior management roles at that time.

"I'm probably like many, many other women in that I spend more mental energy on my job than I do on my personal remuneration," she observes. "This is one of the differences between all the men I know who are my peers and me.

"My female friends and I are all of a generation, and I think our focus was very much to get the task done. When I was 25, I was having to focus on acceptance and credibility issues when I walked into a room filled with guys who thought I should be in a junior position. It's only as you get farther along that it becomes more natural to spend the time and energy thinking about what I'm getting out of this besides promotion and success; whereas I think, for the men who were my peers, the financial part was the driver for them from the start.

"This may be a woman's perspective," she adds, "but I think you pick your career path for what gives you satisfaction, not just financial benefits. I wasn't financially driven. I felt I could make a difference, and I did, in three companies where I had senior management influence. Now I'm looking at remuneration."

In my experience, many successful women are very much like Janice. Work and family obligations often come well before personal financial considerations. One enticing career opportunity follows another, and the thrill of advancement and personal challenge can overshadow the concrete realities of salary, benefits and perks. Janice has become a skilled negotiator and she'll share some of her hard-won wisdom later on in this chapter, but she knows she should have paid more attention to the financial realities earlier in her career.

We'll discuss some of the important things you need to know to get more into your pocket at the end of the day. You need tax planning savvy, an understanding of your benefits and their tax ramifications, a strategy to manage your risks, and the motivation to take action on all these things. Take care of your financial side now because it will fuel your power going forward. As Janice says, "Power is both a mental and financial thing. The less you need the job, the more power and confidence that gives you to negotiate."

Chances are you are going to have a lot of opportunities to gain and use this power. A study by U.S. management consultants McKinsey and Company says that the average executive will work in five companies. (Janice has worked in six different corporations.) They predict that in ten years, if the trend in labour mobility continues, executives will have worked their way through seven different companies before retiring. That's a lot of benefits packages to weigh, and perhaps even a severance package or two to negotiate.

The study also says the supply of executives is not keeping up with the demand: "The number of 35- to 44-year-olds in the United States will decline by 15% between 2000 and 2015. Moreover, no significant countervailing trends are apparent." [1] You're going to be in demand and ever busier, so make the most of your time now to get as solid a financial base as you can.

Tax planning a salary

Tax breaks are singularly few for those earning a salary. You have to sharpen every dull tax planning tool, because the expense deductions that self-employed people enjoy are not available to you. Of course, there are things you can do. Let's run quickly through some of the tried and true planning tactics to make sure you're making the most of them.

Max out your Registered Retirement Savings Plan (RRSP)

You may have heard that RRSPs are a thing of the past. Not so. Lower personal taxes and capital gains rates do not make RRSPs obsolete. The tax rebate from RRSP contributions is just too advantageous to ignore, especially for someone on a salary who is eager for ways to save taxes. Contribution limits are set at $13,500 for 2002 and 2003, but will rise by $1,000 a year for 2004 and 2005, at which point the contribution limit will be indexed to inflation. (You do have to be careful about which assets you hold inside your RRSP and which you hold outside. New research has found a flaw in the common wisdom, but we'll talk about this in the investing chapter.)

Use a spousal RRSP

Spousal RRSPs are one of the few ways left to split income between spouses, and even though they're not immediately advantageous, they are quite worthwhile. A spousal RRSP is simply an RRSP set up in your spouse's name, but to which you and you alone contribute. You get the tax benefit of an RRSP contribution, but your spouse gets the capital, thus reducing your taxes while putting money in your partner's name. It'd be even better if your spousal contributions didn't affect your own RRSP contribution limit, but unfortunately they do. Your spousal contributions are deducted from your overall limit, so a $7,000 spousal contribution, for instance, would mean you have only $6,500 in contribution room for your own RRSP if you have a $13,500 limit. Your spouse's contribution limit, on the other hand, is completely unaffected by your spousal contribution.

When you retire and start receiving income from your retirement savings, you and your spouse will pay less tax if your income is more evenly split between the two of you. A senior couple with two incomes of $25,000 pays about $6,000 in income tax in Ontario, compared to $7,200 for a retirement income of $40,000 for one spouse and $10,000 for the other. With greater disparity between the two incomes, and at higher income levels, where government clawbacks kick in, the total after-tax differences can be more extreme.

Here's a chart that illustrates the potential benefits of retirement income splitting using a spousal RRSP.

Tax Savings through Use of a Spousal RRSP

	SPOUSE A	SPOUSE B	TOTAL
Couple 1—No Spousal RRSP			
Retirement income	$40,000	$10,000	$50,000
Less taxes*	$7,235	$0	$7,235
Net income	$32,765	$10,000	$42,765
Average tax rate	18%	0%	14%
Couple 2—Spousal RRSP			
($15,000 of RRSP income is switched from spouse A to spouse B)			
Retirement income	$25,000	$25,000	$50,000
Less taxes*	$3,094	$2,871	$5,965
Net income	$21,906	$22,129	$44,035
Average tax rate	12%	11%	12%

Taxes calculated based on 2001 Ontario tax rates for 66-year-olds who are eligible for the age exemption and the pension income credit on RRSP income.[2]

Splitting retirement income more evenly between partners can reduce taxes. In this example, couple 2 used a spousal RRSP to balance retirement income for a more than $1,200 annual tax savings over couple 1 with the same total before-tax income.

Spousal RRSP accounts can be opened for married spouses, common-law partners and same-sex partners. They're great things, but there's one restriction you should keep in mind. Spousal contributions have to be kept in the account for at least two calendar years following the year the contribution was made before being withdrawn or the withdrawal is attributed to you, the contributor, as income. In that case, you will have to pay tax on this withdrawal at your marginal rate, which means you will have gained no tax advantage in the contribution and you will have lost that contribution room. (Once a contribution is made to an RRSP, that contribution room is gone forever unless withdrawals are done under a program like the Home Buyers' Plan or the Lifelong Learning Plan that allows repayments.)

What a Difference a Day Makes

If you think you might need to withdraw funds from a spousal RRSP, consider the timing of your contributions carefully. A contribution made on December 31, 2002, with no subsequent contributions, will be available for withdrawal without attribution on January 1, 2005. A contribution made only two days later, on January 2, 2003, would not be available for withdrawal free of attribution until January 1, 2006. A day's difference in contributing can make a whole year's difference in withdrawing without attribution.

Do as much income splitting as you can

The self-employed can do things like paying their children to shovel snow or design their Web site, but salaried people have to resort to more common income-splitting methods. Beyond spousal RRSPs, apportioning non-registered investments is about as daring as it gets.

As you know, any investment housed in an RRSP stays there without requiring you to pay any tax on its income or growth until it is withdrawn. Investments held outside registered accounts are not similarly sheltered from tax. These unsheltered investments generate tax liabilities when they pay interest or dividends, or when they are sold and give rise to a capital gain. The best you can make of this situation is to ensure that the spouse with the lower marginal tax rate buys and holds the non-registered investments in his or her name. That way, less tax will be paid on the investment income and gains, which improves your after-tax return. To make this possible, though, the higher-income spouse should pay the bills and the taxes so the lower-income spouse has the money to buy the investments.

GIVE INVESTMENTS TO YOUR FAMILY

You can also give money (or investments) to your spouse or partner to achieve some income splitting in a roundabout way. The income and capital gains generated by your gift are attributable back to you, and you must pay tax on that as though that income was actually paid to you; however, income on that income (otherwise known as second and succeeding generation income) is not attributable to you. Second and succeeding generation income can accumulate in your partner's name and be taxed at your partner's marginal tax rate.

LOAN MONEY TO YOUR SPOUSE

A slightly more sophisticated tactic involves loaning assets to your spouse or minor children to invest in their name. As long as the loan is at the rate prescribed by CCRA—or a commercially reasonable rate—at the time the loan was made, and interest is actually paid on the loan every year, the income and gains from those investments will not be attributed back to you. You also avoid the attribution if you sell your assets to your partner at fair market value, but you have to pay the capital gains tax when you transfer the assets to your partner's name. Because of this, it's usually better to sell assets to your spouse that have little or no accrued gain in order to limit tax liabilities at the time of sale.

When you sell investments to a spouse or partner at fair market value but have a capital loss on the transaction, your loss is unfortunately deemed to be zero. In other words, you can't use a capital loss generated through a sale to a spouse to offset other capital gains. Your spouse, however, can add back your capital loss to his cost base for the investment. If you bought a stock for $100 and sold it to your spouse for $75, you have a capital loss of $25. Your spouse's cost base for that investment is $75, but the rules permit him to add your $25 loss to that cost base. When he subsequently sells the investment, his capital gain or loss will be calculated from $100, not $75, which means he'll pay less capital gains tax when he does eventually sell the asset in an arm's length transaction.

GIVE ASSETS THAT GENERATE CAPITAL GAINS TO YOUR MINOR CHILDREN

Thinking of giving an investment or other asset to a minor child? If the asset generates capital gains instead of interest or dividends, you might want to consider it. First, though, you'd have to pay capital gains tax, if applicable, on the transfer, since giving assets to minor children triggers a deemed disposition. If you made money on the asset, you would have to pay the resulting capital gains tax, but once the assets are in your child's possession, capital gains are not attributable back to you. It's just one of those interesting tax oddities. While interest and dividend income are still attributable back to you, capital gains are taxed in the hands of your minor child.

The investment income attribution rules chart shows how these relationships work.

Investment Income Attribution Rules

If you give a **gift** to:
- *Your spouse,** income and capital gains generated are taxable in your hands
- *Your minor child,* income, but not capital gains, is taxable in your hands
- *Your adult child,* income and capital gains are taxable in the child's hands

If you make an **interest-free loan** to:
- *Your spouse,* income and capital gains are taxable in your hands
- *Your minor child,* income, but not capital gains, is taxable in your hands
- *Your adult child,* income and capital gains are taxable in your hands if the loan was made to avoid taxes

If you make an **interest-bearing loan*** to:
- *Your spouse,* income and capital gains are taxable in the spouse's hands
- *Your minor child,* income and capital gains are taxable in the child's hands
- *Your adult child,* income and capital gains are taxable in the child's hands

* Spouse includes a common-law partner of the same or opposite sex
** The loan must be made at CCRA's prescribed interest rate or higher, and interest payments must be made at least once a year

---

Avoid tax refunds

Don't celebrate a tax refund. You've received a refund because you've been giving the government a tax-free loan. Most people get a refund because of RRSP contributions. If you make your RRSP contributions on a regular basis, you can have your employer reduce your taxes at source by completing a source deduction waiver (form T1213) so you're getting the tax benefit of those contributions with every paycheque.

Consider debt swaps

Debt swapping is a way to make your debt tax-deductible. It goes like this: You take your non-registered investments, cash them in and use that cash to pay down a debt—a mortgage or loan, for instance. Then you get an investment loan to buy back an equivalent investment portfolio. Interest on money borrowed to earn taxable income is tax-deductible. You've instantly converted non-deductible debt from your mortgage or consumer loan to deductible debt in the form of an investment loan. The rules stipulate that the investments must be held for the purpose of earning income.

It sounds simple, but leveraging is riskier than many people fully appreciate. Should your investments fall in value, you are still responsible to the lender for the full amount you borrowed. If interest rates spike up at the same time, you could be making expensive payments on assets that may have dwindled in value. This is a calculated risk some are willing to take, but it's not for me.

On the other hand, if all goes well with a leveraging strategy, you could multiply your investment growth by a sizable factor. Even with a conservative leveraging strategy and modest assumptions, you can increase your return by 50%. More optimistic assumptions or more aggressive borrowing can pump your returns up by 200% or more. You have to decide if the potential returns are worth the risk—and the risks are real. If you just match your own capital with borrowed money and borrow no more beyond that, a 50% decline in the value of your portfolio will wipe you out completely. I'd have a hard time sleeping at night with that range of possible outcomes, but that isn't to say leveraging should always be avoided. It has its place if you have the risk tolerance, financially and psychologically. (Our discussion of leveraging in the investing chapter will illustrate the risks and potential benefits in more detail.)

Make good use of allowable deductions

In addition to trying to minimize your tax burden by income splitting, you must look diligently for legitimate deductions from your income. Using your car for business is often a good source of deductions, so long as you can prove, if asked, that these expenses were allowable deductions under the tax rules. Unfortunately, getting to and from work is not a deductible expense for salaried employees.

When you use your own car for business purposes, you are allowed to deduct the gas, repair and car wash costs in proportion to your business use of the car. You can also deduct interest on the car loan to a maximum of $300 a month, and depreciation—known in tax circles as the capital cost allowance (CCA). Monthly lease payments are also deductible to a maximum of $800 but again in proportion to the business use of the car (and a maximum car value of $30,000 before provincial sales taxes and GST). These deductions are available to you as long as your employer doesn't reimburse you for these expenses or pay you a reasonable allowance. You are strongly advised to keep a log in the car to record your business mileage, because your expenses can be denied by CCRA if you don't have proof of them.

Business travel expenses can be another source of deductions. Generally, expenses you incur while travelling for your employer that aren't reimbursed or compensated for in some other way are deductible. Salespeople who earn commissions, pay their own expenses and work away from the employer's office have more latitude for deductions than salaried individuals.

An overseas posting could result in a tax break, too. Depending on the nature of the industry you are in, you may be able to claim a tax credit of up to 80% on the first $100,000 of income made while you live overseas. That may make a transfer all that much more attractive, but make sure you check with a tax professional if you might be posted out of the country, because the rules for this credit are complicated.[3]

Professional membership dues and many courses and seminars you take relating to your employment are deductible if they're not paid for by your employer; however, your course fees in one 12-month period must come to more than $100 per institution.

Getting to deduct expenses relating to your work is logical and completely reasonable. What follows next is not so self-evident. Plenty of benefits your employer pays for could very well be taxable to you as a benefit. You need to know about these to anticipate your tax liabilities and understand your total after-tax compensation.

Taxable benefits

When you find yourself with a nice set of benefits, you might be dismayed at the associated tax bill. Some things you probably see as a perk, CCRA often sees as a taxable benefit, frequent flyer credits among them. Having to pay out hard-earned cash for non-monetary perks makes many of us a little resentful, but it's CCRA's way of making sure we all pay our fair share of taxes.

The cost to your employer, or the deemed value of these benefits, is attributed to your income. You pay tax on that bumped-up income. It hurts, but it's fair. KPMG's *Tax Planning for You and Your Family 2002* suggests having your employer pay for non-taxable benefits while you pay for taxable benefits, but you'll probably find most corporations have already figured this tax optimization strategy out on their own.[4]

Here is a partial list of the taxable benefits most likely to affect your situation:

- Stock option plans
- Loans from your employer[5]
- Life insurance premiums paid by your employer
- Frequent flyer credits obtained through employer-paid business travel but used personally
- Travelling expenses paid by your employer for your personal travel or for your spouse to accompany you on a business trip

- Employer-paid parking, with certain exceptions for the disabled
- Personal use of a company car
- Non-cash gifts or awards over $500 in one year, and all cash gifts and awards
- Employer-paid holiday trips, prizes and incentive awards
- Tax equalization payments (paid to employees who relocate to a higher tax regime)[6]

How Janice learned the fine art of negotiation

Janice moved to Regal in 2000 from a position as Senior Vice President, Strategic Planning and Investor Relations at the company that owned Regal, MDC Corporation Inc. She negotiated a healthy salary, a selling bonus and a severance package to transition Regal's sale to Eos International Inc., a company listed on the New York Stock Exchange. For undertaking to remain at Regal for a three-year term after the company's transfer, she negotiated an equity position and another severance package.

Janice says she always negotiates a severance package before accepting any job. "I assume every company I'm ever in is going to be acquired, merged or downsized, because that's been my history."

In 1988, Janice was working for Tambrands Canada Inc. Like many companies, Tambrands began to downsize its middle managers with the introduction of free trade. As a senior middle manager, Janice was downsized, too. "Being downsized shook my value system because it had nothing to do with anything I had done," she recalls. "It was a decision made in the U.S. head office." Knowing her job was being eliminated, Janice was asked to stay on to help the company through the transition. "Because I continued to do a good job through the downsizing and managed to get my emotions under control, I actually negotiated a very generous severance package at the time."

Her next job was at Griffith Laboratories Ltd., a privately owned American company that began merging its Canadian and U.S. offices in favour of the U.S. location. Janice was asked to play a major role in that process until she was faced with the necessity of going to the States herself. For family reasons, she chose to stay in Canada and was severed. "But the company still needed me, so I negotiated a little more and ended up with a windfall. The day after I was severed, I was hired back as a Toronto-based consultant, so I had a severance package and an income. I learned the fine art of negotiating in the era of downsizing.

"For a long time after the Tambrands experience, my negotiation was focused on protecting myself," she says. "As I moved up the ranks, I realized that I needed to be negotiating my share of the pie. And I realized it is common practice to approach the CEO or the board and ask for compensation for the value I produce. The more I drive the value, the more the shareholders make, so why shouldn't I be rewarded, too? It is expected, though it won't be volunteered. It's perfectly acceptable to negotiate your compensation, and it's your responsibility to do so."

Early on in her career, she negotiated an upgraded car lease and converted a health club membership she would never use into a clothing allowance. Over time, the stakes have gotten bigger.

"The best time to negotiate is before you walk in the door," says Janice, but she points out that junior executives have a lot less negotiating room. Much of the compensation is set for the director, associate VP and VP levels. Nevertheless, she tells people to try for the best possible salary, because bonuses are linked to it. Even if the bonus is a non-negotiable percentage of salary, the salary itself can usually be negotiated within a fairly broad range, she notes. She also suggests people leverage their former job benefits for a better salary. If you had a company car in your former position, for instance, and your new company does not have company cars, she suggests negotiating a car allowance into your salary. "You can always open negotiations again," advises Janice, "once you've got a good track record or when you're asked to do something extraordinary or exceptional."

To be effective in bargaining, she says, "You need a pretty good sense of what you're valued for and what you're being hired for. You also have to have a sense of what's fair and reasonable. I have a network of recruiters and peers in a lot of industries whom I can phone. They tell me the going market rate."

Her advice? "Be consistent with precedent. Build on your track record. Don't be afraid to ask, and make sure you deliver results."

Lump sums

A plump cheque over and above your regular salary is a pleasant sight, but a tax worry. Here are some of the common sources of lump-sum payments and how they're taxed.

Bonuses and commissions

Bonuses and commissions go straight into your taxable income. As disheartening as it is to see a long-awaited cheque nearly cut in half by taxes, there's not much to be done about it short of contributing it to your RRSP within your allowable contribution limit.

Retiring allowances

All sorts of things are considered "retiring allowances" by CCRA, which is a good thing because it means at least some of the lump-sum payment may be transferred into an RRSP over and above your normal contribution room. Severance pay, termination awards, retiring allowances, unused sick leave, even wrongful dismissal settlements are classified as retiring allowances for tax purposes. There are numerous qualifications on the RRSP sheltering opportunity, however. This is how KPMG's guide sets out the limitations: "The amount that can be transferred is normally limited to $2,000 for each calendar year (or part year) of employment before 1996, plus $1,500 for years of employment before 1989 for which employer pension contributions have not vested."[7] (Pension benefits "vest" when you can carry your contributions *and* your employer's with you should you leave your employer. We'll talk about pensions later in this chapter.)

You should know that retiring allowances are calculated from years of employment with a company related to your current employer. Many employees have faced a change of employer just by virtue of merger, acquisition or consolidation.

Let's take a look at an example.

Alice receives a retiring allowance in the amount of $25,000 when she leaves her employer. She worked there between 1986 and 1997. In 1986, her employer contributed $2,000 to a registered pension plan (RPP) on her behalf.

How much can she roll into her RRSP tax-free?

$2,000 per year that she worked for the company up to 1995: $2,000 × 10 years

Plus $1,500 per year before 1989, less any year during which her employer contributed to her pension plan: $1,500 × 2 years

Total amount she can roll into her RRSP: ($2,000 × 10) + ($1,500 × 2) = $23,000

It doesn't matter how much the employer contributed to Alice's pension: If any amount is contributed in a given year, Alice cannot claim the $1,500 for that year.

Sometimes retiring allowances are paid in the year after your employment ended. If the amount is at least $3,000, you can attribute the allowance to the tax year in which you left your employer or you can take it into income in the year it's received—whichever is more advantageous to you.

What you can't put in an RRSP you are required to pay tax on at your marginal rate unless some of that allowance is for a wrongful dismissal settlement that is partly compensation for mental distress. Damages for wrongful dismissal are generally taxable, but damages for mental distress are usually not taxable.

You can see this gets complicated quickly. It is always best to see a professional when significant money or tax liabilities are on the line. This recommendation is underscored for our next topic, stock options.

Stock option and share plans

Stock option plans are used by companies to attract and retain valuable talent, but coveted as they sometimes are, stock options have to be treated with care. The tax liability that results from exercising them can be punitive if not properly managed.

A company stock option is simply the option to buy the company's shares at a given price for a certain period of time. Typically, a number of options will be granted to you that will "vest" over a few years. You might, for instance, get 20,000 options, with 5,000 vesting each year over four years. A stock option "vests" when you gain the right to exercise it. You exercise your options when you use them to buy the company's stock, and that's when the tax liability comes into play. Your company or your accountant will be able to advise you on the tax implications when you choose to take advantage of your stock options, but here's a sketch of what's involved.

> Congratulations. Ruthenium Chip Company Inc. has granted you the right to buy <u>10,000 shares at $10 each</u>.

> Ruthenium is a publicly traded company, and $10 was the fair market value of the shares on the day the options were issued. The options vest in 2002 and expire in 2004.

> In 2003, Ruthenium's shares double in value and you exercise your options. You buy and immediately sell <u>10,000 shares at $20 each</u>.

> Your profit is $100,000 ($200,000 proceeds of sale − $100,000 acquisition cost).

Under old CCRA rules, that $100,000 profit is a taxable benefit and would be included in your taxable employment income when the options were exercised whether or not you subsequently sold the shares. (Under certain conditions, a deduction equal to 50% of the taxable benefit was allowed.) Because of the hefty tax bill that ensued from exercising these options, you'd most likely exercise your options only when you intended to sell your shares.

New rules introduced in the February 2000 federal budget give you more breathing room. You can now defer tax on publicly traded shares until you actually sell the shares—which has always been the case with private company shares. The deferral is limited to an annual maximum of $100,000 worth of the shares at their fair market value when the options were granted. Anything over the number of shares that originally represented $100,000 you still have to include as profit in your taxable income and is subject to a possible 50% deduction. The deferral also depends on a subtlety about when the options vest. If $150,000 vests each year for four years, $100,000 could be deferred each year and $50,000 would have to be included in income. Had the $150,000 vested over two years, the entire amount could be deferred. Your employer will be able to explain when your options vest, as this depends on the terms of your employment.

And the new deferral rules apply only to what's known as an "eligible employee." Basically, this means you are a Canadian resident, you don't own more than 10% of the company's shares and you deal at arm's length with your employer and related companies.

It's important to note that you need the tax deferral only if you are going to buy the shares without immediately selling them. There's a big risk in exercising your options without immediately selling the stocks. If the 10,000 Ruthenium stocks you bought at $20 subsequently go down to $15 and you sell them at that lower price, you are nevertheless liable for the taxable benefit on the $100,000 profit you would have had on the day you exercised the options ($200,000 market price − $100,000 option strike price). The fact that you reaped only $50,000 on the transaction is of no consequence. The $50,000 you lost qualifies as a capital loss, but that can be used only to offset capital gains, not general tax liabilities. So take a good hard look at the benefits of the tax deferral. It may not be worth the risk.

You can qualify for a 50% tax deduction on the taxable benefit of stock option profits if the shares you buy are common shares, the exercise price was no less than the fair market price of the shares at the time the option was granted, and you deal at arm's length with the corporation that granted you the options. The effect of the deduction is to make your tax liability the same as it would be if the proceeds from your options were treated as capital gains.

Considerations here do get thorny, so consult an accountant before you exercise your options, and get advice on how best to manage the tax consequences and how to register your request for a tax deferral. At the time this was written, requests for tax deferrals had to be made by letter to CCRA every year the deferral is required; namely, until you sell the shares, become a non-resident of Canada or die.

If your stock options have vested, you may or may not take them with you when you leave your employer, depending on the conditions of your departure. Being fired for cause may instantly cancel your options, but typically you have a few months to exercise them once you leave your employer. Each company has its own rules and time frame for this, and may well leave it open for negotiation during termination. Upon retirement, you generally have a more generous window to exercise your options, maybe even a few years. Should you die with vested options, they will pass to your estate, where your executor will have a limited time to exercise them. Options that are not exercised expire worthless.

What Janice learned about stock options

"Either you have a really good stock option plan or you have a strong pension. In my experience, it's weighted either-or," says Janice. "There's a lot of compensation benefits hidden in your medical, dental, drug and optometry plan. Club memberships are often given on the understanding that you keep that membership for life. There are huge subtleties in the pensions, too."

Janice has observed that those who have done well with stock options have been in established businesses for a long time. "To make a lot of money on stock options in the short term, it helps to be in a business that has some sort of merger and acquisition activity, because that's what makes the stock price move quickly," she says. "You can only vest so many at a time, and you have to sell them within a certain period of time, so that business has to be moving quickly to make those options pay off."

Janice says stock options have never been a big part of her compensation, but she does have some opinions about what to look for in a plan, based on her experience. "Whether a stock option plan is good or not so good is totally dependent on the nature of the business and your career plan," she says. "If I wanted to move up the corporate ranks in a big company, a stock option plan that gives me so many options a year would be great because it's a large company and has been growing every year since its inception. I would want a plan with a three- to five-year vesting so I could maximize the value of my stock, because it should go up every year and I'm there for the long term. If I had a short employment horizon with a company, I'd have to keep in mind that I would be required to sell my stocks the day I left the company, or very shortly thereafter, because membership in an option plan is conditional on employment. Ideally, a plan structure should be aligned to your own career aspirations."

Share plans

Stock option plans seem to be falling out of favour because stocks no longer seem to be going up regularly enough and some companies have issued close to the maximum number of options allowed by stock market rules (10% of outstanding shares). Instead, companies can grant shares outright to employees, or arrange to pay them the price increase as though they had given them the shares. A vesting period and some performance requirements are frequently tied to a share plan.

About one-third of Canada's 100 largest companies have a stock plan of one sort or another.[8]

Pensions

Many small companies can't afford pension plans and provide their own shares or stock options instead of a steady cheque at retirement. Large companies, on the other hand, not only provide a standard pension, they also have topping-up arrangements for their most well-paid employees.

Pensions are expensive to administer and are complicated to run. Fortunately, the internal complexities of pension plans can be left to the actuaries, but there are two basic kinds: defined benefit plans and defined contribution plans. Large companies—and especially the most highly paid employees of large companies—frequently have defined benefit plans. This kind of plan guarantees your benefits when you retire. The responsibility for providing this retirement income belongs to the company, which must manage the underlying investments well enough to fund your pension. If the plan runs short, the company has to put its own money in to make good. In a defined contribution plan, you are taking the risk for the performance of the underlying investments. The pension is funded by fixed contributions by you and/or your employer. It is only the contributions that are guaranteed, not what becomes of them once they've been invested. With a defined contribution plan, your pension income ultimately depends on the assets in your plan when you retire.

All registered pension plans max out at around $60,000 in retirement income—which comes nowhere close to being adequate for high-earning employees and executives. To get around this government-imposed limitation, large companies frequently provide their senior management with topping-up arrangements broadly known as supplemental executive retirement plans (SERPs) that are intended to help high-earning employees come close to the standard retirement income goal of 60% of their working income and may include what's commonly called RCAs, or retirement compensation arrangements. Simply, these plans are apart from the registered pension plans and are designed to augment pension payments but are not subject to contribution limits. The payout formula on SERPs is not necessarily related to the company's registered pension plan and can have more generous terms—such as two years of credited service for every year of continuous service—and may include bonuses as well as base salary in their benefit calculations.

Pensions "vest" when the value of your pension plan (including your employer's contributions) accompany you if and when you leave your employer. Pension funds transferred out of a company pension plan have to be put into a "locked-in" RRSP. The locking-in feature means you can't access the money any sooner than you would have been able to had you continued to be a pension plan member with that employer— typically only within ten years of your official retirement date under the plan—to ensure that money earmarked for retirement stays available for retirement.

Should You Participate in Your Company's Pension Plan?

Advantages
- Your employer pays for part of your pension
- The pension provides a guaranteed income for life (defined benefit plans only)
- Income may be indexed to keep up with price inflation (defined benefit plans only)
- Pensions are creditor-proof
- Pension contributions qualify for tax deductions
- Pensions grow free of taxes

Disadvantages
- Having a pension reduces your allowable RRSP contribution room
- There is no flexibility with respect to contributions; you cannot skip a contribution if you are going through a difficult period financially or if the money would be better spent paying down debt
- Your money is tied up until retirement (unless you have a group RRSP or you leave before vesting)
- Investments within the plan may not meet your objectives
- You may not get much of your employer's contributions if you quit before retirement

A company's pension plan could be a major benefit for those who choose to join it, and the generosity of the whole retirement compensation package can be a big factor in evaluating the attractiveness of a job offer. Given the intricacy of pension programs, how can you evaluate a pension plan? Malcolm Hamilton, a well-known pension actuary with Mercer Human Resource Consulting in Toronto, offers these tips.

Size: Evaluate the size of your projected pension compared to that provided by other companies. Executives will find that a defined benefit plan will generate a bigger final pension than a defined contribution plan. Pay attention to the terms of the top-up arrangement, too. Sometimes they are subject to non-compete clauses and may not vest until you are 55 years old. Is your final pension calculation based just on salary, or does it include bonuses and commissions as well?

Age: At what age are the benefits payable without reduction? The earlier, the more valuable the pension. According to Hamilton, standard arrangements generally permit unreduced benefits when the plan holder is from 60 to 62 years old. Compare this feature of your plan to other pension plans in your industry.

Security: Standard pension funds are held in trust by the employer, but top-up arrangements are often not funded or secured in any way. Hamilton says about two-thirds of top-up plans in Canada are not secured, so if the company goes bankrupt, your pension top-up goes right down with it. Retirement compensation arrangements are a secure way for a company to provide a topping-up mechanism, but tax considerations make these much more expensive for companies than pension plans.

Indexation: Defined benefit pension plans can have an inflation adjustment mechanism and you should know how it is calculated. For those with a supplementary pension plan, Hamilton says there are special concerns: "If pensions in the registered plan are indexed on an ad hoc basis, are benefits in the supplementary pension plan similarly indexed (the best case), unindexed, or is the indexing of the registered plan clawed back from the supplementary pension (the worst case)?"

Managing your risks

We don't often think of risk management as something related to our personal health, but the Canadian Life and Health Insurance Association provides an arresting statistic that should change our outlook.

> *"At age 42, you're four times as likely to be disabled as to die before age 65."*

We associate risk with an investment strategy or a career venture, but hardly with our own bodies. In fact, though, the body we groom and dress every day has a huge potential to betray us. Illness, injury and disability are not rare events that happen only to others. They are disturbingly common occurrences that need to be anticipated and provided for despite the deceptive internal psychology that makes us think nothing bad will ever happen to us. That's our innate optimism at work, but those who make their risk management decisions on this basis will be playing with the odds stacked against them.

Your human and financial capital are on the line. Moshe Milevsky, a professor of finance at York University, has popularized the term "human capital" as a measure of our future productivity. The younger we are, the more human capital we steward within ourselves. As we age, our human capital diminishes, but with prudent management, our financial capital should increase. At some point in middle age, our

Your Lifetime Financial and Human Capital

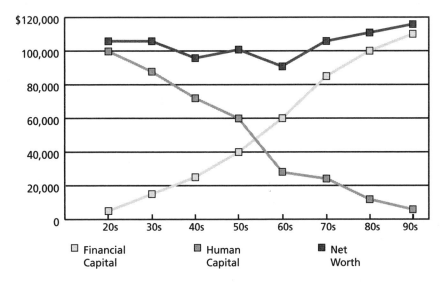

Source: *Professor Moshe A. Milevsky,* Insurance Logic

At some point, your human and financial capital are momentarily equal. As your human capital declines, your financial capital should be in ascendance to maintain your standard of living.

financial and human capital meet, and as our human capital declines, our financial capital should continue to climb.

When you are young, you invest in your human capital by getting an education, learning your business and so on. In the natural course of things, your investment will change from investing in yourself to growing your financial capital, but what will happen if circumstances prevent you from realizing your human capital? Naturally, your financial capital will suffer; hence the need for insurance.

Most likely, you're a member of your employer's benefits program. You may even have a supplemental executive benefits package. But you still may not have enough insurance coverage to protect both your human and financial capital. We'll look briefly at the varieties of insurance and how much of it you should have. Those who are thinking of becoming self-employed or sit on corporate boards will also find this information useful.

Disability insurance

Disability insurance is the most expensive to buy because it is the most likely to be used. It is important for that very reason. The cost of disability insurance is also related to the type of "disability" you want to be covered for. Surgeons and other highly skilled professionals typically want to be insured should they become unable to do their very specific jobs. Known as "own occupation" disability insurance, this is a pretty narrow concept of disability. Most of us would consider ourselves disabled when we couldn't do any job for which we are reasonably trained, which is the definition used in "any occupation" disability insurance. As you might expect, policies using this definition are less expensive than those covering "own occupation" disability.

All disability insurance is designed to replace your after-tax income and is usually limited to replacing a percentage of your income up to a fixed maximum monthly payout until age 65. If your monthly employment income after tax exceeds your group plan maximum, you will have a shortfall. You should check the income ceiling on your group disability plan. If the monthly payment would pose a hardship for your family, you can buy supplementary disability insurance privately.

As a general rule, you cannot insure 100% or more of your pre-tax employment income. If you buy a private disability policy before joining a group plan, you can circumvent this restriction, but it doesn't work the other way around. Private disability insurance purchased after you are already a group plan member will reduce the benefits when your group plan also pays out. It is still useful to have private insurance, however, because group plans generally have more restrictive definitions of disability and it's quite conceivable that your group plan would not consider you disabled when your private plan might. Before you buy supplemental disability insurance, make sure you check the policy on benefit payments when other disability insurance is in place.

Check out how long your group disability lasts and under what conditions. Group plans will generally pay disability benefits for two years when you can't do your own job. After that, they may pay only if you are unable to do any job that you are qualified for by training and experience. A private supplemental plan is most useful when it doesn't have a provision like that, and it's a good idea to see that it doesn't or you may not be getting the protection you need.

Other critical variables to look for in disability insurance include the elimination period and options to renew or cancel the coverage. The elimination period is the amount of time you have to wait before your insurance benefits kick in. The longer the elimination period, the less expensive the insurance. You will often see policies with elimination periods of 90 days, but if you have enough of a cash cushion put aside, you might consider a six- or even 12-month elimination period.

Understanding some insurance jargon, such as "renewable" or "non-cancellable," will help you better evaluate these policies. A guaranteed renewable policy will never be cancelled, but your premiums may increase. A non-cancellable policy will never be cancelled, nor will your premiums go up. This, of course, is a more expensive feature.

Disability insurance is a specialized area, and if you need to top up your coverage, you should consult with a qualified disability insurance specialist. There is no shortage of options, and with them a range of costs, which make this kind of insurance particularly complex. Will your benefits be indexed to inflation? Are common mental illnesses covered? Does it cover vocational rehabilitation expenses? Will you be penalized for returning to work part-time? Can you buy more insurance in the future? Will your premiums be automatically paid if you become disabled? As long as you are willing to pay for it, there is an insurance option for just about any contingency, but don't pay for "bells and whistles" you don't really need and might not even have known about without a careful reading of the policy.

Canada Pension Plan (CPP) and Quebec Pension Plan (QPP) disability payments are taxable. Disability payments from an employer-paid plan are also taxable. You will not be taxed, however, on payments from a plan you pay for yourself or payments from an employer's plan in which the premiums were treated as a taxable benefit to you.

Critical illness

If the disability statistic didn't shock you, this one from the Heart and Stroke Foundation of Canada almost certainly will:

"One in four Canadians will contract a serious illness by the age of 65."

Sixty-five hardly seems old anymore, yet a quarter of the people this age have serious health problems.

About 12 years ago, something called critical illness insurance made its appearance in Canada to fill the gap between disability and life insurance. This type of insurance will pay a tax-free lump sum if you are diagnosed with—and survive—a variety of major illnesses, such as stroke, cancer, Parkinson's, multiple sclerosis, Alzheimer's and specified others. You must survive for a specified period, usually more than 30 days. (With most plans, a full refund of premiums is available should you die within the 30 days.) The benefit money can be used without restriction, and the amount you wish to insure for is limited only by what you care to pay in premiums.

Sometimes thought of as lifestyle insurance, you can also see critical illness insurance as a way of financing medical treatment in the United States or alternative therapies not covered by your province. The younger you get this insurance, the better, because your family history will probably reveal fewer illnesses. As you age, your family members are more likely to develop an illness that will increase the cost of your insurance or make you ineligible for coverage for those familial illnesses. The ailments covered by critical illness insurance vary from policy to policy, as do rates. On average, men are more expensive to insure than women of comparable age.

This type of coverage shouldn't be confused with disability insurance. Disability will replace a portion of your income when you can't work. It will not give you money to build a wheelchair ramp, pay for medications or hire a physiotherapist, for instance. A prolonged illness can impose onerous additional expenses on your family, and it's quite possible a serious illness will not keep you out of work long enough to collect disability benefits but may nevertheless seriously change your lifestyle. Imagine the havoc a mild heart attack could wreak on your life.

Life insurance

I've found, in my experience anyway, that women tend to underinsure themselves. We easily underestimate the importance of our financial contribution to the family, especially those women who stay at home. Just because you may be a member of a group benefits plan, don't assume your insurance needs are fully addressed. Group plans set a foundation of insurance coverage, but that doesn't mean that's where it should stop. The amount of life insurance you need varies through your life as your financial responsibilities to your loved ones rise and fall. Your group plan may set your life insurance based on a multiple of your salary, perhaps one or two times your salary, but the most accurate way to determine your life insurance needs is to look at your financial responsibilities.

You want to protect those who depend on your income should you die before you reach financial independence. You should consider your mortgage, education for your children, support for a stay-at-home spouse, nursing home care for your parents, and the numerous other financial responsibilities you have. It is not unreasonable to want all your debts paid off on your death, with enough cash left over to fund the ongoing expenses of your dependants. Two times your salary might do that, but maybe it won't. You'll find many on-line calculators that can help you assess your life needs; TD has one at **www.tdcanadatrust.com/insurance**.

Should the calculators indicate you're falling short, it is easy and usually quite competitive to buy additional insurance through your group plan. The big advantage to buying private insurance rather than adding to your group coverage is portability. Whereas your group coverage ends when you leave your employer, your privately arranged insurance carries on and gives you some protection between jobs or through the transition to self-employment. A good place to look for supplementary insurance is through your professional association, which will often offer well-suited insurance packages at competitive rates.

But before you dash off to check your coverage, you should give some thought to the kind of life coverage you want: term insurance, whole life or universal life. Permanent insurance—that is, insurance that is anything but term insurance—has complicated features and you may want the help of an experienced insurance advisor to help you assess.

TERM INSURANCE

Term insurance covers you for a fixed term, usually in 10- to 20-year increments. It is the least expensive kind of life insurance because it does not have an investment component and it comes with many variations. Term insurance can be guaranteed renewable so that you can renew your coverage without further evidence of insurability. (Expect a premium hike on renewal, though.) It usually comes with an option that allows you to convert to some form of permanent insurance, so it is flexible as well as inexpensive. Except for term to 100, which covers you for life even if you live beyond 100, term insurance is not recommended for estate planning purposes, since it gets increasingly expensive as you age and generally won't cover anyone beyond age 80.

WHOLE LIFE

Whole life is permanent insurance with a guaranteed savings component to it. As long as you pay your premiums, the insurance will not expire, nor will your premiums go up. Over time, the policy will build up a cash value from which you can borrow. If you do borrow from the policy and die before repaying it, your death benefit is reduced by the amount of the loan. You can also obtain the cash value by cancelling the policy. Whole life is often used for estate planning purposes, since you can't outlive a permanent insurance policy in good standing. Both the insurance and the investment component are paid out at death, and because they are both considered part of the death benefit, they are not taxable.

UNIVERSAL LIFE

Universal life is another form of permanent insurance, which means it doesn't expire and your premiums will not go up. Universal life also has a tax-sheltered investment component, but that component is not necessarily guaranteed. In fact, depending on the nature of the investments you select, you could lose money. Like whole life, however, you receive both the death benefit from the pure insurance portion of the policy and the investment component tax-free.

DEATH AND TAXES

Death and taxes, they say, are inescapable, but the insurance industry seems to have been able to hold at least one of them at bay. The death benefit from virtually all forms of life insurance is non-taxable. That fact makes life insurance with an investment component very attractive because the investment element compounds and is paid out at your death tax-free. You can access this money at any time by cashing in your policy, but the gain in the policy is taxed as income. Leaving your money in the plan until your death allows it to avoid tax altogether. Remember, though, that life insurance premiums are not tax-deductible. Insurance premiums are paid with after-tax money. (As we'll see later, permanent insurance is very useful for offsetting estate taxes.)

Most people aren't aware of this, but permanent life insurance will generally pay you a discounted settlement while you are still alive should you contract a terminal illness. This is arranged either by an interest-bearing advance on the policy or with what's known as a "viatical settlement," which is an outright sale of the policy at a discount. Viaticals are not legal in all provinces, however.

These are unfortunate ways of getting access to your life insurance money, but it's good to know the options exist.

WATCH THE MANAGEMENT FEES

If you want some form of permanent insurance, scrutinize the management fee the insurance company charges for managing the investment portion of your premiums. These can be quite high by mutual fund standards, so you have to weigh the benefits of tax-free compounding with the annual management fee, which, of course, also compounds. In some cases, it can take 20 years for the tax sheltering to overcome the drag of a high management fee, so ask your insurance advisor to show you those numbers before signing on the dotted line. You may be better off buying term insurance and investing the difference in the premiums in some solid mutual funds if you don't feel you need the protection of insurance that lasts until you die.

SHOULD YOU BUY TERM AND THEN CONVERT?

Robert Aggio, Vice President, Estate Planning Solutions with TD Private Client Group, says he generally advises clients with high incomes to buy a lot of term insurance while they're young. "Then, when you've maximized your RRSP and paid off all your non-deductible debt," he says, "you can convert to universal life with no medical exam and sock money into the tax-sheltered policy as an estate planning tool." Your money will compound tax-free until you pass away, at which point the money can go directly to your beneficiaries, tax-free and without having to go through the estate. Avoiding the estate means avoiding probate fees, too. (See the estate planning chapter for more details.) Aggio also suggests asking for a preferred rate on your insurance quote if you're in exceptionally good health. Not all types of life insurance offer preferred rates, but he says it never hurts to try, because the marketplace is always changing.

USING PERMANENT LIFE INSURANCE AS COLLATERAL FOR LOANS

If waiting until you die to get hold of your money requires more patience than you possess, you can use your policy as collateral for a loan. Depending on the nature of the investments in the policy, you can borrow as much as 90% of the investment value of the policy. You get your cash and the lender waits steadfastly for you to make your exit. You will have to pay interest on the loan, of course, but it is possible to have those interest payments added to the loan balance. Compare the interest cost to the money you save by not having to pay tax on this money, and you may find this is one interest payment you don't mind making. Many older investors supplement their retirement income this way.

LOOK AT THE RELATIVE COST OF AN INSURANCE PORTFOLIO

A topped-up insurance portfolio may appear to have high monthly payments, but it's important to look at the expense as a percentage of your total income. The absolute numbers may strike you as high, but as a proportion of the salary you are trying to protect or replace, a well-designed insurance plan should not be a significant percentage of your total salary.

Severance packages

Many, many good people lose their jobs through no fault of their own. Companies downsize or decide to refocus and talent is trimmed, often to be squandered on the competition. Unless you've been dismissed for cause, there is no reason at all not to try to get the most favourable severance package you can. Frequently the severance amount and the payment options are open for negotiation, most especially for senior management, but to have any stomach for it, you have to get beyond the pride and the emotions.

"The face you show the world has to be calm and unemotional," says Janice, a veteran of a few such negotiations. "You can't make the managers feel guilty. Show them you understand it is a business decision and they will be so grateful for your professionalism that you will be able to have a really productive conversation about a severance package."

Should you find yourself having to pack up your desk earlier than you would have liked, an employment lawyer can help you evaluate the terms of the package you're offered, though you may prefer to do the negotiating on your own. Severance packages are typically based on some formula tied to the number of years you were with the company, your earnings, your age and likelihood of finding another job, and local standards. An executive might be offered, for instance, one month's pay for every year of service, with a minimum of six months' pay. If the employer who is now releasing you encouraged you to leave your previous job not so long ago, you might have a case for a more generous settlement, as might be the case if you're older and unlikely to find suitable work soon.

Keep in mind that severance packages are fully taxable. You might prefer a lump-sum payment or the continuation of your salary over the course of a year, but either way you will be paying tax on that money. Lump-sum payments are usually most attractive to those who are reasonably confident of getting another job quickly. Continuing payments have the advantage of building up pension contributions, but they have the disadvantage of being lost if you get another job before they expire. Often these payments are structured to give you 50% of the remaining payments when you find other employment while the former employer keeps the rest.

Your negotiations should take into account all your benefits, even some you may not currently have. You'll want to look at continuing your life insurance and health benefits after you leave, the longer the better. If you can't get them extended, you will have to get private insurance, so keep that cost in mind when negotiating. Clarify how your pension and stock options will be affected by your departure. Is your pension vested? Is your (former) employer willing to top up your pension in some way if you're 50 or older? Are your stock options vested, and if so, when do the options expire on your termination? It's possible your former employer will pay for career counselling, a résumé service and other services that will help you find suitable employment more quickly.

Don't be in a hurry to invest your entire severance package until you know you've got another job. You will have taxes to pay, and you will need access to your money to see you through to the next day on the job. Having your money buffered from short-term market variances will help to lessen your overall anxiety levels until your employment situation is sorted out.

Sitting on a board

At some time in your advancing career, you may be asked to sit on a board or become a director of a company. If you haven't made it to the chief executive level just yet, don't feel your chance of pushing up to a board table is remote. Women are having an increasingly large presence in the boardrooms of Canada's biggest companies. A recent study shows

7.4 % of those seats are held by women, up from 6.2% three years ago.[9] It's an encouraging trend, and one that will continue to escalate, but it's not just large companies that need directors. A community organization, a cultural group or a large charity could ask for your help. Not so long ago, board positions, big and small, were seen as prestigious perks, a chance to rub elbows with the social elite. Now we know they are accompanied by the possibility of liability—even if you're just trying to help out your local youth orchestra.

"In Canada, there's still a little of the feeling that if I'm doing good, how can anybody sue me?" says David Griffiths, Senior Vice President of the Financial Services Group at Aon Reed Stenhouse Inc. That's very much mistaken now, he says, and not-for-profit organizations see a disproportionate number of legal suits. If the organization you join as an officer or director does not have the financial wherewithal to indemnify you for lawsuits, then you would be wise to make sure they provide directors and officers with liability insurance. One suit from a fired employee is all it could take to make you personally liable for settlement costs and legal fees in a small organization.

Griffiths says anyone contemplating becoming a director should do vigorous due diligence. He recommends learning the organization's agenda, finding out the background and experience of the other directors, studying the governance rules and standards, checking out the financial condition and employment practices of the organization, and getting legal counsel.

"Once you accept the responsibilities and potential liabilities, are you sure you can participate in the decision making? If you walk in and accept a directorship blindly," he says, "you could get a sad awakening." One of the biggest risks, and the most common, Griffiths says, are the statutory liabilities in bankruptcy. Directors can find themselves liable for taxes and the vacation pay and wages owed to employees.

As daunting as it sounds, plenty of people find sitting on boards rewarding and satisfying. At its loftiest, it's a chance to give something back to the community while expanding your business network and perhaps even paving the way for a gentle transition from employment to retirement. Just be careful that when you sign on, you do it with eyes wide open.

Other considerations

Not diversifying

Many managers can be considerably overinvested in their company, and not just from an emotional perspective. Between stock options and share purchase plans, it's easy to get overconcentrated in the company you work for. Imagine what would happen if you lost your job. First, you'd lose your salary. Then, because things are pretty tight financially in the company (which is why you were laid off), the company's stock price starts to plunge. Your stock options become worthless. You lose your group benefits. And, suddenly, much of the security you thought you had has vanished.

Recent history has shown the vulnerability of even top-flight companies. Diversifying your investments will buffer you at least a little from this harsh scenario. It's bad enough that your job, your house and your retirement monies are in one country. Don't exacerbate the concentration by placing so much of your financial capital in your employer. Much of your human capital is already there.

Not delegating

Thinking you have the time to do your own investing is another common problem. You're empowered, forceful, authoritative and in charge. Why would you let someone else handle something so vitally important to your future? But face it. Many people let their financial planning objectives slide because they simply don't have the time to follow their investments, track transactions and rebalance their portfolios when they're out of kilter.

Here's a test. How much time did you devote to your investments in the last three months? (Don't count the time it takes to file away your statements!) If that number is close to zero, either you have to make room for more active supervision of your money or you have to give the job to somebody else. Procrastination about your finances will undermine your long-term goals.

Here, too, Janice has some experience. She neglected her personal financial planning until the age of 40 and attended to it then only because she had to take over her ailing mother's finances. "I had to arrange to get her a regular monthly income and keep her money safe. I knew I couldn't do that by myself," she says.

In the investing chapter, we'll discuss finding the right solution for you on the investing continuum, whether you want to go it completely alone or with some combination of advice, but this decision has to be realistic in light of your time constraints and your ability and interest in managing your investments. This decision is also far from irreversible. Allowing an advisor or a group of advisors to work on your portfolio now doesn't mean you can't reclaim it in the future when you have more time or interest in doing it yourself. I see many high-powered, high-income people neglect their finances because they always intend to get to it on the weekend. Don't leave your financial security to a free weekend, because one day that rewarding, satisfying, engaging job will be over and retirement will be upon you.

> *"Why is it we always expect better and better results by doing the same things over and over again?"*
> Dr. Jeffrey Pheffer, Stanford University

The best employers are the ones who stretch you, who give you a big job before you expected it, who keep you challenged and involved every minute. With this high-powered life comes, fortunately, a serious compensation package that has to be managed so there will be something to show for it all at the end of the day. You have to maximize the limited tax planning available to you, augment group benefits to give you flexibility and manage your risks, and avoid common money management mistakes. Get professional help to make the right choices. The biggest difficulty of all is finding the time and motivation to do it—but do it you must.

Notes

1. Elizabeth G. Chambers, Mark Foulon, Helen Haudfield-Jones, Steven M. Hankin, Edward G. Michaels III. "The War for Talent," *The McKinsey Quarterly* 3 (1998): 44–57.
2. Thanks to Robert Murray, CA, CFP, FMA and Manager of Financial Planning Advice at TD Waterhouse Financial Planning for this chart.

3. Wayne Tunney, Sandra Bussey and Joseph Petrie, eds., *KPMG, Tax Planning for You and Your Family 2002* (Toronto: Carswell 2001), 150.

4. KPMG, 137–55. Much of the tax information in this section was drawn from the chapter entitled "If you are employed."

5. In the case of a loan to buy investments or a vehicle needed for your work, you may be able to claim an offsetting deduction. See KPMG 141–42. KPMG's book has a further caution about employer loans: "If you are a shareholder of the company as well as an employee, or if a member of your family is a shareholder, you must be especially cautious. It is possible for the *entire* amount of the loan, rather than the imputed interest, to be included in your income for tax purposes, unless stringent conditions are met [emphasis theirs]," 142. Talk to an accountant about taxable benefits so you can plan your tax liability.

6. See KPMG 139 for a more extensive list of taxable employment benefits.

7. Ibid., 149–50.

8. Janet MacFarland, "Share plans gaining favour," *The Globe and Mail*, 23 April 2002.

9. Elizabeth Church, "Enron ills seen as boost for women on boards," *The Globe and Mail*, 26 March 2002.

For Further Reading

Brem, Marion Luna. *The 7 Greatest Truths about Highly Successful Women: How You Can Achieve Financial Independence, Professional Freedom, and Personal Joy* (New York: Putnam Publishing Group, 2001).

Collins, James C. *Good to Great: Why Some Companies Make the Leap…and Others Don't* (New York: HarperCollins, 2001).

Johnson, Spencer, and Kenneth H. Blanchard. *Who Moved My Cheese?: An Amazing Way to Deal with Change in Your Work and in Your Life* (New York: Zebra Bouquet, 1998).

4 Marriage and More: Separation, Divorce, Living Together, Widowhood

"Some people ask the secret of our long marriage. We take time to go to a restaurant two times a week. A little candlelight, dinner, soft music and dancing. She goes Tuesdays, I go Fridays."
HENNY YOUNGMAN, COMEDIAN

As insensitive as it may sound, affairs of the heart often become concerns of the chequebook. From the closest lifelong marriage to the brief live-in relationship, money and emotions entwine themselves tightly. This chapter will give you an insight into some of the financial entanglements with the hope of helping you escape those that are avoidable.

My first husband and I decided six months in advance that we would separate and ultimately divorce. Ours was an amicable breakup, and when everything was final, our total bill for the divorce was negligible. But it still had its challenges.

We had time to prepare our two children so they would understand that Mom and Dad's decision to stop being married had nothing to do with them and that we both still loved them very much. I had time to get a credit card in my own name, open my own bank accounts, transfer ownership of the car and calmly tally and divide our assets.

Once separated, my world changed. Suddenly, I was applying for a mortgage and realizing that I alone was responsible for making those payments. I had to plan vacations carefully and budget for Christmas presents, and for a good part of the time, I was a single parent. No amount of planning could have prepared me for how hard that is.

So I've been there. It's no picnic. The biggest pitfall in a marriage breakup is letting feelings of hurt, guilt, anger or exhaustion influence your perception of a fair settlement.

Despite the hardships of a failed first marriage, I strongly believe in marriage and the importance of building strong relationships. I know I beat the odds, but I knew my way around the financial world if I needed to protect myself. That's what I hope this chapter will lay out for those who have experienced the disappointment and pain of a failed relationship or the death of a spouse and have to deal with decisions that can lead to managing significant wealth.

Separation: A parting of the ways and means

While your separation may entail a division of sizable assets, for most women, it means a sharp decline in their financial comfort. In 1997, Statistics Canada reported that women and children who received support had suffered a median decline of 33% in their standard of living one year after their separation. That same study showed that men who paid support had a 20% to 25% improvement in their lifestyle.[1] Support payments have been increasing, so this disparity is probably less glaring now, but separation remains a financial hardship for most women and their children. Quoting Statistics Canada, **DivorceMagazine.com** says 46% of children living in poverty are in single-parent families.[2]

Even if your situation is far more comfortable, there's still the potential for a noticeable cut in your accustomed standard of living. Your best defence against a deteriorating lifestyle in the event of a separation is good preparation. Although it may sound extreme and combative, Michael Cochrane, a seasoned divorce lawyer, says, "Anyone who breathes a word to anybody about separating without first talking to a family lawyer is making a big mistake." Cochrane practises in Toronto and is the author of three books on family law, including the excellent *Surviving Your Divorce*. "With strategic advice, you can change the outcome of a separation," he says, and it doesn't have to get adversarial or ugly.

A lawyer can help you structure things so that you are more likely to get custody of the children and spousal support, and perhaps even keep more of your assets, but this requires careful planning before the separation. If you want to initiate a separation, or even if you suspect your spouse might be thinking of it, see a family lawyer before the situation is upon you.

Unfortunately, not everyone has the luxury of forethought in these matters. Many of us just suddenly find ourselves thrust into a whirlwind of surprise and emotion and don't know what to expect or what to do. Cochrane says most people haven't any idea of the financial consequences of a separation. Suddenly, it seems everything in your life is at stake and on the table—the children, the home, your income, your savings, a business you may have built up over the years, you name it. But, as we'll see later, there are a few assets that can be kept from being drawn into this vortex.

In all the turbulence, it's good to know there is an order to addressing the issues. Cochrane says custody of the children and child support are the first to be dealt with, followed by an agreement on property division, then spousal support. We'll look at the financial aspects of these issues in that order, too.

Custody and child support

Children can easily suffer a huge trauma when their parents break up. Sometimes they have to leave good friends and a familiar school to start a new life where they're complete strangers. The courts do everything they can to protect children from avoidable upset. Cochrane says the spouse who stays in the couple's home is likely to get custody of the children because it is close to the children's friends, schools and activities. (Having the home brings with it the added likelihood of spousal support to take into account mortgage payments and home maintenance, but more on that later.)

The wisdom of the law has also taken child support payments out of the realm of negotiation and made it a simple matter of a calculation based on gross annual income. Lawyers refer to federal child support guidelines that spell out the amount of money to be paid for child support per month, based on the payor's annual income and province of residence and the number of children to be provided for.[3] Some negotiation can still take place if the parents have joint custody, but by and large the amount of child support is no longer a contentious issue. However, the payments get considerably more generous as incomes climb, because judges use considerable discretion in high-income situations.

In a ground-breaking ruling in March 2002, the Ontario Court of Appeal ordered a wealthy businessman to pay a staggering $36,000 a month in child support for his four children. The case, known as *R. v. R.* to keep the identity of the individuals confidential, shattered the previous child support record in a British Columbia case in which three children were awarded a total of $25,000 a month. The Ontario businessman and his wife separated in 1997, when he was making about $1 million a year. Not long after, his income rocketed to $4.1 million. Mrs. R.'s appeal of the original $20,000 a month child support had asked for almost $81,000 a month for her children and double her $5,000 a month spousal support. While her spousal support was not changed,[4] family law commentators take this case as a good indication that the courts are increasingly willing to award substantial support payments in high-income cases.

Property division

"Once the children are dealt with and the emotional stuff is finished, then it is just about money. It's all about money," says Andrew Freedman, an accountant and chartered business valuator with Cole and Partners in Toronto who specializes in valuing assets in family law cases. Recognizing this regrettable truth is your first defence.

Determining Your Assets

Harden your determination, roll up your sleeves and figure out just what you have to work with by making a complete list of all the things you and your husband own, what you owe money on and its current value. This should include:

- House, cottage, vacation property
- Registered Retirement Savings Plans (RRSPs)
- Registered Education Savings Plans (RESPs)
- Public and private pensions

- Life insurance with or without cash value
- Stocks, bonds, GICs, savings bonds, mutual funds
- Stock options
- Interests in trusts
- Chequing and savings accounts
- Vehicles
- Business assets and interests
- Antiques
- Household possessions
- Jewellery (except that excluded as gifts)
- Loans and notes payable
- All debts:
  –Mortgages
  –Loans on life insurance policies
  –Lines of credit
  –Credit card balances
  –Other loans (e.g., car, renovation, RRSP, furniture, etc.)

This document is a financial statement—a balance sheet—and is compiled by the lawyers, based on information you provide.

You need to draw up a financial statement, and the information you need will depend on what province you live in because the division of property is governed by provincial law. (Divorces and child support are under federal jurisdiction.) The biggest difference among the provinces is in the treatment of business assets. Some provinces deem business assets "non-family assets" and don't divide them at all, while other provinces, such as Ontario, do include these in division. In either case, income can be sheltered in a company business, so it is important to know just what the business income and assets are when it comes time to calculate support payments. (A worksheet to help you prepare a financial statement is available on-line at **www.ontariocourts.on. ca/family_court/forms/english/pdf/f-13.pdf.** This one is used by Ontario courts and is very comprehensive.)

Be sure to scrutinize the accuracy and completeness of the financial statement very carefully. It must be updated to reflect the value of the assets and liabilities at different times, depending on the province that has jurisdiction over the property settlement. Alberta, for example, generally divides the property based on the value of the assets on the date of the trial for divorce. In Ontario, on the other hand, the property settlement depends on what the assets are worth on the date of separation. In the case of an investment portfolio or a business interest, the valuation date can have a huge impact on how much money is finally divided.

Given the importance of the financial statement, Cochrane insists that both parties in the cases he deals with swear to its truthfulness. That's a good idea, especially if you believe there is reason or room for deceit. Cochrane also notes that the financial statement in some provinces, such as Ontario, shows the disposition of assets for the past two years, which effectively prevents spouses from hiding or stripping away assets in anticipation of a parting. Your lawyer should ask for this anyway. The financial statement is filed with the court and so becomes public record. In some circumstances, and in certain provinces, your lawyer may be able to shield the financial statement from public view, so ask if and how some privacy can be retained.

Apart from business assets that may or may not be included in what is considered family property, some other kinds of property are usually left out of property settlements. Generally, the provinces try to divide assets acquired during a marriage and obtained because of the contribution of both spouses. The property usually left off the table includes inheritances received during your marriage, family heirlooms, proceeds from an insurance settlement, assets owned before the marriage and assets excluded through a marriage contract. These assets have to be traceable, however, and that means they have to be held separate in some way. Many people use inheritances and insurance proceeds to pay down the mortgage or renovate the house. If that money were held apart in separate investments, it would not form part of the family property, but once it's put into the house, it becomes subject to division. Your lawyer will know for sure what should be included.[5]

Once you've got everything listed, you'll find putting a value on it is not always straightforward. Some provinces specify how all assets are to be valued, such as "fair market value," while other provinces allow "current market value," "cost," "book value," "liquidation value," or value with or without costs of disposition. Again, your lawyer can advise you on the valuation method, and, of course, you can have an accountant do much of this for you.

It is important to come to an agreement with your spouse on the exact date of separation. This probably won't come as a surprise, but sometimes the official date of separation is itself contentious. Was it when you stopped sharing a bedroom or when you finally walked out? Not only is the value of family assets sometimes pegged to this date, but some provinces impose a time limit on the right to claim property and spousal support from the date of separation, so you shouldn't delay deciding on the property division, or at least registering a claim. (There is no specific time limit on application for child support, but it isn't indefinite.)

THE HOUSE YOU SHARED

The house you lived in with your spouse is called "the matrimonial home." In some provinces in Canada—for instance, British Columbia, Saskatchewan and Ontario—the value of your home is evenly shared in a marriage breakup, even if one spouse owned the house before you were married. Other jurisdictions divide only the value that accumulated after you were married. Alberta, Quebec and the Northwest Territories are among these. The courts, of course, have discretion to address inequities that may result from these rules of division. No province lets one spouse mortgage or sell a matrimonial home without the other spouse's permission, and just to be sure this doesn't happen, you can file a notice of interest at your local registry office to that effect. After your divorce, however, that protection ends—another reason not to delay registering a claim for property on separation. Any debts you have on the property, such as mortgages and liens, are equally shared and deducted from the value of the home.[6]

If you own only one residence, taxes on the sale of your house shouldn't be an issue. (Things can get more complicated with a vacation property, so we'll leave that aside for a moment.) The profit you make on the house that is known technically as your "principal residence" is not taxed. The rules let a couple declare only one dwelling as their principal residence for tax purposes, so your separation agreement needs to specify who gets to keep the principal residence designation. Once divorced, you are no longer a couple and you can both declare your own principal residences.

You can transfer a cottage or another dwelling to a spouse at its original cost when you separate and no capital gains tax will need to be paid until that property is sold.

But if you neglect to spell out who has the principal residence for tax purposes, the spouse who first sells a residence, be it the home or the cottage, can claim that as the principal residence and eliminate capital gains tax on the entire appreciation of the property. This would leave the other spouse to pay capital gains tax on the other property's appreciation from the day of purchase to the date of separation when the property is sold. After the first calendar year of a couple's legal separation, the property can be designated a principal residence so that, when it is eventually sold, capital gains tax will be calculated only on the appreciation up to the date of separation and no later. After the first calendar year of separation, each party can claim the principal residence designation on any one home that he or she sells.

PRIVATE PENSIONS

By now, you must be getting the feeling that nothing much about separation is uncomplicated. A look at pensions won't contradict this impression.

The value of private pensions you've accumulated during marriage is generally shared upon separation, but not automatically. If you live in British Columbia, Alberta, Saskatchewan, Manitoba, Ontario, Quebec or P.E.I., your pension and your spouse's pension will be shared. In the other provinces and territories, pensions are not specifically listed as property, which means the court must decide whether and how they can be shared.

Dividing a pension may sound deceptively easy, but it is fraught with pitfalls. You may have heard bitter spouses say, "She's divorcing me? Fine, I'm retiring tomorrow and she'll get nothing." Among other things, this is a strategic error. It's best for the pension plan member, says Cochrane, to assume retirement at age 65, because the value of a pension increases the earlier the benefits begin to be paid out. In any event, a pension evaluator (whom you can expect to bill between $600 and $1,000) is required to determine a pension's value if it is being shared on a lump-sum basis.

There are three approaches to sharing a pension and which is used depends on your jurisdiction. You can share the pension benefits when and if they are paid out on retirement; you can take a lump sum from your spouse without waiting for his retirement; or the pension account itself can be split into two separate pensions if the province you live in and the pension plan allows this. Your lawyer must be careful that your choice is permitted by your provincial or federal pension legislation.

Pensions can also have what are known as survivorship benefits. This is money paid to the surviving spouse of a pension plan member after the plan member's death. It is called a "joint and survivor" pension. This means that a plan member is able to elect to receive a smaller pension in exchange for survivorship benefits so the surviving spouse will continue to get a payment, usually 50% or 60% of what the plan member received during his lifetime. Pay special attention to a pension's survivorship benefits, especially if you divorce close to retirement age. As lawyer Linda Silver Dranoff warns:

> To have a chance at survivor's pension, a spouse must make sure the pension settlement is resolved before the divorce. Once divorced (and, in some jurisdictions, once separated), the non-member may lose status as a "spouse" for the purposes of the pension plan, and with it the rights to surviving spouse benefits or death benefits.[7]

There are other fine points, too. Malcolm Hamilton, a pension actuary with Mercer Human Resource Consulting in Toronto, explains that the survivor benefit goes to the person the member was married to when the member's pension began. "If the member's marriage breaks down after the pension commences," he says, "the parties can agree to divide the pension asset as they choose, subject to any constraints imposed by the law or by the plan. If a member wants to qualify a spouse acquired after the pension commences for a survivor pension, the member should check with the pension plan administrator to see if this is permitted by the plan (usually, it is not). If it is, the member's pension will usually be actuarially reduced, and the reduction can be significant if the spouse is much younger."

CANADA PENSION PLAN

Canada Pension Plan (CPP) and Quebec Pension Plan (QPP) benefits have rules of their own, but there's still some provincial variation. CPP benefits accumulated during marriage must be divided upon marriage breakdown unless you live in a province that allows spouses to contract out of this division. British Columbia, Saskatchewan and Quebec allow contracting out, and other provinces may pass legislation in the future to permit this. Where there is no opting-out legislation, you and your former spouse are obliged to share CPP benefits with each other.[8]

REGISTERED RETIREMENT SAVINGS PLANS (RRSPs)

RRSPs, Registered Retirement Income Funds (RRIFs) and other registered accounts can be divided and/or transferred to a spouse tax-free upon separation as long as it is done properly, i.e., by taking the assets from one registered account and transferring them directly to a similar account in the spouse's name. The transfer must lead directly from one registered account to the other to avoid taxation.

Suppose your spouse has an RRSP worth $300,000. You might be tempted to split that by asking for $150,000 in cash as an equalization payment. That seems reasonable until you take into account the woeful tax implications of that division. Withdrawing (otherwise known as deregistering) $150,000 from the RRSP would trigger tax at the highest marginal rate, somewhere around 46%, depending on your province. It's unfair to your spouse to have to swallow $69,000 in tax, so after you take the tax hit, you'd be left with $81,000. That hurts—which is why it is generally better not to deregister assets to make equalization payments. A simple transfer of assets from one registered account to another is a far more tax-efficient option, though, of course, tax will eventually have to be paid when those transferred assets are finally withdrawn from the account. In the meantime, you are growing and sheltering from tax a much larger asset base than you would have had otherwise. To twist an old adage, a penny in tax deferred is a penny in tax saved temporarily.

Spousal support

A lot of money in legal fees is consumed in disputes over spousal support. Many lawyers advise their clients to do everything they can to avoid spousal support because they fear that, once it starts, it may never end. Recent court rulings seem to be bolstering this fear.

You may be wanting to receive spousal support or you may be the one being asked to pay it, but let's start by supposing you're requesting support. The first thing you need is a thorough understanding of your current expenses, in other words, a detailed budget. Once you know exactly how much you spend and on what, you can accurately gauge how much income you'll need for yourself and your children. Even though child support is calculated on fairly rigid guidelines based on income, thoroughness doesn't hurt and could be a help when negotiating spousal support.

Trouble is, to get the degree of real-life detail you want, you need to review your actual spending over the past year. It's tedious, but it has to be done for big things and small. Car repairs and maintenance? Entertainment? Dry cleaning? Mortgage? Insurance? Gifts? If you might have to move out of your home, investigate moving costs, rents and other tenancy expenses. (See the worksheet in the appendix for help constructing an historically accurate budget.)

Don't put off making a claim for support. There are no time limits for claiming child support, but spousal support is a different matter, although those time limits differ from jurisdiction to jurisdiction and are not clear-cut. "Bottom line is, if you want to ensure you don't lose any rights to support, see your lawyer in a timely fashion," says Robert Micheli, a lawyer in Oakville, Ontario, who adds, "We can't tell you what a 'timely fashion' is exactly, but we can say don't waste any time at it."

If you're the one trying to fend off a claim for spousal support, you may consider making a generous property division or a lump-sum payment instead of ongoing spousal support, but be forewarned that this may not save you from having to pay spousal support for your spouse's lifetime. Current cases before the courts are reopening some cases where a spouse is in need despite receiving what was thought to have been a large lump-sum payment.

Be completely frank with your lawyer, too. Talk about every worry, concern or potential problem you see. Separation agreements can touch on any and all aspects of your marriage, including the division of property, support obligations, custody and visitation of the children, the education and religious instruction of the children, and whatever else needs to be laid out. Things assumed and left unspecified can often lead to emotionally draining and costly disputes later on. If you are worried that your spouse might not fully disclose or sell assets, your lawyer can send your spouse's lawyer a letter to confirm that no assets will be altered without your consent.

Tax considerations

Taxes play a big part in an efficient separation, so let's take a closer look at how they affect property division and support payments.

DIVISION OF PROPERTY
CAPITAL GAINS OF SPOUSAL ROLLOVERS

Normally, when one person gives or transfers an asset to another person, the transaction is considered a sale at fair market value (a.k.a. "deemed disposition") and CCRA starts totalling up capital gains tax. Fortunately, when property is divided between a couple as a result of a settlement agreement, the transfers do not attract tax. Dividing up your property should not have any immediate tax consequences for you or your former spouse because the property is transferred at its original cost base. In other words, there are no realized capital gains or losses in the division of property unless you elect to claim them, which may sometimes be useful.

Here's a situation where you might consider electing to realize capital gains or losses. Suppose you have a mutual fund you lost money on, but you also have a stock Aunt Sally recommended that actually made you a profit. You might elect to treat the transfer of your mutual fund as a sale at fair market value so the capital loss can be used to offset the capital gain on your stock. On the other hand, if you are also transferring the stock to your spouse, it may be more advantageous to transfer that—and any other asset with a capital gain—at its original cost base if your spouse is in a lower tax bracket. That way, less tax goes into CCRA's coffers overall.

A word of caution, though: Once a divorce is final, these spousal rollovers stop being tax-free and are treated like any other deemed disposition.

TAX ATTRIBUTION RULES

There's one other tax rule that can work in your favour, but only with a written separation agreement or court order. It has to do with the tax attribution rules. Attribution rules were put in place to prevent income splitting in families. A family member in a high tax bracket used to be able to give or loan securities or other assets to a family member in a lower income bracket and pay less tax on that investment income but still have the benefit of actually owning it. The attribution rules short-circuit this ploy by requiring the person gifting or loaning an asset to a spouse to pay tax on the income and capital gains from that asset—unless the transfer is arranged through a loan with a prescribed interest rate.

Two kinds of attribution are at work here, capital gains attribution and income attribution. "Income" refers to the interest and dividend from an investment. "Capital gains or losses" refers to the profit or loss from the sale of an asset. When you have a written separation agreement or a court order, income attribution ends. Capital gains attribution, however, continues until the separated parties file an election to waive the capital gains attribution or become divorced. Without a written separation agreement or court order, the attribution rules for both income and capital gains continue as they would for a couple that is still together.

This sounds pretty theoretical, but it can have very concrete consequences that are easy to stumble over. Suppose in your division of assets your spouse wants to transfer some mutual funds to you. Unless you agree otherwise, the transfer will be non-taxable and you'll get the mutual funds along with their capital gains liability (if they've made money since they were first purchased). You will have to pay tax on the interest and dividends—the income—the mutual funds generate, because income attribution ends with a formal separation. But if you sell these mutual funds before the divorce is final, your spouse will have to report the capital gains and pay the tax on it. Capital gains attribution doesn't automatically end at separation, which is why you must consider explicitly waiving the capital gains attribution.

SPOUSAL RRSPS

If your eyes aren't completely glazed over by attribution rules yet, get ready for the eye drops. There's one more.

Spousal RRSPs have an attribution rule of their own that also changes with a written separation agreement or court order. A spousal RRSP is an RRSP in which the contributor is different from the person whose name is on the account (the annuitant). These registered spousal accounts are used by couples to equalize their retirement savings and make a better division of their income in retirement. Rather than the higher-income earner always having the larger RRSP, and consequently a higher retirement income, spousal RRSPs allow a spouse to contribute to an account in his or her partner's name but still claim the tax deduction at the contributing spouse's marginal tax rate. This is a good thing, and one of the very few income-splitting devices left to Canadians. (We'll talk more about spousal RRSPs in the investing chapter.)

There is a catch. The contributing spouse will be taxed on any withdrawals from a spousal account that happen in the calendar year of a contribution and in the two calendar years following a contribution. That means a contribution to a spousal RRSP normally must remain in the account, with no other intervening contributions, for the year in which you contributed it and the two calendar years thereafter. If you break these rules, the withdrawal is treated as income for the person who originally contributed the money, regardless of who actually took the money out. The person whose name is on the account may actually be enjoying the benefit of that money while a spouse is paying the tax bill. It seems unfair, but this attribution rule is needed. Without it, couples could contribute to a spousal RRSP, deduct the contribution at a high tax rate, then quickly take the money out in the name of the lower-income spouse and subsequently pay less tax on the deregistration than the deduction gained from the contribution. You can imagine a spousal contributor getting some unpleasant surprises if this rule were still in force through a separation. Once you're separated, you have to pay the tax for the withdrawals from your own account, regardless of who made the contributions in the first place and how recently those contributions were made.

In an aggravating but necessary technicality, spousal accounts always show the name of the contributor even after divorce. Unfortunately, there's just no getting away from it.

SUPPORT PAYMENTS

There are two kinds of support payments—child support and spousal support. And this shouldn't surprise you by now, but they have different tax treatments as long as certain conditions are met.

First of all, these payments must be designated as spousal or child support in the separation agreement or court order. They also must be made as a result of an agreement or order. And, finally, you and your spouse must be living separately and apart (though the courts sometimes have a peculiar interpretation of what exactly that means).[9] If these conditions aren't meet, CCRA will consider all payments as child support, which is not a great outcome for the person paying the support. Child support is non-deductible for the person paying it and completely non-taxable for the person receiving it.[10] Spousal support, on the other hand, is deductible to the person paying it and taxable to the person receiving it. Since the person paying spousal support is often in a higher tax bracket than the person receiving the payment, the taxation of spousal support often results in an overall tax savings.

To capitalize on this, some experts have suggested classifying as much in spousal support and as little in child support as possible. Their argument goes like this.

Let's assume Bob is paying support to Alice. Bob is in a 45% marginal tax bracket. Alice is in a marginal tax bracket of 30%. Assume Bob pays Alice a combination of spousal and child support payments totalling $40,000 a year. Here are three different ways they could arrange their payments and how taxes will affect the payments.

How Taxes Affect Spousal and Child Support Payments

PAYMENT TYPE	TAXABLE / NON-TAXABLE	TOTAL CASH PAID	NET AFTER TAX AT 45% FOR BOB	NET AFTER TAX AT 30% FOR ALICE
Scenario 1 (50:50)				
Spousal support	Taxable	$20,000	$11,000	$14,000
Child support	Non-taxable	$20,000	$20,000	$20,000
Total cash paid		$40,000		
Net			$31,000	$34,000
Scenario 2 (75:25)				
Spousal support	Taxable	$30,000	$16,500	$21,000
Child support	Non-taxable	$10,000	$10,000	$10,000
Total cash paid		$40,000		
Net			$26,500	$31,000
Scenario 3 (25:75)				
Spousal support	Taxable	$10,000	$5,500	$7,000
Child support	Non-taxable	$30,000	$30,000	$30,000
Total cash paid		$40,000		
Net			$35,500	$37,000

> Alice wants to maximize her total support payments, while Bob wants to minimize his after-tax payments. Tax planning can help them both win.

Naturally, Bob wants the lowest after-tax cost. At a marginal rate of 45%, it's best to have more of his payments as spousal support (scenario 2), since $40,000 in payments gives an actual out-of-pocket expense of only $26,500.

On the other hand, Alice wants the highest after-tax income, which means she wants more of the payments as child support (scenario 3). The lower the tax bracket Alice is in, the more money she keeps. If Alice were in a 45% marginal tax bracket, she would keep $35,500. If Alice pays tax at a marginal rate of 30%, she keeps even more: $37,000.[11]

The difference between these arrangements is dramatic. Bob stands to reduce his total cost by 25% in his most favourable scenario (scenario 2), but Alice's take is reduced by 16% from her most favourable scenario. If level heads prevail, it is possible for Alice and Bob to negotiate a fair after-tax cost for both of them.

There are a few cautions in this arrangement, however. If the money deducted as spousal support is actually intended for child support, the deductions stand a chance of being retroactively disallowed. Telltale signs of the real intended purpose for the money include stopping or reducing payments when a child finishes school, moves out or gets married, so give thoughtful attention to how support payments are intended and structured.

Since May 1, 1997, child support payments have been calculated based on a federal formula pegged to the non-custodial parent's income. Unless you and your spouse can agree to set the formula aside, or you can show good reasons for why this formula would be unfair in your situation, there isn't a lot of room to maneuver between what is classified as spousal and what is paid as child support.

Whether or not you have some flexibility in how you structure support payments, at the very least be sure they meet all the conditions to make them support payments in the eyes of CCRA, especially if you are the one paying spousal support. Don't ignore inflation either. Separation agreements usually include an automatic cost-of-living increase, so make sure your agreement has one if you are the one receiving the payments.

LUMP-SUM SUPPORT PAYMENTS

Sometimes support payments don't materialize even though they've been ordered by the court or agreed to in a separation agreement. When support payments fall into default, they can be paid back in a lump sum. Fortunately, the spouse getting the money from defaulted payments doesn't have to declare it all in one year and take a big tax hit. CCRA has a form (T1198) that allows certain lump-sum payments to be averaged over past tax years so the recipient is no worse off for having received a lump sum rather than regular instalments.

Unless they are from already registered assets, such as an RRSP or a RRIF, lump-sum support payments cannot be sheltered in an RRSP above and beyond the normally allowable contribution limit. If your spouse is transferring assets to you from a registered savings account, you can roll these into a corresponding account of your own. If the money is not from a registered account, you can put it in your RRSP only insofar as you have available contribution room in your account.

Generally, lump-sum payments are not deductible for the person who pays and are not taxable for the person who receives them; but as you might expect, there are some exceptions to this general rule. When it comes to taxes, when large amounts of money are at stake—and a proportionately large potential tax liability—it is always best to consult an accountant. This book should help you ask the right questions and save you time and fees, so bear with the tedious tax material in this chapter just a little longer.

TAX CREDITS AND BENEFITS THAT MAY BE AFFECTED BY SUPPORT PAYMENTS

Tax rules are notoriously complicated. Apart from the tax consequences of dividing property and negotiating support payments, there are other, smaller tax considerations that may affect you—some of them good.

If you are separated but taking care of a child, infirm parent or grandparent, you may be able to claim an equivalent-to-spouse tax credit.[12] This meant up to $1,400 in tax credits in 2001.

You can also usually claim childcare expenses as a deduction to your income even if you share custody of your child with your spouse. In a married household, the lower-income earner must claim the childcare expenses for federal taxes, but in the case of separated couples who have been living "separate and apart" for at least 90 days and continued to be separate and apart at the end of the year, the higher-income earner may be entitled to claim the childcare expenses. Once a separated couple has been apart for a whole year, each parent may claim childcare expenses (to the extent that they are incurred by the respective parent) for the same children. In 2001, the maximum deduction limit was $7,000 for each disabled child or children under seven years old and $4,000 for each child between the ages of seven and 16.

Child tax benefits that are paid monthly go to the parent with the primary responsibility for the care of the children. A benefit is paid for each child, depending on the age of the child, and the number of children in the family. The maximum benefit in 2002 for the first child was

$93 (unless you live in Alberta, where the payments rise as the child ages to top out at $108 for children 16 or 17 years old). These payments start getting clawed back when net family income reaches $32,000. Families with one or two children and a net income over $75,000—or families with three children and an income over $99,000—won't see any cheques in the mail for them.

CAN LEGAL FEES BE DEDUCTED?

Many people mistakenly believe that legal fees to get a separation or divorce are tax-deductible. They aren't, and unfortunately, that's where the clarity ends on this issue. Andrew Freedman's professional guide, called *The Tax Principles of Family Law*, says recent court decisions have made the tax deductibility of legal fees unclear, but this much is fairly sure:

Legal fees relating to the following are not tax-deductible:
- Obtaining a divorce or negotiating a separation agreement;
- Establishing a right to spousal support after divorce, even if subsequently provided for under a court order or written agreement; and
- Lump-sum spousal support amounts.[13]

It does seem that fees for enforcing a pre-existing right to spousal support can be deductible, as apparently they are incurred to defend against a reduction in support (spousal and child). Petitions to *increase* spousal or child support are not deductible, but legal costs to get an order for child support generally are. Just to be sure, you should check with your accountant for the latest CCRA interpretations on the deductibility of legal fees and have your lawyer break out the fees separately for work related to spousal and child support.

What happens should one of you die during separation?

It's a terrible prospect and one I hope you don't have to face, but the possibility of a spouse dying during separation brings up important estate planning issues that need to be considered.

Suppose you and your spouse recently separated but you haven't yet worked out a separation agreement and neither of you have wills—

hardly a far-fetched situation, in my experience. Suddenly your spouse dies. Do you know what will happen to his/your estate? In Ontario and Quebec, his estate will be transferred to you just as it would for a surviving spouse. In other provinces, though, a separation may disentitle the surviving spouse from claims to the estate.

If there was a separation agreement in place, his estate would be divided according to the agreement. Separation agreements usually release the spouses from claims on each other's estates, so the separation agreement will take precedence over the will unless the will was made in the knowledge of a separation and/or a divorce.[14] A gift to a former spouse that is made in a will must say that the gift is being made in light of the separation and/or divorce; otherwise, the gift could be invalidated. It's a good precaution to update your will when you're separated.

We'll talk more about the importance of a will in the estate planning chapter, but by now it should be clear that a written separation agreement is a critical piece of protection for both you and your spouse.

Health insurance

Health insurance is easy to overlook, but it, too, must be reviewed on your separation. In most cases, separated spouses can continue to be carried on their partner's policy until they are divorced, but it may not be a good idea. Doing so could leave you unknowingly without coverage if it's your spouse who is the health insurance plan member. His plan probably lets him opt for single coverage or substitute a common-law spouse in the coverage without notifying you. You could have insurance one day and be without it the next. Your lawyer might require your estranged spouse to give you notification whenever a beneficiary designation is changed, but as this is not exactly a beneficiary change, it could slip through the cracks.

What happens when a common-law partner enters the picture during separation?

Apart from the caution about health insurance coverage, there are a few other things to watch out for when a common-law partner enters the equation during separation. Life insurance, pension plan and RRSP beneficiaries could be changed without your knowledge. Of course, this could happen at any time, but it is most likely to happen with a new partner in the picture.

If you are the one with the new partner, there may be tax ramifications you didn't anticipate. The friendly equivalent-to-spouse credit and the childcare expenses may be affected. As we said before, if you are not married but are supporting a minor child, someone infirm, or a parent or grandparent, you can claim the equivalent-to-spouse tax credit. Childcare expenses are tax deductible for you, too, but these tax breaks could be affected by the start of a common-law relationship. As far as CCRA is concerned, a common-law relationship takes one year to establish unless there is a child. If someone with a child enters a relationship and becomes financially dependent on a new partner, he or she could lose the equivalent-to-spouse credit for the child even within the first year of the relationship. If the new partner has a lower income than you do, you will not be able to claim the childcare expenses. Your common-law partner will have to claim them and you could very well end up paying more tax because of the relationship. In addition, all payments and benefits that are pegged to family income, such as GST/HST (QST in Quebec) rebates and child tax benefits, could also be affected. And remember that only one partner can designate a principal residence for tax purposes.

It's not all bad news, though. Common-law partners can transfer disability credits, charitable donations and tuition, age, education and pension credits between themselves.

What Constitutes a Common-law Partner?
CCRA has this handy definition:

For income tax purposes, a common-law partner is a person of the opposite or same sex who at that particular time is living with you in a common-law relationship and is the natural or adoptive parent of your child, or who is living with you in a common-law relationship and has been living common-law with you for at least 12 continuous months, or lived with you previously as your spouse or common-law partner for at least 12 continuous months. This includes any period that you were separated for less than 90 days because of a breakdown in the relationship. You still have a spouse or common-law partner if you are living apart for reasons other than a breakdown in your relationship.[15]

Tax laws in Canada try to be completely neutral with respect to married, common-law or same-sex common-law arrangements. Other areas of the government are not as uniform. Common-law partners may claim spousal benefits from the Canada Pension Plan as long as there is no legal spouse to claim priority, but here the definition of common-law partner is slightly different: "For the purpose of the Canada Pension Plan ... [a] common-law partner is a person of either sex, with whom you have been living in a conjugal relationship for at least one year."[16] Having a child involved in the relationship makes no difference to the CPP definition.

Actually, the definition of common-law spouse or partner varies from jurisdiction to jurisdiction. The tax people have their own definition, CPP another, and the provinces each have their own again. The provinces get involved because the division of property, separation and common-law relationships are dealt with in provincial legislation. Divorce, which applies only to married couples, falls under the federal *Divorce Act* and is dealt with federally. Who said this would be easy?

Separation of common-law partners

Common-law arrangements don't foster as many rights as commonly believed. In most provinces, when a common-law relationship breaks down, the partners walk out with what they brought in. Neither partner has a statutory right to property apart from that brought into the relationship. There is no immediate claim to the matrimonial home, for example, as in a married relationship. Sure, the courts will divide some property if one of the partners can prove a contribution to it, but, as you can imagine, that can get pretty messy and expensive to put before a judge. Saskatchewan and Nova Scotia courts have found that this state of affairs was discriminatory and that common-law spouses should be entitled to property rights similar to those of married spouses. At the time of writing, this issue was pending before the Supreme Court of Canada.

People may not have the right to much by way of property in a common-law relationship yet, but some provinces do seem to recognize the right to support. Here it is important to know your province's criteria for determining a common-law partnership. To give you an example of how varied these definitions can be, Ontario and Saskatchewan stipulate three years of cohabitation, or a child and a relationship of some permanence. British Columbia, on the other hand, requires only two years of cohabitation (with no mention of a child) to recognize a common-law relationship.

Recognizing a relationship and giving it legal consequences when it breaks down are two different things, and some provinces have yet to enact legislation extending rights of support to common-law partners. Alberta, Quebec, P.E.I and the Northwest Territories do not give partners entitlement to support when a common-law relationship ends.

Divorce

In Canada over one-third of marriages eventually end in divorce. The chart on the next page shows how divorce statistics break down across the country. It's not a pretty picture.

A divorce can be granted quickly on grounds of adultery or cruelty, but most couples simply wait out a year of separation. It's not an easy year, but at least most of the upheaval should be behind you, unless you haven't been able to arrive at a separation agreement. In that case, you may be proceeding to court for a judge to decide the outstanding issues.

It is very easy to lose a significant portion of your net worth going through divorce court, and my view is that lawyers should do everything they can to keep their divorcing clients out of court. Furthermore, the final settlement is very often not all that different from an offer made earlier in the conflict but when the parties were in a less rational—or perhaps less realistic—state of mind.

The best advice on every front, emotionally and financially, is to settle your differences as amicably as possible so you don't have to see the inside of a court. If you have children, this is doubly important.

In his family law book, Michael Cochrane is outspoken about how damaging, wasteful and unproductive divorce conflicts can be, but he's

Percentage of Marriages Expected to End in Divorce within 30 Years

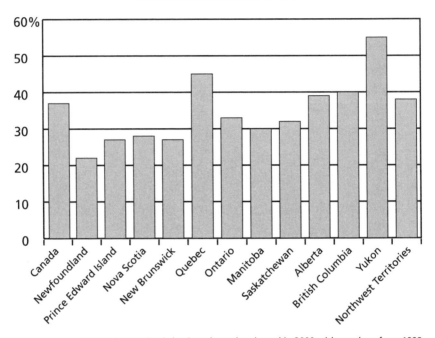

Source: From a Statistics Canada study released in 2000 with numbers from 1998.

Newfoundland and the Yukon are Canada's extremes in matrimonial success.

found that some of the emotions that lead to these unfortunate conflicts can be managed with some understanding of the natural progression of feelings in a marriage breakdown. Cochrane believes the stages of grief over the breakdown of a family relationship parallel Kubler-Ross's stages of dealing with death: denial and isolation, anger, bargaining, depression and acceptance. Understanding this grieving process, he says, may give "a rare cue to a person's motivation when instructing his or her lawyer."[17]

What that means in practice for him is that a reasonable settlement put before a client still in the anger stage stands a good chance of being rebuffed, while the same terms would be more rationally considered in the acceptance stage. Cochrane warns particularly about the bargaining stage, where he often sees unrealistic promises made to put off the unpleasantness.

The bargaining may manifest itself in overly generous settlement proposals—"She can have everything." Sometimes the offer is no more than a weak attempt to ease guilt or to prove to the other spouse that "I'm not so bad after all." "I'm the one who left. He can keep the house." Unfortunately but not surprisingly, such promises are rarely wise or kept. The client's interests have not been advanced, in fact they may have been harmed.... Lawyers and clients alike must be alert to these motivations and recognize that instructions during this phase of false bargaining are unlikely to produce lasting settlements. They will however produce a legal bill...and you will wonder later what you are paying for."[18]

Cochrane says lawyers can manage their client's emotional responses by giving them time to work through the stages of the grieving process. Delays are not always bad in these circumstances.

Perhaps you're wondering if you should even take the next step to divorce. Why not stay separated indefinitely? People do, but most often spouses want to disentangle themselves from each other. Much of what needs to be done upon divorce can be done during separation, but here's a list of important things that should be reviewed by the time the divorce becomes final.

Life, health and dental insurance: You will probably want to change the beneficiary on your life insurance. Minor children cannot be life insurance beneficiaries, so if you want your children to get your death benefits you may want to consider a trust arrangement for them, which you can do with the help of your lawyer. (You'll find more on trusts in the estate planning chapter.) If you were a member of a group plan through your spouse's employer, you will need to take out a new policy for yourself and your dependants, as it is highly unlikely you will be permitted to continue on as a single member in your former spouse's group coverage once you are divorced. (During separation insurance companies consider the separated spouse a dependant and continue coverage.) Many group life insurance policies come with a convertibility feature that allows you to convert to individual life coverage at any time without proof of insurability. This isn't necessarily the best course, because insurance companies often figure people convert because they don't qualify for individual coverage elsewhere and the price of coverage reflects that added risk.

Evaluate the medical and life coverage you have through the group coverage and decide what benefits need to be replaced. You can approach the company providing the group coverage for a cost and qualifications break on individual insurance in light of your divorce. You may not get any concessions, but it's always worth asking.

RRSPs, RRIFs and pension plans: With these, again, examine the beneficiary designation. Your beneficiary on these plans is most likely your former spouse. You'll probably want to change that, but be careful about designating your estate as the beneficiary. Doing so could subject your RRSP to unnecessary probate fees. (See the estate planning chapter.) Your survivorship benefits under your former spouse's pension plan could be affected by your divorce. It is the spouse at the time the pension commences who is entitled to survivorship benefits.

Credit cards, bank and investment accounts, and lines of credit: You should have your own credit card(s), savings and chequing accounts, line of credit and an RRSP account during your marriage. This is a good time to talk to your financial services provider and get to know the full line of services it can offer you. It is very important to establish your own credit history. Otherwise, you can find yourself without a credit card and unable to rent a car or make purchases over the Internet. You will also need an investment account to manage the money from your settlement that you can't shelter in your RRSP.

Registered Education Savings Plans (RESPs): These accounts pose something of a problem if your child does not use the money for further education. RESP plans generally have a mechanism to let you reclaim your capital contributions. Under certain conditions, the growth on these contributions can be put into your RRSP, up to a maximum of $50,000, as long as you have enough unused contribution room to shelter this money. Since the subscriber is the one who gets to harvest the RESP money should your child not be eligible to receive those funds, you and your former partner will have to decide who will be the subscriber.

Mortgage, house insurance, utilities, household bills, credit cards and other debts: Your mortgage was mostly likely held jointly. That will probably have to be changed, based on how you've decided to divide the house, and you will have to notify all the utility companies of the change in billing, if there is one. Other bills and accounts also have to be changed from joint to single, especially credit cards. Couples commonly have two credit cards for one account, which makes them both responsible for the debt on that account.

Car and car insurance: If ownership of the car changes, the car's registration and insurance will have to be changed.

Will and power of attorney: You probably don't still want to give your former spouse your estate on your death, nor do you likely want your former spouse to have control over your finances and/or personal care if you are incapacitated, so these documents should be redrafted. Divorce can invalidate wills, but separation doesn't necessarily do so.

Passport: If you intend to change your name, don't forget to apply for another passport, and update other pieces of identification.

It's a lot to deal with, but in the future you may be able to call upon the services of a "certified divorce planner." These are financial advisors with extra training to help clients deal with the financial details of separation and divorce. This designation is more popular in the United States but a version of the certification program has recently been introduced to Canada and you could see this designation becoming more widespread here in the next few years.

Another word on spousal support

In recent years, judges have appeared quite willing to revisit the terms of separation and divorce agreements. In 2000, an Ontario Superior Court judge ordered Mr. P., a wealthy stockbroker, to pay his former wife $5,000 a month in temporary support pending trial.

Mr. P. had been married to Ms. B. for 20 years. The couple split in 1985 with a generous division of assets. Mr. P.'s spousal support payments ended in 1990, and since then, Ms. B. had been unsuccessful in establishing herself in a business while Mr. P.'s career has flourished. Just before trial, the parties agreed to settle on $7,000 a month for life.

This case and others like it indicate that separation agreements are not necessarily final. It's a good thing to remember, whichever side you are on. Agreements, it seems, need to be fair and remain fair.

Marriage or remarriage

Having money makes romantic involvements more complicated. You'll likely be torn between the optimism of a solid, lifetime relationship as a team in which everything is shared, and knowing that protecting your wealth is prudent and wise. Somehow, thinking about a marriage contract seems crass, materialistic, mistrustful and opposed to all the values that make you want to marry in the first place. It's almost impossible not to feel this way, but in the end it's misguided and downright harmful. Given the grim divorce statistics, no one could blame you for wanting to protect yourself with a marriage contract. Statistics Canada says 36% of marriages are likely to end in divorce within 30 years of the vows. A good marriage will not be affected by a marriage contract, but it will protect at least one aspect of your life from a bad one. Think of it as a kind of insurance: You don't need it when times are good, but it's a good thing to have when things go wrong. And, if you have older children from a previous marriage, they'll be able to relax and perhaps accept your new partner more easily if they know their interests have been looked after.

Marriage contracts

"A marriage contract is the most sophisticated financial planning tool that most couples can use. It's a financial planning device, not a divorce device," said Cochrane in an interview. "It can do lots of things. You can put your will and your marriage contract all in one document. You can protect a business, protect yourself from creditors, protect your estate, children and assets from a first marriage—all kinds of things."

Despite all these tremendous advantages, people remain reluctant to use marriage contracts because they have a sense of defeat about them, an underlying pessimism that lawyers and financial planners should do more to dismiss.

Most commonly signed before the big day, a marriage contract can be made any time before or after marriage. (Perhaps it's best to avoid bringing it up on an anniversary.) The courts, it seems, will enforce such a contract so long as it doesn't contradict general terms of contract law and your province's family law. In those provinces where a spouse has a right to possession (but not necessarily ownership) of the matrimonial home, for instance, a party cannot waive that right in a marriage contract. It is possible to waive a claim to ownership of the matrimonial home, but not the right to live in that home when the marriage breaks up.

SOME OF THE THINGS A MARRIAGE CONTRACT MIGHT TOUCH ON

- Division of property upon separation and death
- Duration and extent of spousal support after separation
- Financial obligation to stepchildren during and after the marriage
- Religious instruction and schooling preferences for children
- Financial responsibilities of each spouse during marriage

You and your partner must negotiate the contract with full financial disclosure because being less than completely honest can invalidate the contract. You should both have independent legal advice if you want the contract to have a better chance of standing up in court, and neither side can be pressured into it under "duress" or with "undue influence"—legal terms that may not be easy to prove in court, but you get the idea.

One thing a marriage contract can't address is child custody for the children from your marriage, because the courts have final say over what is in the best interests of the children when a marriage breaks up.

Marriage contracts and your will

Working out a marriage contract is an ideal time to make a new will for a number of reasons and not just convenience. For one thing, marriage invalidates your old will unless it was drawn up in anticipation of your marriage and says so. If you die with an old will that does not recognize your marriage, the courts will treat your estate as though you died with no will at all, which means your estate will be distributed in keeping with standard rules for those who die intestate and not necessarily according to your wishes.

Marriage contracts and wills are best designed together. Since a marriage contract can be changed only with the written consent of both parties whereas a will can be changed privately at any time, property division on death should be spelled out in the marriage contract and not left to the will. Your new spouse will have to be written into your will as a beneficiary, but, at the same time, you might want your marriage contract to call for your spouse to release all claims to your estate (insofar as provincial family law allows) in the event of a separation and to accept the terms of your will without change. There is no general rule as to which document takes precedence in the case of a discrepancy between a marriage contract and a will, but you can imagine that it could be messy and costly to sort out once the person who made the will dies.

When couples separate, the law tries to achieve some sort of fair division of assets, but when one spouse dies, the surviving partner can actually be considerably worse off financially than a separated spouse. Most people give the majority of their property to their spouse in their wills. The children have to wait until their last parent dies before they come into the bulk of their inheritance. Some people, never happy with the natural order, have been known to skip this step and give just about everything to the children or some favourite charity while leaving the surviving spouse with meager financial resources.

A number of provinces have addressed this problem by imposing provincial property division rules on married people's estates. Alberta, Saskatchewan, Ontario, Quebec, Nova Scotia and Newfoundland have laws to this effect.[19] Ontario allows a bereaved spouse to accept the inheritance as set out in the will or have the estate divided as it would have been had the couple separated. Opting to have the estate divided by provincial rules means other beneficiaries will be affected and the original intention of the will overthrown.

Drafting your will and your marriage contract together means you are less likely to run afoul of family law provisions and have your spouse challenge your last will and testament. Individuals can apply to the courts for a variance to a will, which is essentially an application to have the terms of the will changed. This is good to know if you are the one feeling shortchanged, and it's also an incentive to make sure your will is properly drafted so your wishes have a better chance of withstanding a challenge.

How to Help Your Partner Accept a Marriage Contract

According to author and divorce lawyer Michael Cochrane, three times more marriage contracts get drawn up than are implemented. Here are three things to do to improve your chances of getting your partner to agree to co-operate.

Step 1: Make sure you clearly understand why you want a marriage contract. Saying your family wants one or you think it's a good idea likely wouldn't be terribly persuasive. Set out what you expect a contract to do for both of you and be able to explain why you think it's a good idea.

Step 2: Gather the advice of professionals to generate a number of options. There are different ways to hold and structure assets, and some of them have tax advantages too. You may find you can do your will and your contract in one document, which will also help you with step 1.

Step 3: Now broach the idea with your future partner. Do it sensitively and leave plenty of time for consideration. A month before the wedding isn't enough. Your partner will need time to consult his own lawyer and give some thought to his own estate planning needs.

Life insurance

You'll also probably need to revise your insurance coverage, since there's one more person added to your family whom you have to provide for in the event of your death. If you have children from a previous marriage, they might even be willing to pay for this insurance, as it will leave more of your estate for them. Be sure to include them in any discussions.

Other cautions

Have an open discussion and exchange of information with your future partner about money, your financial positions, and your spending and saving habits. Lots of people have a hard time talking about money but no problem at all fighting about it later. On a decidedly unromantic note, you might consider exchanging your personal credit reports with each other. It's free, and it will give you a good insight into your future partner's money management skills.[20] You can contact one of the two personal credit rating services in Canada—Equifax at 1-800-465-7166 or Trans-Union at 1-800-663-9980—for a copy of your own credit report, but you can't get a report on someone else.

This brings up another money management caution. You should always have your own chequing account and a joint chequing account to pay household and living expenses. This not only protects your money, it helps you budget how much of your monthly income goes into the joint account.

Living together

Marriage is a big step. The legal entanglements when it doesn't work out are daunting, so it's no wonder more and more people are living together before walking down the aisle. For some, living together is a test; for others it's a more permanent arrangement. But you'd be mistaken if you think living together exempts you from a lot of the obligations married couples owe each other. Here, again, you need some protection if things don't work out.

Get a cohabitation agreement

As we have already seen, each province sets its own definition of a common-law partner. Some require only one year of living together whereas others require as much as three. But once you've met the conditions of a legally recognized common-law relationship, responsibilities ensue. Although it is not yet widely done, it's a good idea to get a cohabitation agreement in place well before achieving common-law status to set out the rights and obligations of the partners should the relationship end. If it doesn't and the relationship advances to marriage, a cohabitation agreement automatically becomes a marriage contract.

If you're considering a relationship with a partner who brings a child into the relationship, do consult a family law lawyer. You could become financially responsible for a stepchild after the end of the relationship. A cohabitation agreement may not protect you from this, but it can set out terms that would make it less likely for a court to subsequently order child support payments.

CPP benefits and common-law partners

Common-law couples (which include same-sex couples) are entitled to the same benefits as married couples. But CCRA has this warning:

> It is important that couples record their marital status in the same way for all benefits. If you do not report your common-law relationship for the Guaranteed Income Supplement (GIS) or the Allowance, it may affect your or your partner's eligibility for other benefits in the future (e.g., CPP survivor benefits).[21]

The government also urges couples to notify Human Resources Development Canada when their marital status changes to avoid being overpaid benefits and having to repay them.

Common-law partners can get spousal support, too

As we discussed before (and subject to a pending Supreme Court ruling), common-law partners do not have an automatic right to "family" property when the relationship ends. Each partner is entitled to what that person brought into the relationship and what he or she can prove was contributed to during the relationship. Some provinces do, however, recognize the right of common-law partners to spousal support once the relationship ends. Common-law partners seeking spousal support are generally out of luck in Alberta, Quebec, P.E.I. and the Northwest Territories because these provinces do not currently recognize the right of common-law partners to such support.

Widowhood

The sad truth is that most of us will end our lives alone. And the anguish of losing your husband is not made any easier by the confusion of new and possibly unfamiliar financial responsibilities. I always urge couples to keep each other informed about their money decisions. Not only does it make for greater peace of mind throughout the marriage, it avoids the painful confusion of trying to put together all the financial pieces of a lifetime.

The estate generally

Most likely, your husband appointed you or a trusted friend as the executor of his will and directed the bulk of his estate be passed to you. The executor is the legal owner of the estate on behalf of the beneficiaries and must identify all the assets, make sure they're secure and gain control over them. The executor is responsible to the beneficiaries for the assets at the date of death and may have to buy insurance to protect the value of real estate, issue cease trading orders on discretionary accounts and generally do everything possible to preserve the value of the estate, including keeping a mindful eye on triggering capital gains tax liability.

Business interests

If your husband owned a business, you will have to see a lawyer to deal with the business promptly. Its fate will depend in great part on its legal structure—a sole proprietorship, partnership or corporation—and the succession arrangements already in place. The estate's executor will have to wind up or sell a sole proprietorship. In a partnership, the estate assumes ownership of the deceased's partnership interest, which is typically bought out by the remaining partners. The disposition of a private corporation's shares is dictated by the terms of the shareholders agreement, if there is one. If there isn't, the shares could be bought by other shareholders, bequeathed to a spouse or someone else, or go into the estate to be subsequently sold or retained within the estate.

Naming new guardians for your children

Your minor children will need to be looked after in case of your death so you should appoint a guardian for them. This is done in your will, which can also be, but doesn't necessarily have to be, wholly revised at that time.

Apply for CPP death and survivorship benefits

You should also apply for CPP death and survivor benefits. A death benefit is generally paid directly to the surviving spouse. Survivorship benefits are paid to your husband's estate but not automatically; you have to apply for them.[22] Common-law and same-sex spouses are also entitled to these CPP benefits.

Change beneficiary designations

You'll likely need to change all your beneficiary designations on RRSPs, pensions and insurance.

A terminal tax return is important

The tax returns for someone who has died can be quite complicated and, for the knowledgeable, there's a chance to do some tax planning. Seek out a good accountant to do the returns, especially the terminal return. Although an executor cannot make an RRSP contribution on behalf of the deceased, it is possible to make a spousal contribution within 60 days of the end of the year in which your spouse died if he had contribution room available. This will save the estate taxes and give you a better retirement income.

Don't be in a hurry to give money away to your children

Giving money to your children or putting money in trust for them is not necessarily a bad idea if you are confident you have enough for your own future, but don't give money thinking you will be able to call it back when you need it. Giving it away means losing control of it legally and quite often practically. Joint accounts aren't necessarily the answer, either. Each joint owner has a claim on 100% of the assets in a jointly held asset. If your child has financial difficulties, what you hold jointly could be sought by your child's creditors. (See the estate planning chapter for more information on transferring your wealth to your children.)

Also be sure all taxes are paid on the estate before giving money away. An unexpected tax bill could leave you with a lot less money than you may have anticipated.

"Knowledge, combined with action, is power."
Anonymous

Falling in and out of love, living together or being married, finding ourselves suddenly alone—these emotional circumstances can have profound financial consequences. It's hard not to be buffeted by these changes in our lives, but a good grasp of the fundamentals could help you structure your finances in a way you might not have considered otherwise. A marriage contract or a cohabitation agreement, for instance, could end up saving you money and grief. The same is true for a separation agreement. It is always best to negotiate from strength, and being aware of what is on the line financially is a big part of that strength.

Understanding some basic tax and family law considerations will also permit you to use professionals more efficiently and advantageously when you need them. Manage the tax and family law implications of your personal arrangements, and you can protect your wealth and the financial foundation for your future happiness. Without this savvy, your wealth could be as deeply hurt as your heart. There's a lot to consider, and it's important to make informed choices and do what makes sense for you.

Notes

1. As reported in Linda Silver Dranoff, *Everyone's Guide to the Law: A Handbook for Canadians*, rev. ed. (Toronto: HarperCollins 2001), 238. The StatsCan figures were derived from an examination of tax files from 1987 to 1993.
2. "Canadian Divorce Statistics, 1998." **DivorceMagazine.com**, 24 July 2002. **www.divorcemagazine.com/statistics/statsCAN.shtml.**
3. You can find these guidelines at the Department of Justice's Web site, **www.canada.justice.gc.ca/en/ps/sup/grl/ligfed.html.**
4. Kirk Makin, "Child-Support Case Sets Record." *The Globe and Mail*, 26 March 2002.
5. For a detailed province by province discussion of property division on separation and divorce, see Dranoff, 272–81.
6. For a brief discussion of the matrimonial home, see Michael G. Cochrane, *Surviving Your Divorce: A Guide to Canadian Family Law*,

2nd ed. (Toronto: John Wiley & Sons 1999), 63. Thanks go to Philip M. Epstein, Q.C., for providing his paper, "Matrimonial Property Law in Canada" (unpublished) as background.

7. Dranoff, 280.

8. For more information on CPP benefits, see www.hrdc-drhc.gc.ca/common/income.shtml#pp.

9. A court case involving a couple living under the same roof but with very separate lives found the couple to be "living separate and apart" for tax purposes, but it isn't a good idea to try your luck with a similar domestic situation.

10. The tax treatment described is for child support payments made as a result of a separation agreement or court order on or after May 1, 1997. Child support payments made as a result of agreements or orders on April 30, 1997, or before are deductible for the payor and taxable to the payee—unless the amounts have been changed since May 1, 1997, in which case the new tax treatment applies.

11. Thanks to Robert Murray, CA, CFP, FMA and Manager of Financial Planning Advice, TD Waterhouse Financial Planning, for this chart and explanation.

12. The federal equivalent-to-spouse tax credit is not available in Quebec.

13. Andrew J. Freedman, Paula G. White, Vivian M. Alterman and Sue Loomer, *The Tax Principles of Family Law, 2001*, self-published (Toronto), 31. A very valuable guide, but distributed to lawyers and accountants only.

14. Dranoff, 241.

15. Definition of common-law partner by CCRA, 23 July 2002. www.ccra-adrc.gc.ca/eservices/tipsonline/infotax/mess303-e.html#303-01%20-%20Definition%20of%20the%20term%20spouse.

16. Who is a common-law partner according to the CPP, 23 July 2002. www.hrdc-drhc.gc.ca/isp/cpp/retire_e.shtml#sharing.

17. Cochrane, 3.

18. Ibid., 18.

19. This information from Cochrane, (*Surviving Your Divorce*, 202), was current as of 1999. More than six provinces may now have

provisions for property division on the death of a spouse, but sources did not state definitively whether that number has changed.

20. This idea thanks to "Ready to Remarry? Take a Vow to Avoid the Financial Pitfalls," www.msn.ca, 12 March 2002. www.money.msn.ca/articles/planning/wills/article8.asp.

21. "Are You Living in a Same-Sex or Opposite-Sex Common-Law Relationship?" 23 July 2002. www.hrdc-drhc.gc.ca/isp/common/inpay_e.shtml.

22. Contact Human Resources Development Canada at 1-800-277-9914 or www.hrdc-drhc.gc.ca for an application.

For Further Reading

Cochrane, Michael G. *For Better or for Worse: The Canadian Guide to Marriage Contracts and Cohabitation Agreements* (Toronto: John Wiley & Sons, 1999).

——*Surviving Your Divorce: A Guide to Canadian Family Law*, 2nd ed. (Toronto: John Wiley & Sons, 1999). A third edition is due out in fall 2002.

Dranoff, Linda Silver. *Everyone's Guide to the Law: A Handbook for Canadians* rev. ed. (Toronto: HarperCollins, 2001).

Tunney, Wayne L., Sandra Bussey and Joseph Petrie, eds. *KPMG's Tax Planning for Your and Your Family 2002* (Toronto: Thomson, 2001).

5 Insurance Settlements, Inheritances, Lottery Winnings and Other Lump Sums: How to Deal with New-Found Wealth

"The gratification of wealth is not found in mere possession or in lavish expenditure, but in its wise application."
MIGUEL DE CERVANTES, *DON QUIXOTE* (1547–1616)

Coming into money is like falling into a deliciously comfortable feather bed. The immediate effect is heavenly, but after a short while the feathers start to prick and you begin to sneeze. Money buys freedom, opens up new horizons, releases you from many tiring daily worries and can give you the luxury of choosing your own work, be it for pay or personal satisfaction. In short, money is great—but it comes with some responsibilities of its own. For some, it is a once-in-a-lifetime opportunity that is, sadly, too often squandered. This chapter will discuss the normal emotional upheavals, some tax and legal considerations and show you how to weigh a few investment options that arise with receiving a substantial lump sum, all with a mind to helping you preserve and protect your new-found wealth.

The "chute of emotions"

First there's the responsibility of having to look after this money, which means figuring out how to preserve it while still enjoying it. Unlike other sources of wealth, which can replenish themselves in the right circumstances, seldom does anyone get a second chance to replace a squandered inheritance, insurance claim or lottery win. The responsibility of overseeing a windfall wouldn't be so bad if it weren't also usually accompanied by some other less productive emotions. Susan Bradley, an American chartered financial planner who has written a book entitled *Sudden Money*, lists a gamut of emotions that those who come into money can experience. She calls this the "chute of emotions," and they include:

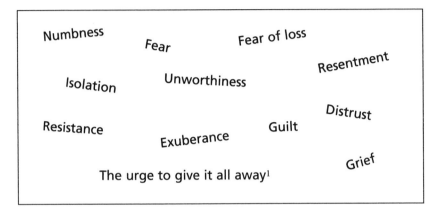

Numbness   Fear   Fear of loss

Resentment

Isolation   Unworthiness

Distrust

Resistance   Guilt

Exuberance

Grief

The urge to give it all away[1]

Gerry Smith, a Senior Vice President with Toronto-based Warren Sheppell Consultants, which provides employee assistance programs to corporations, has a lot of experience dealing with the "chute of emotions." Smith leads training sessions to help employees cope with change, and one of the exercises he estimates he's conducted with over 12,000 people requires them to imagine they have just won $10 million in a lottery. "The results are astonishingly consistent," he says. People go from "elation, relief, a feeling of great opportunity, no worries about the future, to an anxiety attack and feelings of depression." They imagine being removed from their loved ones, becoming suspicious of others, worrying about having their children kidnapped, needing to watch out for fraud and having to deal with pushy relatives.

Smith says that people who actually find themselves in this situation can turn to deliberately self-defeating behaviour, such as spending binges. Certainly we've all heard stories of lottery winners spending their winnings with wild abandon, only to wake up to more debt than they had before their windfall. There are no concrete statistics in Canada on what's known as the "dissipation rate," but a somewhat dated American study seems to reinforce much of the anecdotal evidence.

Shocking statistics

The study found that within two months of receiving a lump sum, 25% of recipients had nothing left. By the end of the first year, half of them had gone through their money. That percentage rose to 70% at the end of two years, and within five years, 90% had nothing left.[2] I'd like to think that North Americans generally have become more financially sophisticated in the 25 years since the study was done. Those are very bleak numbers that represent a wasted opportunity for long-term comfort and security, something a large lump sum gives you the chance to achieve if you manage it properly.

Part of that, of course, is recognizing the opportunity and seizing it. Sometimes it takes a while to realize just what the money can do for you. One of our clients, Kathy White (I've changed her name to protect her privacy), received over $1 million in an insurance settlement when her 54-year-old husband died suddenly. This was in addition to an already established investment portfolio. Yet even with that financial security behind her, Kathy says, "I didn't accept that I didn't have to work anymore and so I did work at some jobs that weren't very much fun." It took her six years to grow into the realization that she could stop working and pursue her interests. She's now taking a history course so she can get more out of her travels.

Although it's too bad she had six years of less than enjoyable employment, Kathy actually acted prudently. She didn't change her life impulsively. She didn't go on a spending spree. She sought out and interviewed financial advisors, invested her money and sat on it until she was ready to accept its possibilities. Seven and a half years later, her children and most of her friends still don't know the extent of her wealth, and she wants to keep it that way. She lives in a modest apartment she can leave without worries for extended periods, and, at 59, she looks forward to many more years of travel and learning.

Don't be in a hurry

As it happened, it was a good thing Kathy sat on her money for a while. It turned out there were numerous unresolved issues with her husband's business and his personal tax situation, some of which required Kathy to pay legal expenses. Only last year, six and a half years after the death of her husband, CCRA asked her to pay tax that her husband's estate was unable to pay. Thanks to a good estate lawyer, Kathy knew she had no legal obligation to pay this tax and refused, but it is not unknown for tax problems—even someone else's—to come back to affect you years later. Tax experts say that even when CCRA's legal window to reassess a taxpayer's return has expired, you may still not be off the hook for the joint and several liability for the deceased's estate tax in certain circumstances.

But that isn't the only reason to exercise patience. Many people who come into sudden money may give too much of it away or find themselves with possessions they don't have the cash to maintain. The best advice for anyone who comes into money is to take a deep breath and put it away for six months or so in a safe and liquid investment such as a Government of Canada Treasury bill, a money market fund or a term deposit. That will give you time to settle in to the situation, work out the emotions, plan the best use of that money and investigate the possibility and implications of a tax bill.

That sounds eminently reasonable, but what about a little celebration? Some writers on this topic suggest budgeting 2% to 5% of your windfall for immediate gratification. Nothing wrong with that, as long as you are disciplined enough to stop spending after that initial splurge and don't become impatient with your former lifestyle.

Receiving death benefits, insurance settlements and legal awards

Death benefits

Every year, between $2.5 and $3 billion is paid out in death benefits to Canadians.[3] That's a tremendous amount of money. Insurance death benefits are generally tax-free and are usually paid within 30 days from the time the insurance company confirms the death of the insured. This doesn't give you a lot of time to make financial plans. You may be approached by the insurance company to purchase an annuity with the money being paid to you. We'll talk about this choice shortly.

Insurance settlements and legal awards

Although awards are not nearly as generous in Canada as they are in the U.S., they can still be sizable and take years to finally win. Fortunately, money awarded to you in compensation for personal injury or a crime is generally not taxable, though the interest that accrues on the settlement money before (and after) it is paid to you is taxable unless you are under age 21.

If you agree to it, you can receive your awarded damages for personal injury or death through periodic payments rather than a lump sum. The periodic payment option is arranged through a specially designed annuity and is known in the legal field as a "structured settlement." Unlike other annuity payments, which are taxable, the annuity used in structured settlements results in 100% non-taxable income to the person receiving the payments. Under the structured annuity option, payments cannot be assigned, transferred or commuted. The payments must go to the original recipient or her heir, but this doesn't mean that, once paid, they're not subject to claims by creditors.

Structured settlements are especially advantageous for the parties having to pay the settlements because they require less up-front capital than a lump-sum settlement. Some advocates of these arrangements also believe they are advantageous to the recipient because the investment growth accumulating in the annuity is distributed without tax. This is true, but the distributions are predicated on the growth that occurs within the annuity. Without that growth, the recipient would be getting less than the agreed-on settlement. A lump-sum payment, on the other hand, would generate taxable income from the investment growth only, but that growth would be genuine growth and not part of the initial settlement.

Anyone weighing the pros and cons of a structured settlement should talk to a lawyer and an accountant. As with any annuity, you have to carefully scrutinize the terms of the annuity being offered. Does it have a guarantee period? Will it pay your survivor, and for how long?

What's the interest rate on the underlying investment? Could you do better investing a lump sum on your own? Is there a chance you could dissipate your money without using an annuity? Once any annuity is purchased, the terms cannot be changed. It is a decision you must be content to live with no matter what changes in your life.

Later in this chapter, we'll look at how to calculate the present lump-sum value of a proposed annuity so you can better weigh your options if you are presented with a choice.

Getting an inheritance

Inheritances are rife with emotions: honour, fondness, sadness, guilt, unworthiness, and sometimes bitterness and resentment, too. Some people grow up expecting an inheritance; others are surprised to learn they are the beneficiary of an elderly relative who lived modestly. An inheritance is a connection to the person who has passed away. Which ever way an inheritance comes to you there seems to be a strong sense of responsibility for the money that lottery winnings, for example, don't often provoke. People worry that this good fortune may have come by way of somebody else's sacrifice, a life cut short or less full, or that some-one else is somehow more deserving. It's not always easy to accept that the deceased really and truly wanted you to have this money over all other possibilities. Once you accept that, it is easier to treat the money objectively as just another financial asset to be enjoyed, not necessarily a sacred trust.

How Many Inherit How Much?

A study done in the U.S. in 2001 by *Financial Advisor* magazine in 2001 surveyed 388 people who had inherited at least $1 million in the last three to five years. Here's some of their findings. [I've added the *Gilligan's Island* references to make it easier to follow.]

- 56.4% inherited between $1 million and $2.99 million [we'll call these the Gilligans].

- 32.5% inherited $3 million to $5.99 million [the Professors].
- 11.1% inherited over $6 million [the Howells].
- 70.4 % of the inheritors had portfolios of under $500,000 before the inheritance.
- 25% of the inheritors said their lives had "changed dramatically" for the better. The larger the inheritance, the more likely they were to agree with that. Only 7.3% of the Gilligans agreed with that statement vs. 95% for the Howells.
- 25% said their inheritance caused family conflicts. The bigger the inheritance, the more likely it was there were conflicts.
- Fewer than 20% of those receiving $1 million to $2.99 million left their day jobs.
- Only 11.3% spent at least half their inheritance on luxury items [the Gingers].[4]

Taxes

There is no such thing as an inheritance tax in Canada because the estate giving rise to your inheritance has already been taxed—and those taxes can be brutal. For tax purposes, capital assets including personal property owned by the deceased are deemed to be sold at fair market value as of the date of death. As a result of this deemed disposition, the estate has to pay tax on all previously unrealized capital gains and take all registered holdings into income (unless a surviving spouse, common-law partner or certain other dependants elect to implement a tax-free rollover). When RRSPs, RRIFs and other registered monies are taken into income, that money is taxed at your marginal tax rate, which can exceed 48%.

Even with this ultimate financial reckoning, an inheritance can still be encumbered with a tax liability. The estate is responsible for paying tax on the assets within it. Should the executor erroneously release assets without deducting tax or without leaving enough money in the estate to pay the taxes on them, CCRA can go after the executor and you, the inheritor, for the taxes owing.

This has been known to happen with RRSPs, for instance. When there is no spouse or financially dependent minor child or handicapped adult child to roll the registered account over to, the registered account is treated as though it were completely cashed in just before death. All the fair value proceeds, real or deemed, are taken into the deceased's income in the year of death and are taxed at the deceased's highest marginal tax rate. This usually means close to half the value of a registered account can be lost to tax. The money to pay that tax usually comes from the estate, and not necessarily from the registered account, when the beneficiary is other than the estate of the registered plan's annuitant/owner. CCRA requires the estate to pay the tax owing, but if the estate has no money to do so, CCRA could turn to both the executor and the inheritor of the RRSP for its tax.

As we've just seen, executors can make mistakes that have tax consequences. CCRA issues a clearance certificate to certify that all taxes owing on the estate have been paid. This protects the executor, but it can give you a measure of comfort, too, so it's a good idea to check with the executor when you receive an inheritance to see if the estate has received a clearance certificate from CCRA.

Receiving the assets

An inheritance usually comes to you in bits and pieces and at different times, sometimes over a fairly prolonged period during the administration of the estate and its assets. One day you'll get a cheque. Another day you'll get some stocks. Yet another day you might get the proceeds of a registered account. You must keep track of what you expect to receive and its source so you can check it off against what you have actually received. This is a good discipline because it will keep you organized, help your advisors marshal your assets more efficiently and help you plan your disbursements. The estate's executor will be able to give you a list of assets and their value, though it's not always easy to tell how long it will take to transfer those assets to you.

Contesting a will

There are many grounds for contesting a will, and part of a lawyer's job in drawing up a will is to make sure the document has a good chance of standing up in court should it be contested. A will has to be properly witnessed and should not have any material factual mistakes or it may be challenged.[5] The mental competency or physical condition of the person making the will, the testator, could also come into question as grounds for contesting a will. If the testator was of unsound mind or under undue influence, the will can be challenged. Dependants can also make a claim against the estate for support if they are left out or given inadequate recognition. Adult children left out of a will have contested wills and sometimes won. A will can also be easily contested if it was drawn up before a marriage or divorce without recognizing the impending change in marital status.

If you want to contest a will, you must see a lawyer promptly so the executor and beneficiaries, the court, insurance companies and other involved financial trustees can be notified before the assets are distributed.

Winning the lottery

You can almost feel the tropical breezes on your face and you long for that new-car smell. But before you pick up the cheque, think about who in your family should actually claim your lottery winnings. If it's a sizable prize relative to your financial circumstance, you should consult with an accountant, lawyer or trust company, because included with that windfall are tax, creditor and family law issues to consider.

Taxes
Lottery winnings aren't taxed in Canada, but the income they generate certainly is, which is why you should also do some tax planning up front before collecting your winnings. Of course, your strategy will depend on the size of the winnings and your personal tax situation, but you should know there is some flexibility in how the lottery cheque is made out. You might want to consider having the cheque in your name and your spouse's name so the investment income from the winnings will flow equally to you both. Or you could have the cheque made payable entirely to the spouse with the lesser income so more of the investment income stays within the family and less gets paid in taxes.

Minor children can't collect lottery prizes, so you can't have your young children's names added to the cheque. You can add your adult children, but it's probably best to give your money away after you've had time to consider all your options. Opening a formal trust for your adult children, for instance, might be a better idea than just handing them the cash.

Creditors and ex-spouses

Although lottery winnings in Canada are beyond the reach of the tax department, they are not protected from creditors. If you are worried about creditors, you should speak with a lawyer and an investment advisor. The law doesn't look kindly on those deliberately trying to avoid their debts, but some investments are designed to be creditor-proof if you don't go into them to avoid a current or impending creditor.

For family law purposes, lottery winnings are likely to be considered family property. That means your winnings would be divided between you and your spouse should you separate or divorce. Winnings that result from gifts, however, aren't considered family property so long as the money is kept separate and apart from other family monies and assets. If that lottery ticket in your birthday card from Aunt Sue strikes pay dirt, you should think twice about renovating the house or paying down the mortgage with it if you're uncertain about the future of your marriage, as that money will likely become part of the family assets up for division.

What if you win money in the U.S.?

If Vegas has been good to you, you should know that Canadians pay U.S. tax on their stateside winnings. Federal and/or state taxes may be due. Fortunately, no Canadian tax is due on these winnings.

U.S. citizens and residents winning Canadian prizes

Because U.S. citizens and residents have to report and pay tax on their worldwide income to the U.S. government, U.S. citizens and residents winning Canadian lotteries do have to pay U.S. taxes on their winnings.

Interest and settlement options

Lottery corporations do not pay interest on unclaimed prizes, so there is no benefit in waiting to collect your winnings, just so long as you've had time to consult with an accountant and/or a lawyer beforehand.

Depending on the nature of the lottery, very large prizes can sometimes be collected as a lump sum or as fixed regular payments for life, known as an annuity option. The Cash for Life instant game in Ontario, for example, awards a lump sum of $675,000 or an annuity that pays $1,000 a week for the rest of the winner's life.

If you are attracted to the annuity option, remember that a life annuity may not necessarily have a guaranteed period, which means that if you died the year after winning it, your estate would get nothing and the remainder of the prize would be lost. Some life annuities allow you to bequeath them to a beneficiary but with restricted benefits. The Cash for Life annuity option, for example, gives a beneficiary payments for 20 years from the time the prize was originally claimed or until the 91st birthday of the original winner, whichever comes first. A winner 71 or older might want to consider the lump sum instead of the annuity. And there's nothing stopping anyone from in effect creating their own annuity by buying a portfolio of guaranteed bonds.

Watch out for the taxes, too. Whereas the lump-sum option is not subject to tax at all, the annuity payments are partially taxed. An annuity is a contract issued by a life insurance company that pays out interest and principal for a prescribed period and the interest portion of an annuity payment is taxed. The Ontario prize withholds the tax and pays $1,000 in after-tax dollars. According to the Ontario Lottery and Gaming Corporation, out of 38 winners to date, 31 opted for a lump sum and seven chose an annuity.

Your choice of payment will depend on your age, health and how well you think you could do investing the lump sum. Your accountant can help you sort out the variables. Whatever you do, you'll want to avoid becoming another dissipation statistic.

A Lottery Winner's Game Plan

Whether you've won $100,000 or $10 million, you should have a game plan for making the most of your good luck.
Step 1: Don't delay, but before you claim your winnings, see an accountant about tax planning. This advice may determine who in your family should claim the prize. If your prize is a significant one, in your estimation, it's a good idea

to also consult a lawyer to discuss family law and estate planning considerations.

Step 2: Consider paying off your non-deductible debt, such as your mortgage, car and consumer loans, credit cards, lines of credit, etc. Lottery winnings arising from a gift that are kept apart from family assets, will probably not be subject to division in a separation or divorce. Paying down the mortgage with this lottery money will cause it to become family property and subject to subsequent division if your relationship breaks down.

Step 3: Live a little! Set out a relatively small, fixed amount for a celebration.

Step 4: Put the money aside in a safe and liquid investment to give yourself time to explore your options and adjust to your new situation.

Step 5: Interview financial advisors. Look for qualifications and experience and get references from friends. Make sure this person can help with insurance and estate planning. Ask to see an (anonymous) example of a statement, a financial plan and an estate plan. (See appendix 4 for help choosing an advisor.)

Step 6: Get a financial plan, taking into account what you want to do with your money. Then stick to it. You'll want a written financial plan, which should include an investment strategy, cash flow projections and tax liabilities from your portfolio. Pay attention to fees and tax planning strategies.[6]

Annuity or lump sum?

You've just been offered the choice of a lump-sum payment of $500,000 or annual payments of $36,000 for 25 years. Which is better? First you have to sort out the tax implications of the annuity. An annuity arranged through a structured settlement should generate non-taxable payments. Payment from other annuities will be taxable at least in part.

You also need to know the interest rate the annuity is earning, in this example 6%.

Then you have to do the math to make sure the numbers are equivalent in value. A financial calculator would help here, but you can do it by hand with some patience. A dollar today is worth more than a dollar tomorrow because having a dollar today means you can collect interest on it starting today. Now you have to determine what all those annuity payments would be worth if they were given to you today as a lump sum.

The present value of money can be worked out using this formula:

Present Value (PV) = $\dfrac{FV}{(1 + r)^n}$

Here FV = the amount of money you will receive

n = the number of periods you plan to let your money grow

PV= the value of that future value payment today

r = the interest rate per period

You can solve this equation for each of the 25 years of annuity payments, then add those all up to get the present value, but it's much easier to use a formula specific to annuities:

Present Value of an Annuity = $PMT \left[\dfrac{(1-(1/(1+r)^n))}{r} \right]$

Where PMT = the amount of money you receive each period

n = the number of periods you will receive the payments

r = the interest rate per period

Present Value of an Annuity = $\$36,000 \left[\dfrac{(1-(1/(1+0.06)^{25}))}{0.06} \right]$

= \$460,200

Plugging the numbers into the formula, it turns out that a $500,000 lump sum is slightly bigger than annual payments of $36,000 from an annuity earning 6% over 25 years.[7]

Even if the annuity option is identical or better than a lump-sum offer, there could still be reasons for preferring a lump sum. You may want to have more flexible access to the money, or you might believe you could achieve better investment results by investing a lump sum and not tying your money up in an interest-bearing instrument such as an annuity would use. There's always the possibility that inflation could seriously erode the purchasing power of your annuity payments. Also, those in poor health or the elderly may find a lump sum a better choice without crunching the numbers because they may not realize the full benefit of an annuity.

Of course, before committing to an annuity, you should be clear on the terms of the contract. Some annuities guarantee an income for life no matter how long or short your life turns out to be. While this sounds great, just think what happens to your money should you die shortly into the contract. You will have collected only a fraction of what you put into the annuity but your estate gets none of the remaining money. That goes to the insurance company for assuming the risk you might live a long time. For this reason, many people prefer buying a life annuity with a guaranteed period. If you die within that period, your estate or beneficiary will be paid the value of payments to the end of the guaranteed period.

Should you invest all at once or a little at a time?

It has often been said that the best time to invest is when you have the money. That means you shouldn't try to second-guess the market: When you're ready to invest, do so without trying to find a market trough to step into. At least a few studies have shown that this strategy has worked pretty well in the past. A U.S. study that tracked lump sum vs. systematic investments over 780 12-month periods from 1926 to 1991 found lump-sum investing coming out on top 64.5% of the time.[8] With two-year periods, the superiority of lump-sum investing would have been higher still. Lump-sum investing has worked well because the stock market has gone up over time.

The problem is that the market may not trend up just when you're ready to entrust your money to it. And if you need to draw on those investments before a market rebound, you will likely lose money. With this very real worry, a more gradual approach is sometimes recommended. Investing smaller amounts periodically spreads the risk of buying at a market high or leaping full tilt into a declining market. Systematic investing is also known as "dollar-cost averaging," a term you hear more often applied to buying mutual funds on a regular basis. In periods of market declines, this investing strategy will lessen your losses compared to a lump-sum investment, but it will also lessen your gains in a rising market.

Those erring toward caution or with a short investment horizon will probably find a dollar-cost averaging approach more attractive than a single lump-sum investment even though the historical record has shown lump-sum investing has more often given superior returns.

Find a mentor

Finding a mentor to help guide you through your new lifestyle might sound like a funny idea, but don't dismiss it entirely, especially if you feel ambivalent about your wealth. In the business world, mentoring relationships are not at all unusual. Less experienced entrepreneurs, for instance, often seek out more established entrepreneurs for guidance in growing their business and managing their many personal demands. The same can be said for executives. In fact, many organizations exist to facilitate mentoring relationships in business.

Rest assured that whatever is happening to you because of your new wealth has indeed happened to others. If you can find someone who has put his or her money to use in a way similar to your own aspirations, it might not be all that difficult to strike up an informal mentoring. More formally, you might want to contact organizations who could put you in touch with others in similar circumstances. Do you think a foundation might one day be in your future? Contact some small foundations and see if you can speak to the founder. Want to sail around the world? Contact a yacht builder or dealer to see if he or she can put you in touch with someone who has. There's no end of ways to find people with money who have done what you would like to do. If they are willing to share their experience and their insight, it will help you get a little closer to your ultimate goal, and maybe even help you manage a few other things along the way.

> *"When a person comes into money, it amplifies their basic personality, their basic self. If they tend to be curious, they can travel the world. If they're intellectual, they can go to school for the rest of their lives. If they're hypochondriacs, they can be fabulous hypochondriacs. If they know how to enjoy life, they can certainly do that with intensity."*
> Myra Salzer, president, the Wealth Conservancy[9]

It's been called the sudden money syndrome—the unhappiness and anxiety that come with a windfall. It doesn't happen to everyone who comes into money suddenly but enough people have experienced it to make it the topic of books and studies. The best advice is to take some time to consult with professionals, think seriously about what's best for you and be patient with yourself while you resolve the many emotions that might stir inside you.

You need to understand the tax consequences and future tax liabilities your new-found wealth brings along with it. Understand, too, some family law and estate planning considerations. Compare regular payments vs. an annuity. Could you do better managing a lump sum yourself? To best answer that question, you need to be aware of all your investment choices—which brings us to our next chapter, investing strategies and options.

Notes

1. Susan Bradley, with Mary Martin, *Sudden Money: Managing a Financial Windfall* (New York: John Wiley & Sons, 2000), 39–50.
2. John P. Weir, *Structured Settlements* (Toronto: Carswell, 1984), 18. Prof. Weir was quoting from R. Somers, "The Structured

Settlement—A Better Way," *Journal of Insurance* (March/April 1979). The Somers information was based on pre-1975 U.S. data.

3. Statistics Canada, "Life insurance benefits payments," from 1993 to 1997.

4. As reported by Marla Brill in *Windfall: Managing Unexpected Money So It Doesn't Manage You* (Indianapolis: Alpha Books, 2002), 74–75. I have added the references to *Gilligan's Island*.

5. Not all wills have to be witnessed. A handwritten and unwitnessed will, known as a holograph will, is valid in most provinces. According to Linda Silver Dranoff's, *Everyone's Guide to the Law*, rev. ed. (Toronto: HarperCollins, 2001), 330, Alberta, Manitoba, New Brunswick, Newfoundland, Saskatchewan, Ontario, the Northwest Territories, Nunavut, Yukon and Quebec recognize holograph wills. In British Columbia, Nova Scotia and Prince Edward Island, only holograph wills made by a member of the armed forces are valid.

6. This "Game Plan" owes a lot to Susan Ferrier Mackay, "Sudden Wealth," *IEmoney Magazine*, 26 (December 2000).

7. In doing these calculations, it is critical to match the compounding period to the interest rate period. Monthly payments require you to calculate a monthly interest rate and a compounding period in months. If you wanted to do our example for monthly annuity payments, the number of compounding periods would be multiplied by 12 and the interest rate divided by 12. In our example that would mean:

r = .005 (6% divided by 12 periods)
n = 300 months (25 years multiplied by 12 months)
payment = $3,000

8. Peter Bacon and Richard Williams, *Journal of Financial Planning VI*, no. 2 (April 1993), 13–15.

9. As quoted by Lucy Larzarony, in "Sudden wealth can leave you rich—and miserable," **www.bankrate.com**, published in 2000, viewed 3 June 2002. Myra Salzer is President of the U.S.-based Wealth Conservancy, a company that specializes in financial advice to inheritors.

For Further Reading

Bradley, Susan, with Mary Martin. *Sudden Money: Managing a Financial Windfall* (New York: John Wiley & Sons, 2000).

Brill, Marla. *Windfall: Managing Unexpected Money So It Doesn't Manage You* (Indianapolis: Alpha Books, 2002).

Gudgeon, Chris, and Barbara Stewart. *Luck of the Draw: True-Life Tales of Lottery Winners and Losers* (Vancouver: Arsenal Pulp Press, 2000).

6 Making Your Money Work for You: Investing Strategies and Options

"A good plan, executed now, is better than a perfect plan next week."
GENERAL GEORGE PATTON, U.S. MILITARY

Your goal is simple: You want to find the best way to protect and grow your money. The challenge is sorting through the crowded financial offerings to find the best solution for you. Unfortunately, the huge selection of investment products and account options intended to provide a bounty of consumer choice can end up being confusing.

In this chapter, we'll start with an overview of investment vehicles using a straightforward framework of asset classes that instantly organizes the ever-expanding universe of products. Once you've set out your investment goals and your appetite for risk, you can use these asset classes to design a personal investment strategy.

We'll explore the asset classes and how to use them to structure your portfolio's asset allocation, including new work on the perennial question of what should be in your RRSP and what should be held outside it. Then we'll look at the three basic investment solutions to see where you fit on the investment continuum. Deciding on the kind of investment account that best suits you may be one of the most difficult investment decisions of all, so I want to clearly set out what you can expect from the different relationship options. If you choose to work with an advisor, we'll also discuss what to look for when choosing one. And, finally, we'll talk about borrowing to invest. Low interest rates provide opportunities for leveraging, but it may not be right for you.

But before we begin, let's look at some unconventional arguments for why establishing a deliberate investment strategy and sticking to it is so very, very important.

Are you your own worst investment enemy?

If academic research is anything to go by, our behaviour as investors regularly undermines our returns. The good news is that women seem to have a natural investment advantage.

Terrance Odean, an assistant professor in the graduate school of management at the University of California at Berkeley, has made some surprising discoveries about investor behaviour. In a series of studies that looked at nearly 200,000 trading accounts for at least five years, Odean has found that the more investors trade, the less money they make. Furthermore, investors, to their peril, just don't seem able to resist jumping on the top movers. Now comes the biggest blow to our egos: The stocks we sell systematically do better than the stocks we buy. By a lot. Not counting trades that were made for non-speculative reasons, Odean calculates that after 504 trading days, the stocks that had been purchased went down by 1.3% whereas the stocks that had been sold appreciated in value by 7.3%. "Trading is hazardous to your wealth," he concludes. That's a resounding endorsement for a prudent buy and hold strategy and a well-defined investment plan.

If buying and selling securities is so damaging to our bottom line, why do we continue to do it with such vigour? Professor Odean believes it is because investors are overconfident in their own abilities. Investors generally—and men in particular—have an illusion of market knowledge and control.

Men trade 45% more and earn a return of 1.4% less than women, according to Odean. Single men fare even worse. They trade 67% more frequently and have 2.3% lower returns than single women. "Overconfidence," he says, "gives investors the courage of their misguided convictions." The professor's study, aptly entitled "Boys Will Be Boys," was based on data from 35,000 household accounts at a large U.S. discount brokerage firm, where information about the common stock investments of men and women was collected from February 1991 through January 1997.[1]

Other sources show similar gender differences. A 2002 survey commissioned by U.S.-based OppenheimerFunds Inc. found that 34% of the female investors surveyed had bought a stock based on a tip from a friend, compared to 51% of male investors. The survey also reported that 29% of male investors surveyed had lost half of their investment in a tech stock in the last three years, while only 20% of female investors had experienced a similar loss.[2]

While it's easy to understand why patient, prudent investing pays off, it's less easy to change our aversion to loss. All investors, male or female, hate loss. We seem to hate loss so much that we regularly sell winners and keep losers. A $1,000 loss weighs far heavier on us than a $1,000 gain makes us happy, so we typically delay setting our losses in stone and instead let our portfolio sink with the stone.

Not only do we hate loss, we secretly believe we won't have to confront it. Research has shown we are all, in a way, born optimists. It's often said that 80% of drivers think they are better-than-average drivers. Many of those people really have to be mistaken, but they are also optimists. Optimists believe bad things won't happen to them. They underestimate the role of chance in their lives and believe games of raw chance can be affected by skill.[3] Add optimism to overconfidence and you've got an investor who thinks, mistakenly, that he can predict the market.

This illusory predictive power leads to market timing, the practice of making investment decisions based on market conditions. If that doesn't

Investing's Emotional Roller Coaster

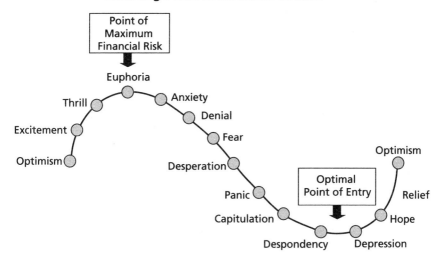

Source: Westcore Funds/Denver Investment Advisors LLC

sound like such a bad thing, you should know that market timing is very seldom successful. Instead, it usually seats us squarely on a roller coaster of emotions.

Nobody has a watch good enough to time the market

Dalbar Inc., a financial services research firm, tracked the cash flows into and out of mutual funds in the United States from January 1984 to December 2000. They found that mutual fund investors consistently under-perform benchmark indices by a sizable margin. This, they believe, is because investors put money into funds at the wrong time and pull money out—again—at the wrong time. (On average, U.S. investors hold their funds for 2.6 years, up from 1.7 years after the 1987 crash but down from 2.8 in 1999.) The Dalbar study concludes that a buy and hold investment strategy would leave more money in investors' pockets.[4] (See Emotional Investing in Action chart on the next page.)

But it's not just mutual fund investors who have problems with market timing. Investors generally have faulty watches.

The only way off the roller coaster is by committing to a well-crafted long-term investment strategy.

Buying and holding seems boring, but it works

By now you are probably convinced that trading can be detrimental to your wealth, as Professor Odean says. Okay, you're not going to trade a lot, but you may still be a covert market timer. Have you ever held on to your money or parked it in a money market fund waiting for a better time in the market to invest? That's a kind of market timing, too, and one that's hard to get right.

Markets often move in lunges, and missing just a few days of dramatic movement can seriously undercut your returns. By the time you take notice of a move and get your money into action, it is usually too late.

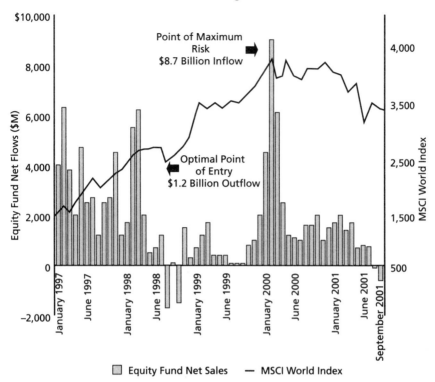

Emotional Investing in Action

Equity Fund Net Sales   — MSCI World Index

Source: MSCI and Investment Funds Institute of Canada (IFIC)

When the Morgan Stanley Capital Index (MSCI), an international equity index, was at its lowest during the Asian crisis, $1.2 billion came OUT of the markets. At its peak, $8.7 billion went IN. The point of maximum risk was at the market peak.

Missing the Best Days

A $10,000 investment in the Standard & Poor's 500 Index (S&P 500) on October 1, 1996 would have been worth $15,500 on December 31, 2001, but had you missed the best 20 days, you would have $7,301. Missing the best 60 days of that period would leave you with a paltry $2,826.

It is better to get into the market even at the worst time than not be in the market at all. Take the case of four coworkers, each representing different approaches to market timing. All four receive an end-of-year bonus of $2,000 each year for 20 years, and all four faithfully invest these bonuses. After 20 years, here's how they fared.

Anita: Invested her money with unerring timing. Every year, she bought at the lowest monthly close. $269,698

Laura: Invested her money every year on December 31. $261,917

Anna: Invested each year at the market's peak. Every year she bought at the highest monthly close. $216,246

Catherine: Never found the right time to get into the market. She bought T-bills instead. $68,639[5]

As you might have predicted, the fleet and flawless timer, Anita, got the best returns of all. Of course, it's highly unlikely anyone would ever be able to time the market as well as our fictional Anita. The surprising outcome, though, is Laura's fine showing. The plodder who simply put her money to work the minute she got it every year earned just $7,781 less than Anita. While Anna, the one who unerringly invested at the worst possible moment every year, will probably not be sharing the same retirement luxuries as Anita and Laura, she, too, had encouraging results. She earned about $147,600 more than if she had never been in the market, disastrous timing and all.

The decided loser in this slow 20-year race was Catherine, who never found the right time to buy into the market. Ironically, even if she had invested at exactly the wrong time every year, as Anna did, Catherine still would have more than tripled her money.

Over long investment periods, procrastination has been worse than bad timing. It has proved much better to invest even at the worst time each year than to be out of the market altogether.

Asset classes

The enormous array of investments can be grouped into just a handful of asset classes. Every kind of investment you can possibly buy falls into one of these classes:

Cash equivalents: Cash; Treasury bills; savings bonds; money market funds

Fixed income: Guaranteed investment certificates (GICs); government and corporate bonds; mortgage-backed securities; bond and mortgage mutual funds

Equities: Common and preferred shares, foreign and domestic shares; equity mutual funds

Tangible assets: Real estate; oil and gas; precious metals; collectibles

These classes are useful not just because they organize an overwhelmingly diverse universe of investments. They also respond in different ways to the same market conditions, which makes them helpful in controlling the volatility of your overall portfolio. Let's look at the effect of inflation on asset classes, as an example. When inflation runs high and interest rates go up, fixed-income investments suffer, but real estate typically prospers. When inflation is under control, interest rates tend to fall, which makes bonds do well. Stocks, on the other hand, may languish during periods of falling interest rates when the interest rate drop reflects a slowing economy. The relationship between the changes in the values of various asset classes under identical market conditions is referred to as "correlation." If investment A rises when investment B rises, and falls when investment B falls, the two are positively correlated. If investment A rises when investment B falls and vice versa, the two investments are negatively correlated.

Ideally, you'd like to have your asset classes negatively correlated, which means that one asset class would go up as much as another goes

Correlation at Work

Positive Correlation

Stock A

Portfolio

Stock B

Stock B

Portfolio

Stock A

Negative Correlation

Source: TD Wealth Management, Media Relations and Investor Communications

Correlation measures how much stock A goes up or down when stock B fluctuates.

down. Unfortunately, no asset classes are perfectly negatively correlated, so the differences that do exist must be exploited as much as possible.

Building a solid portfolio is not just about balancing the risk of one asset class against the others. It is about building returns within the scope of your own risk tolerance and investment time frame.

The greater the risk of an asset class, the greater the potential returns offered by that class. Cash equivalents offer no short-term risk, but they also don't offer much of a premium, if any, over inflation. Stock prices can fluctuate, but they hold out the promise of far better returns than T-bills or money market funds.

Risk and Return

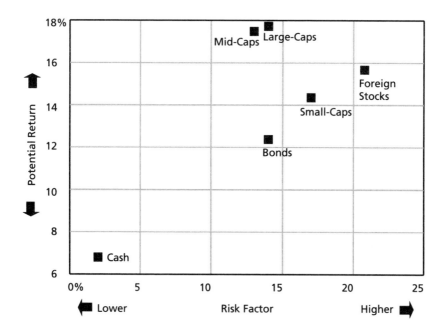

Sources: Standard & Poor's; Frank Russell Company; Morgan Stanley; the Federal Reserve (January 1,1982 through December 31, 2001). Large caps are represented by the annual total returns of the S&P 500. Mid caps are represented by the annual returns of the Russell Midcap Index. Small caps are represented by the annual total returns of the Russell 2000. Foreign stocks are represented by the annual returns of the MSCI EAFE Index. Bonds are represented by the annual total returns of long-term Treasuries (10+ years) and cash is represented by the annual total returns of three-month T-bills. Investors cannot directly purchase an index.

Risk, of course, is a factor of time. Over a short period, stock prices can plunge. Since inception, the S&P 500 has yet to experience a negative return over any 20-year period. The longer you hold stocks, the less risky they tend to become.

Asset allocation

Intuitively, you might think your actual investments are the most important factor in your investment returns, but this is not true. The allocation of your asset classes is the biggest factor in controlling the volatility of your returns. A famous and oft-quoted study found that *asset allocation accounts for 91.5% of the variability in returns between*

The Efficient Frontier

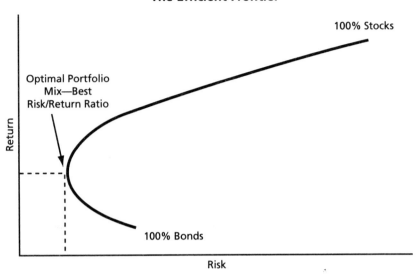

Source: TD Wealth Management, Media Relations and Investor Communications

The efficient frontier quantifies the return an optimized portfolio should yield for a given level of risk.

different portfolios.[6] The amount of money you put into each asset class is the single biggest investment decision you make.

You want your asset allocation to get you the best return for the amount of risk you are willing to take. Modern Portfolio Theory, which pioneered the idea of asset allocation, calls this the "efficient frontier," a term you will hear quite often in investment books and periodicals.

You can start to figure out what proportion of each asset class you should hold by referring to two loose guiding principles. The first is to have a cash cushion for emergencies. I usually suggest three to six months' net salary in a money market fund or something similarly liquid. The other rough guide is to invest a percentage equal to your age in fixed-income assets, so by this light a 40-year-old would have 40% of her portfolio in fixed income. Both these guiding principles are intended merely as a reference point and not as a benchmark chiseled in stone. Observing these "rules" strictly would mean a 50-year-old should have half of her portfolio in bonds or other fixed-income vehicles, and that might be much too conservative for someone who wants to keep working until 70. On the other hand, a 50% allocation to bonds (which might mean a 45% allocation to stocks and 5% in cash) could be far too aggressive a portfolio mix for a 50-year-old who wants to retire at 55, buy a boat and sail around the world.

Although the "age in fixed income" principle works well for retirement savings, it does not work at all for short-term savings earmarked for such things as a house or vacation. This money has to be treated more conservatively because you may not have the time to ride out a market downturn.

Your portfolio has to reflect your investment horizon, cash requirements, risk tolerance and the return you want or need from your investments. Many tools are available to help elicit this information to help you clarify your investment objectives. I've included a questionnaire in the appendix to give you a start. Please work through it, because both your returns and your peace of mind depend on it.

But before you actually get your pencil out to plot your asset allocation strategy, let's take a closer look at those four simplified asset classes to introduce a few subsets you can use to better control the fluctuations in your portfolio.

Alternative asset classes

Instead of looking at asset classes as broad groupings of similar types of investments, as we did in our initial discussion, some financial analysts see asset classes as groups of investments that move in tandem throughout the various phases of the business cycle. This has the interesting result of creating a greater number of asset classes, since investments that act significantly differently from the four basic asset classes are given an asset class of their own. It's important to give some attention to these classes, because adding them to your portfolio can help boost your returns and decrease the overall volatility of your holdings.

Hedge funds: These investments have gained popularity in the past ten years, especially in the U.S. Hedge funds may enhance your returns and reduce the risk in your overall portfolio because their value will not necessarily go up and down at the same time as the stock and bond markets. Hedge funds are like mutual funds in that they pool the money of a number of investors, but they're mutual funds without any of that class's investment restrictions. Hedge funds can take short positions, use leverage and arbitrage, trade options on stocks and indices, and use derivatives freely. If you are considering buying one, you should make sure you know which strategy the fund employs and how aggressive it is. There are many different hedging strategies varying from very low- to extremely high-risk. Funds also vary in how closely they are correlated with equity and bond markets.

Sometimes groups of hedge funds are gathered together in one fund—a "fund of funds" concept—with the aim of getting the benefit of many different hedging strategies with reduced risk.

Royalty and income trusts: These are trusts that pool investors' money to buy an interest in an operating business's cash flow. In exchange for your investment, you receive a proportional share of the business's cash flow. Royalty trusts are income trusts specific to the resource industry where you buy cash flow from the sale of depleting oil or gas or other resources.

Income trusts are designed to generate steady income with high returns, at least initially. They have become a popular alternative to fixed-income vehicles, but they are not guaranteed in any way and the income could dry up or diminish before the trust expires.

Individually, income trusts can be risky because you are betting on just one operating company's cash flow; however, mutual funds that specialize in income trusts buy an assortment of trusts and so mitigate the individual investment risk. Many high-income-oriented mutual funds enhance their portfolios with income trusts, as well.

Because these investments have so many bond-like characteristics, you might think they would suffer when interest rates rise. And they will, to some extent, but not as seriously as fixed-income vehicles, because rising interest rates usually indicate a robust economy, and that should bode well for the income trust's underlying business. As long as the business remains strong, so will the cash flow. The trust may not keep the high relative yield, but the cash flow is less likely to be in jeopardy.

Real estate investment trusts (REITs): Similar to income trusts, a REIT is a pool of money that invests in an array of commercial, residential or industrial real estate. Income from rents and profits from the eventual sale of the properties is passed on to investors. REITs trade on a stock exchange and are quite liquid. A study done in the U.S. found that REITs had fairly low correlations to the Nasdaq 100 Index, a government and corporate bond index, even, over some periods, the S&P 500.[7] Unlike bonds, REITs tend to hold their own during inflationary periods because rents typically keep pace with inflation.

REITs have some tax advantages, too. REITs can deduct the capital cost allowance (CCA, or depreciation), property management fees and certain financing costs. These deductions are passed to investors so the taxable portion of their distributions is reduced. These deductions can be quite significant and may mean more than two-thirds of a REIT's distributions could be tax-deferred. What you defer in taxes goes to reducing the cost base of the REIT, so when you sell it, you must pay capital gains on the difference between the cost base and the proceeds of the sale. For tax purposes, this has the happy result of converting an income stream to a capital gains situation deferred to some time in the future.

Labour-sponsored venture capital investment funds: LSIFs, for short, invest money in unproven companies with exciting new products or technologies. These mutual funds now provide about 40% of all venture capital raised in Canada—an astonishing fact that has to do with the generous tax credits governments give investors in these funds. In exchange for putting your money in a venture capital fund, the federal government gives you a 15% tax credit on an investment up to $5,000 annually, and most provinces match this tax credit depending on the nature of the fund. In an effort to fund research in the province, the Ontario government gives an additional 5% tax credit (over and above the usual 15% provincial tax credit) for Ontario investors in research-oriented funds.

If these funds retain their value, the tax credits make these funds quite a bargain. Here's an example of how the numbers work:

A $5,000 investment in a labour-sponsored fund with a 30% tax credit will cost only $3,500. If bought within a Registered Retirement Savings Plan, the final after-tax cost could be only about $1,200.

Initial investment	$5,000
Less federal tax credit of 15%	($750)
Less provincial tax credit of 15%	($750)
Less RRSP tax deduction @ 46.4%	($2,320)
*Total after-tax cost	$1,180

*Assumes marginal tax rate of 29% federal and 17.4% provincial, the 2001
rate for Manitoba. For your federal and provincial tax rates see
www.ccra-adrc.gc.ca/tax/individuals/faq/2001_rate-e.html.

There is a catch, of course. You have to hold the funds for a minimum of eight years or the tax credits are clawed back. In case you're wondering why these funds are called "labour-sponsored," investment corporations formed by labour organizations were given these tax breaks to help them raise venture capital for Canadian companies that will employ Canadians. The unions have a presence on the funds' boards of directors but don't manage the funds or decide on the ultimate investments.

Apart from the tax savings, these funds give you a chance to diversify your portfolio with small- to mid-size companies with leading-edge technologies and products in software, biotechnology and other promising areas. Most of these companies are not yet public and would not be otherwise available as an investment option to the average investor. Though the investment is risky, the potential returns are great.

When you're looking to buy one of these funds, the manager's experience in venture capital financing and the prospects for the underlying investments are the key considerations.

Other ways to categorize investments

Small caps, mid caps, large caps: "Cap" here refers to market capitalization, which is simply a measure of a company's size. (It's calculated by multiplying a company's outstanding shares by the stock price. Companies with a capitalization of $500 million or less are considered small-cap companies, $500 million to $1 billion makes a mid cap, and over $1 billion qualifies as large cap.) As it happens, stocks frequently move in parallel with other stocks of similar size. Small-cap companies may flourish while large caps are in the doldrums, and vice versa. You should have an exposure to companies of all sizes because they don't necessarily move in tandem.

Foreign stocks: It used to be that foreign stocks moved independently of North American stocks, but with increasing globalization, foreign markets, especially those in Europe, seem to be more in line with North American markets. Less developed markets, commonly known as "emerging markets," are less tied to North American markets, but they, too, are dependent on trade with those now North-American-aligned foreign markets. It is good to get some geographical diversification in your portfolio, but finding markets with low correlations is not as easy as it was in the past.

Tax shelters: These are investments structured to pass income and tax benefits from a commercial operation to investors. The federal government has curtailed the number of tax shelters available by changing the tax rules that originally permitted these inventions; nevertheless, a few do still exist. Certain film production ventures can raise money by selling their tax losses to investors via a tax shelter. Oil and gas companies can issue what are known as "flow-through shares" that allow investors to claim a deduction from their personal taxes for certain exploration expenses incurred by resource companies. Real estate limited partnerships generate rental income that is tax-advantaged by being able to deduct the capital cost allowance (or depreciation) on the property. Profits from the eventual sale of the properties are also passed on to investors (the limited partners).

These vehicles usually provide investors with a long tax deferral, but not always with an ultimate tax savings. When the investment is eventually wound up, much of what has been claimed as deductions is recaptured. In the case of real estate limited partnerships, the capital cost allowance is recaptured if the property is sold for more than the depreciated value. Sometimes, however, dissolving the shelter can result in an absolute tax savings by generating capital gains, which are currently taxed at a maximum of around 25%.

Tax shelters have greater than average risk. As a general rule, they also have little liquidity, which means, once you buy them, you have to hold them until they are wound up by the issuer. In addition, CCRA can and not uncommonly has denied the tax deductions that make these vehicles so attractive.

Mutual funds

A mutual fund is a pool of money run by a professional manager who invests that money on behalf of those who contributed to it. Some mutual funds hold only stocks or bonds, while others may hold both stocks and bonds and an assortment of other things, such as income trusts and REITs. A mutual fund is an investment product that can contain a number of asset classes within it, but it is not itself an asset class. The manager's investments must remain within the stated investment objectives of the mutual fund. Some funds, for instance, invest predominantly in blue-chip stocks, while others concentrate on small-cap stocks or government bonds. If you can imagine an investment objective, there's a good chance you'll find a mutual fund to match it. The breadth and scope of mutual funds is truly impressive.

Active vs. Passive Management

Mutual fund management comes in two broad varieties, active and passive. Active managers buy and sell securities within the fund with the objective of enhancing the return to unitholders beyond that generated by the underlying market. Passive managers, on the other hand, arrange their investments to mirror a market index. Although they will not beat the market, neither will they fall much below it.

Open-end funds—the kind most investors are familiar with—issue units to buyers continuously and handle the buying and selling of their units themselves. This is in contrast to closed-end funds, which issue a fixed ("closed") number of shares that trade on a stock exchange. As it happens, closed-end funds usually invest in a pool of actively managed securities specific to a particular country: South Korea, Russia, Brazil,

Germany, and so on. These funds can have more risk than open-end funds because their price does not directly relate to the value of the underlying securities. With closed-end funds, there is often a discount or a premium on the underlying securities, whereas, with open-end funds, the price is always directly matched to the value of the securities within the fund.

Conventional open-end mutual funds have become very popular with investors, and for good reason. They offer a simple, easy-to-buy product with professional management and excellent diversification. With one single investment, you spread your risk over a multitude of other investments within the fund—investments that have been screened by specialized managers.

The user-friendly features of mutual funds are numerous. You can buy or sell them at any time without a brokerage commission. Depending on the fund company, you can invest as little as $25 a month and you can arrange a regular withdrawal program, too. They allow you to automatically reinvest your dividends without cost. They're independently audited and well regulated, and their returns are posted publicly and are widely available.

You should be aware of three important features of mutual funds: management fees, taxes and sales charges.

Management fees

A fund manager evaluates potential investments and monitors ongoing ones. There's buying and selling and keeping enough cash in the fund to pay for redemptions. In addition to paying the manager for these services, the fund has to pay GST, the expenses of communicating with unitholders, legal and auditing costs, custodial fees and, depending on the fund, a trailer commission to a financial advisor or fund distributor. These expenses, divided by the dollar value of the fund, give you the management expense ratio (MER). The MER is deducted from fund returns before the returns are quoted.

Taxes

Your hard-working fund manager, buying and selling securities to increase the fund's returns, is also generating capital gains on which you must pay tax. Within its investment portfolio, the fund is also collecting dividends and interest that are passed on to investors.

Some funds are more tax-efficient than others because their managers do less buying and selling in the process of managing the underlying portfolio. The most tax-efficient funds of all are index funds. An index fund reproduces the content and proportion of a given index and changes its holdings only when the corresponding index itself makes a change. This extremely low level of trading within the fund means fewer capital gains are realized and subsequently passed on to the unitholders.

Sales charges
Mutual funds also come with a variety of sales charge options ("loads").

DEFERRED SALES CHARGE (DSC)
Most mutual funds you buy through an advisor who offers value-added guidance and works on commission will have a "deferred sales charge," (DSC), which is another way of saying you don't pay a sales commission until you sell your fund, and only then if a few conditions apply. First of all, you must normally take your money out of the fund company altogether to be charged a DSC fee. If you switch to another DSC fund within the same fund company, you will generally not incur a sales charge. The sales charge declines each year you own the fund, eventually diminishing to nothing after about six to eight years, depending on the fund company. DSC funds also typically allow free redemptions of 10% every year.

FRONT-END LOAD
Front-end-load funds—those that charge a sales commission when you buy them—are sometimes favoured by investors with large amounts to invest, as the commission can be negotiable and the MER may sometimes be lower.

LOW LOAD
Low-load funds are a variation on DSC funds. Like DSC funds, there is no sales commission up front and you pay a redemption fee if you redeem the fund within a certain period. But unlike conventional DSC

funds, the redemption fee is fixed and low (around 2% or 3%) and applies only for a short period of time, about two or three years. After that, redemptions do not incur a sales charge.

LEVEL LOAD
Level loads are a relatively new sales charge option that adds the sales charge to the MER. They are not to be confused with no-load funds, because they have an ongoing sales charge that is tucked into a larger MER. The sales charge is constant, or "level," and does not decline over time.

NO LOAD
No-load mutual funds are the kind sold by banks and fund companies who sell directly to investors. These funds do not have a sales charge attached when you buy or when you sell them, though some companies charge a small transaction fee when you sell a fund. Some no-load mutual funds are also available for purchase over the Internet.

TRAILER FEES
Regardless of the kind of load a mutual fund carries, the fund pays a "trailer fee" to the financial advisor as compensation for ongoing service. Certain classes of mutual funds don't pay trailer fees. These are typically known as F-class funds and are sold exclusively through fee-based advisors. F-class funds pay neither sales commission nor trailer fees, which leaves their MERs lower, but the investor pays a fee directly to the advisor structuring a portfolio with these funds.

Mutual Funds Are Not Insured

Because mutual funds are sold through banks (and other financial institutions), people sometimes believe that mutual funds are covered by deposit insurance from the Canada Deposit Insurance Corporation (CDIC). This is mistaken. Savings account deposits and GICs are insured to a specified limit by CDIC, but mutual funds are not covered by CDIC. A mutual fund holds the fund's assets in trust with a custodian on behalf of the unitholders. The assets are audited annually by an independent auditor and fund companies themselves must comply with strict industry regulations.

Management styles

Like all investment managers, mutual fund managers will tend to display a specific style that describes how they approach and select their investments. Many managers say their approach is a blend of different styles, but they almost always favour one or the other.

TOP-DOWN

A top-down manager looks at broad economic trends and indicators, watches for sectors or industries in ascendance and then looks for companies within those industries or sectors that will profit from the larger economic trends. The emphasis is on the broader economy rather than the individual company.

BOTTOM-UP

Bottom-up managers focus on the fundamentals of a company rather than on the larger economic picture. They invest in solid businesses, thinking that a good business will continue to do well come what may.

VALUE

Value managers look for undervalued companies—ones that are out of favour but nevertheless solid businesses. Value investors generally look for companies whose stock price divided by the earnings per share (the price to earnings, or PE, ratio) is under 20.

GROWTH

Growth managers look for companies likely to have large revenue or earnings increases. They are willing to pay higher prices for these companies because they believe the stock price will go up as revenue and earnings increase. At some point, this escalation ends, so it's wise to balance a growth fund with a value fund, though the balance doesn't have to be even. Bull markets generally reward a growth style until, of course, the bears take over.

SECTOR ROTATION

Managers with this investment style try to anticipate the next big sector. They can move from gold to financials to transportation and back to gold or whatever sector looks promising. Sector funds typically carry greater risk and at times can be very volatile.

A word about indexing

Index investments are gaining popularity because they offer instant diversification, little capital gains liability and lower management costs. These products replicate an index or are pegged to an index in some way and in this sense are passive investments because they do not have a manager actively picking and excluding stocks: Everything in the index gets put into the index product, regardless of its prospects as an investment.

An index is simply a collection of securities designed to mirror the behaviour of a defined group of investments. The S&P/TSX 60 Index, for instance, is made up of the stock of Canada's 60 largest and most liquid companies. The movement of this index is indicative of the whole large-cap market in Canada and the Canadian marketplace in general. You can buy investments that reproduce the index of your choice either by way of an index mutual fund or "exchange-traded funds," which are mutual funds that trade through a broker on a stock exchange. Almost all exchange-traded funds (ETFs) track equity indices, but recently some ETFs tracking bond indices have been introduced in the United States. Here in Canada, there are two fixed-income ETFs that hold specific government bonds. These are unusual in that they are not pegged to a bond index.

Even though they are index-based, ETFs can reflect a variety of management styles. There are ETFs pegged to growth indices, value indices, small-cap indices, sector indices such as gold and energy, and so on. Name the permutation and index, and it's likely you'll find an ETF that corresponds to it. The vast majority of ETFs are traded on American exchanges though there are currently 16 homegrown ETFs in Canada trading on the Toronto Stock Exchange. And, unlike U.S.-domiciled mutual funds, Canadians are permitted to buy U.S.-based ETFs, just as they can U.S. stocks.

Some argue that investing in an index, either through an index mutual fund or an ETF, is a better investment strategy than buying actively managed mutual funds because the index will match the market return. Others believe that prudent professional management of a group of well-selected stocks will outperform the market, or at least not follow it down quite as faithfully as an index investment would. It's a point of debate, but there's no doubt that index mutual funds and ETFs have a place in a well-diversified investment portfolio.

Diversification is an investor's best friend

Your asset allocation must be customized to your situation, but let's just say your portfolio allocation turns out to be something like this:

- 50% equities
- 40% fixed income
- 5% cash
- 5% tangible assets

You might have the 5% cash component in a money market fund and the 5% tangibles in some oil and gas flow-through shares. The larger asset classes require much more diversification. Obviously, putting 50% of your portfolio into one stock would be foolhardy, but there's more to diversifying than that. You want to spread your risk among many industry sectors, purchase both large and small companies, seek out growth and value, and try to achieve some geographical reach.

For the fixed-income component, you have to decide if you want instant diversification through a bond mutual fund that holds an assortment of government and corporate bonds of various maturities or whether you prefer to hold bonds outright yourself. You pay a commission when you buy bonds, but the charge is reflected in the interest rate you are offered. Bond mutual funds, on the other hand, may not cost money to purchase, but they do charge an annual management fee. If you buy your own bonds, you'll probably want to stagger the maturities of your investments so you will have money coming due regularly. This reduces the reinvestment risk of your principal. Without staggering the maturities, you could have a large portion of money coming due when interest rates are very low. You'll also want to consider the mix of guaranteed government bonds with riskier but higher-yielding corporate bonds.

Much of this strategy depends on the amount of money you have to invest in an asset class. Small amounts are more easily diversified through a mutual fund. Larger amounts can be more inexpensively managed by investing in the assets directly. But the major point is to spread your risk around different investments in as many asset classes as possible, because no one has a crystal ball. One year, small caps will reign supreme; another year, fixed income will be the stellar asset class. You want to make sure you have some money on many plays. Just how much you have of each depends on your goals, your tolerance for risk and your investing time horizon.

To show you how effective a diversified portfolio is, here's the 21-year performance of a sample portfolio.

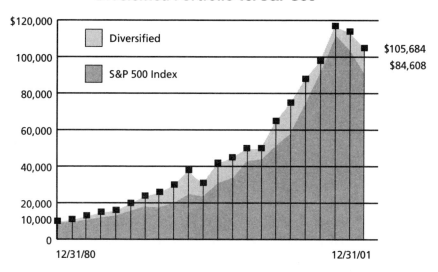

Diversified Portfolio vs. S&P 500

Source: TD Wealth Management, Media Relations and Investor Communications

At no point in these 21 years did the diversified portfolio underperform the S&P 500—and look how the gap widened in 2001.

This diversified portfolio is actually a composite of five indices and shows the return on a hypothetical US$2,000 investment put into a bond index, a foreign equity index, a broad U.S. market stock index, a mid-cap index and the S&P 500 index over 21 years from the end of 1980.[8] You can easily construct this portfolio yourself by buying index funds or exchange-traded funds pegged to those asset classes. The beauty of this portfolio, apart from its superb diversification, is its low maintenance. You simply buy the indices and hold on for the ride. And you can see that diversifying out of even a leading asset class, the S&P 500 in this case, does boost returns.

Indexing as a core holding

Once your asset allocation is established, you can decide whether you would like to index one or all of the asset classes. Indexing guarantees you'll come very close to receiving the overall market return for that asset class, while those who wish to try to outperform the market can buy actively managed mutual funds or individual securities.

Indexing is not an all-or-nothing choice. You can index one asset class and use actively managed mutual funds for other classes, or you can index all the classes and select individual stocks to augment your passive approach. The possibilities are nearly endless.

One approach that has gained favour in institutional money management circles puts index funds or ETFs at the core of the portfolio, with individual securities and some actively managed mutual funds added to the passive position in small quantities. Overall, the portfolio will perform close to the market because most of it is indexed, but there's still the possibility of outperforming the market if the non-indexed investments do well.

To do this yourself in your RRSP, for instance, you might buy an index fund or ETF in Canadian equities and a Canadian bond index mutual fund. Thinking that an active manager might be able to squeeze greater returns out of a less efficient foreign market, you might buy an emerging market mutual fund for part of your foreign content and then perhaps an ETF pegged to a U.S. index. Rebalance your portfolio once a year and you've got a low-cost, low-maintenance portfolio.

Avoiding the pitfalls

You can get too much of a good thing. It is easy to become overdiversified using mutual funds. Each mutual fund you buy should get you an asset or an investment style you don't already have, because duplication doesn't get you any closer to the efficient frontier. To monitor this, you must understand what investments your mutual funds hold and what investment style the fund manager employs. Picking mutual funds and making a solid portfolio out of them does take knowledge, and you can't get around this by simply picking a large assortment of mutual funds. It doesn't work that way.

Common Investing Mistakes

- **Lacking an asset allocation strategy**
  You set yourself up for underachievement without a well-designed investment strategy broken down by asset category. Asset allocation is crucial in getting you the returns you need with the risk you can afford to take.
- **Not setting quantifiable, realistic goals**
  You should work out short (less than 12 months), mid-range (one to five years) and long-range goals (over five years). Quantify these goals and then devise a plan to attain them, working with what you have. If you don't quantify these goals, you can't assess the success of your investment strategy.
- **Not matching investments with personal needs**
  A poor investment is not necessarily one that has low returns but one that doesn't match your goals. Great returns won't do you much good if you can't get your money when you need to. Sometimes, too, your tax situation can transform a great investment to a very mediocre one.
- **Failing to take inflation and taxes into account**
  Your investment strategy must be assessed on the basis of what gets left in your pocket after tax and inflation.

Many investors look at pre-tax returns without consider-ing their after-tax return. If inflation is running at 3% a year, someone with a 35% marginal tax rate must get a 4.6% return just to stay even.

- **Not judging your risk tolerance correctly**
  Risk doesn't have meaning until you've seen its negative consequences on your savings. Many investors have overly optimistic assumptions about their investments and accept more risk than they should because of this. The longer you can stay invested, the more risk you can generally take. But just how long do you have to be invested? If you think it is until retirement, you are mis-taken. It is actually longer. Your retirement assets must support you throughout retirement, which means some equity exposure well beyond retirement for most people.
- **Procrastinating**
  Procrastination turns attainable goals into impossible ones. The best time to start investing was yesterday, but today is better than tomorrow.

Asset location: The RRSP debate

Conventional wisdom has held that highly taxed investments should be sheltered inside your RRSP while lightly taxed investments should be held outside it (assuming you are maximizing your RRSP contributions and have other investments apart from your retirement savings account). And that makes perfect sense, since you want to get the great-est advantage from the tax deferral. Stocks generate dividends and capital gains, which are taxed much more favourably than interest income, so in practice bonds are ensconced within an RRSP while stocks are held outside. (This discussion also assumes these investments are for retirement savings and there is no other, more immediate reason to hold investments outside the RRSP.)

Recent U.S. academic work, however, indicates that this conventional wisdom might be hurting your overall wealth, at least when it comes to the average equity mutual fund over the very long term. Moshe Milevsky, a finance professor at York University in Toronto, has looked at this work as it applies to Canadian investors and concluded that with a 30-year investment horizon, you are better off keeping most equity mutual funds rather than bond mutual funds in your RRSP.[9]

What you lose in taxes from the bond fund you more than offset with growth from the equity fund and the tax sheltering of the dividends and capital gains the fund generates, but only after 30 years. This assumes that your equity mutual fund is of average tax efficiency (or worse), that it grows at a historically consistent rate and that the current level of taxation on interest income and capital gains doesn't fall significantly. Right now, capital gains—the profit on the sale of an investment—are taxed at less than 25%, while interest income is taxed at around 45% for those at

Asset Location
The benefit of holding stocks outside an RRSP

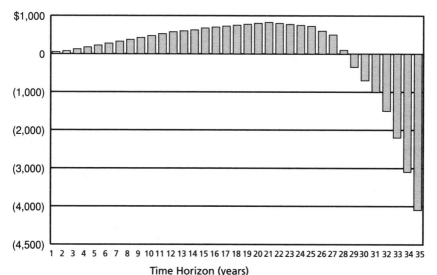

Time Horizon (years)

Source: Professor Moshe A. Milevsky

The *location* of your assets, as well as their *allocation*, makes a difference. Over the short term, equities may fare better outside an RRSP. However, as the chart illustrates, over the long term it may be more beneficial to hold equities inside your RRSP. Assumptions: Equity fund earns 15% annually and has a 50% internal portfolio turnover each year.

the top marginal tax rate. Should the capital gains rate go down, the investment horizon will have to get longer again. If it goes to zero, bonds go back into the RRSP and equity funds resume their unsheltered holding place. Milevsky warns that this location strategy won't work for highly tax-efficient equity investments like ETFs and individually held stocks, which should still be held outside an RRSP if there is a choice of holding places.

"If you are holding your bonds outside the tax shelter (and equity funds inside), and then for some unforeseen reason you are forced to liquidate investments to meet unexpected needs, you are much better off having to sell some bonds, then the other way around," says Milevsky. "Also, from a psychological point of view, having the stocks inside the shelter, when your horizon is long, will force you to stay committed to the long-term nature of the investment. In other words, if the stock funds are sitting outside, you are more tempted to market time by virtue of greater perceived accessibility."

Finding your place on the investment service continuum

Though the permutations seem endless, there are three basic relationship models to choose among: Do it yourself, do it with me, or do it for me.

Investing Options

The "do it myself" model

You might think this is the option for the proactive, confident investor who doesn't want or need the help of an advisor. That's true but also incomplete. Many investors use the help of a fee-for-service financial planner to work out investment goals, risk tolerance and asset allocations. Still others will access the wealth of information available on-line to determine these on their own. Then, equipped with that template, they make their own specific investment decisions and execute their own trades through a discount brokerage. This relationship model works well for those with the knowledge and a desire to invest independently, and also for those with an eye to the bottom line, since this model is the most cost-efficient way of managing your investments.

Opening an account with a discount brokerage is free, and equity trades are relatively inexpensive. (Commissions on bond trades are generally built into the cost of the bond and not charged to you over and above the cost of the bond itself.) You can access your account on-line and trade on-line or with the help of a representative over the phone. Once you've got your detailed asset allocation, deciding on specific investments does take a little research, but the required tools are readily available to you on the Internet or through a discount broker. Though they typically offer little or no advice, some discount brokers can put you in touch with a mutual fund specialist for you to confer with before making a purchase or sale. A representative can also help you understand the credit risk of corporate bonds, tell you the variety of fixed-income products available and even assist you with creating your bond portfolio.

Discount brokers, often referred to as on-line brokerages, used to be clearly distinguished from full-service brokerages in that they offered no advice whatsoever and very little investment or product information, which made very inexpensive trading commissions possible. Now the distinction between full-service and discount is blurring. On-line brokerages are providing their clients with more and more product information and varying levels of service and advice.

The TD Waterhouse Canada site, for instance, (**www.tdwaterhouse.ca**) has a good retirement planning tool that includes government benefits calculations. (You'll also find a portfolio planner tool that can help you build a personalized portfolio of top-performing mutual funds.) The "Markets and Research" section has proprietary and third-party stock and markets research and analysis.

Internet Mutual Fund Information Sites

www.morningstar.ca
www.fundlibrary.com
www.globefund.com

A caution with the "do it myself" option is the risk of falling into thought contagion: "If everyone else is doing this, there must be something to it." Some of the most famous investors of our time have been contrarians who all strongly advise against buying what's hot. Self-advised investors must have a strong sense of purpose in their investment decisions or the chances are great they could fall into the popular investment of the day instead of building a sound, well-diversified portfolio.

Do it with me

When your broker calls or your financial advisor makes an investment suggestion, you're working together to advance your goals. This is the "do it with me" model that represents a more traditional client-advisor arrangement. You and your advisor discuss courses of action and make decisions together, which gives you the benefit of a professional's oversight and care while giving you final say in what happens in your account. That sounds totally uncomplicated, but the variations on this model are manifold.

In the past, brokers worked exclusively on commission, earning their income on the basis of the size and volume of trades they executed on behalf of their clients. This transaction-driven relationship model still exists, but more and more advisors and clients want to be on the same side of the table with their interests firmly aligned. The industry has responded by introducing fee-based programs and wrap accounts.

FEE-BASED ACCOUNTS

Fee-based accounts charge a flat percentage fee based on the size of your account. This fee covers all transaction costs within the account (sometimes to a maximum number of trades), in addition to providing your advisor with a steady stream of income, which in some cases finances her time to look at other aspects of your financial situation.

WRAP PROGRAMS

Wrap programs are designed to bundle or "wrap" assorted fees and services into one comprehensive program for one flat fee based on the size of your account. These programs give you asset allocation, automatic portfolio rebalancing and regular reporting with no ancillary charges.

Wraps come in three varieties—mutual fund wrap accounts, pooled wrap programs and segregated wrap accounts—each targeted to successively higher minimum account sizes.

MUTUAL FUND WRAPS

These accounts are offered by mutual fund companies, financial planning firms and banks. They typically require you to fill out a questionnaire that explores your investment objectives, investment horizon and risk tolerance. Based on this information, you are steered to one of a series of model portfolios composed of selected mutual funds. This portfolio will be automatically rebalanced to your original asset allocation at least annually for no charge, but you pay a small fee to be in the program, in addition to the normally unreduced MERs on the underlying funds. Minimum investments can be in the $5,000 range.

You cannot bring your own investments into this program, nor can you customize your mutual fund holdings, though of course you are free to buy whatever you like outside the program. You must own one of the model portfolios without alteration. On the other hand, many investors find the professional management, ongoing review and automatic rebalancing services useful, since this allows the portfolio to run with virtually no supervision from the investor.

POOLED WRAPS

A pooled fund is a proprietary mutual fund run by investment managers for their clients and is not available to the general investing public. Pooled funds typically have lower MERs than retail mutual funds because they pay no distribution costs, commissions, trailers or other costs associated with retail mutual funds, but they also have high minimum investment requirements, often around $50,000 or more. You may or may not have to select from model portfolios, depending on the nature of the program. Most pooled programs automatically rebalance to your original asset allocation free of charge.

You must watch your total, all-in costs. Sometimes brokerage charges for trading done to manage the pools are charged to you over and above the flat fee. Fees are generally tiered and decline as account size increases. They may also be tax-deductible because investment counsel fees not relating to registered accounts are generally tax-deductible.

A huge variety of pooled wrap programs is available. As with all investments and programs, it is important to read the fine print and know exactly what is included in the "wrap" fee. Sometimes it is not as all-inclusive as you might think.

In addition to the tax deductibility of investment counsel fees, some pooled programs offer other tax savings. Conventional mutual funds distribute tax liabilities equally to all investors regardless of how long any investor has owned the fund. If you buy a fund at the end of December, you will get the same tax bill for the gains in that fund as if you had owned it from the previous January, whether or not you benefited from any of those gains yourself. Some pooled programs have sophisticated software that tracks and allocates an investor's individual tax liabilities so, rather than just equally dividing a pool's liabilities among all the investors in that pool, these programs track the time investors have spent in the pool and allot the tax liability accordingly.

SEGREGATED WRAPS

A third kind of wrap program uses individual securities instead of pooled funds or mutual funds. This is frequently called a segregated program because individual securities are, in theory, segregated from a pool and individually owned. In fact, these programs are frequently managed as pools, but specialized software apportions the securities from the pools to individual investors. You may or may not have the option of including your own investments in the program. Typical minimum investments in these programs run about $150,000. Fees may also include a maximum number of trades.

Do it for me

Formerly the exclusive domain of the extremely wealthy, technology has now made personalized, discretionary management available to those with accounts of $300,000 or more. Your investment counsellor meets with you, learns your objectives and tolerance for risk, then designs a customized portfolio for you. Once you agree to an investment approach, you give your investment counsellor discretionary trading authority over your account. No one will call to ask your permission to sell X to buy Y. You benefit by not missing any opportunities because you couldn't be reached. Your counsellor meets with you periodically, but you will not be involved in the day-to-day investment decisions.

This option allows you to put yourself at a distance from your investments so you can focus on other things in your life, and for many, this is luxurious. Surprisingly, this luxury is a bargain. Discretionary investment management can be the least-expensive professional money management option if your account is $1 million or more. Fees are tiered, and decline as account sizes get larger, but trading costs are often not included in the management fee. Remember, too, that investment counsel fees for non-registered accounts are tax-deductible.

Naturally, you need to look at the experience and the record of the management team you are considering, but keep a keen eye on costs, because the costs are there whether you make money or not.

Don't wait until your portfolio is in the million-plus range to explore the "do it for me" option, because the service itself can create value. By thinking your portfolio may not be big enough, you could miss out on an advisory relationship that shows you not only how to preserve your wealth but also how to build it.

How to choose an advisor

I'm often asked how to choose an advisor or investment counsellor and it's not an easy question to answer. Apart from fundamental competence, a lot depends on chemistry. I believe you have to start with a well-respected company because its advisors will have strong support and guidance. Then you have to make sure the advisor is more than a good salesperson. Look for experience, education and credentials like a CFP (certified financial planner), PFP (personal financial planner) or CIM/FCSI (Canadian Investment Management course/Fellow of the Canadian Securities Institute). If you are looking for a discretionary manager, seek out a holder of the CFA (chartered financial analyst) designation. Ask to see sample statements and a sample financial plan. Find out how often you will meet, how frequently your portfolio will be reviewed, and what fees and charges will be involved. A good advisor will tailor service around your needs. Ask what benchmark your advisor will use to evaluate your portfolio's performance. And before you sign on with anyone, learn the costs of transferring out of the institution and what will happen to your account should your advisor or counsellor leave.

In the appendix, you'll find a checklist for things to ask a prospective advisor that will get you through the factual information you need to help make your decision. It should also help you get an idea of the advisor's attitudes and service ethic.

Borrowing to invest

You might think it odd that anyone would suggest you borrow money to invest since you have probably spent a good part of your life trying to get rid of debt as fast as possible. Well, there is a case to be made for leveraging some of the money you already have with borrowed money to try to boost your investment returns. When interest rates are low, borrowing money for investing is singularly attractive—so long as you have the constitution for it.

Leveraging can be done by borrowing money from a brokerage through a margin account, by borrowing from a line of credit or other private borrowings, or by arranging an investment loan through a financial institution. Typically, a bank will give you one dollar for every dollar of your own you invest. Depending on the institution and the nature of the investments, you might even be able to get two or three dollars for every dollar you put up. The higher the proportion of borrowed money to your own money, of course, the riskier the situation becomes.

With a one-to-one loan, it would take a 50% decrease in the value of your portfolio to eliminate your capital completely. With a three-to-one loan, all you would need is a decline of one-third in the value of your portfolio to completely consume your own capital in paying back the borrowed (but now lost) money, not to mention the out-of-pocket interest expense.

That might be enough to put you and any other reasonable person off, but the attraction of leveraging lies in a tax advantage. Interest on money borrowed to earn investment income is tax-deductible for investments held outside registered plans. This makes borrowing to invest a tax-advantaged strategy. You get to deduct the interest expense and you can buy a portfolio designed to generate a preponderance of capital gains, which means you are getting relatively inexpensive money to increase your wealth while paying little tax on the growth. It's an enticing combination, but a potentially dangerous one.

Leveraging: The Ups and Downs

You have $10,000 and you borrow $10,000 so your total capital to invest is now $20,000.
   You invest the entire $20,000 in JFLO Co. stock.

The upside
- One week later, JFLO Co. is worth $24,000.
- Congratulations. You have made a profit of $4,000, *less* interest costs on your borrowed money.
- If you sell your holdings at that point and pay back the $10,000 that you borrowed, your initial capital would now be worth approximately $14,000. This is a 40% rate of return on the original $10,000 investment, compared to a 20% return that would have been generated had you invested without borrowing.
- But you don't sell. Instead, you hold on.

The downside
- One week later, JFLO Co. sinks to $16,000.
- You now face a loss of $4,000, *plus* interest costs.

- If you sell your holdings and pay back the $10,000 you borrowed, your initial capital would now be worth approximately $6,000. This represents a −40% return on the original $10,000 investment, compared to a −20% return that would have been generated had you invested without borrowing.

Leverage: The Double-Edged Sword

SCENARIO	PRICE OF JFLO CO. (AFTER WEEK 1)	GAIN/LOSS IN INVESTMENT (WITH LEVERAGE)	GAIN/LOSS IN INVESTMENT (WITHOUT LEVERAGE)	TERMINAL VALUE OF INITIAL $10,000 INVESTMENT (WITH LEVERAGE)	TERMINAL VALUE OF INITIAL $10,000 INVESTMENT (WITHOUT LEVERAGE)
1	$12.00	$4,000, or 40%	$2,000, or 20%	$14,000	$12,000
2	$8.00	($4,000), or −40%	($2,000), or −20%	$6,000	$8,000

The bottom line

Although there are significant potential benefits with leveraging, the possible downside to this strategy presents a very real risk that can have a dramatic impact on the value of your portfolio.

> *"If you continue to do as you have always done, you will continue to get what you have always gotten."*
>
> Anonymous

Growing your money requires knowing a lot about yourself, in addition to understanding the financial options available to you. You have to set out your goals in a definable way, recognize how much risk you can afford and how much you feel comfortable assuming, and then make some hard decisions about where you belong on the investment continuum. Are you going to be happy doing it yourself through an on-line brokerage? Or are you the kind of person who always thinks someone else could be doing a better job and feels guilty for not being current with developments in personal finance? Working with an advisor and paying commissions or fees, as needed, or using a discretionary service might have greater appeal, so long as you feel you are getting fair value for your money.

Don't procrastinate. Work out an asset allocation strategy and stick to it. Avoid timing the market. Buy good-quality investments, hold them, rebalance when necessary, and always take into account taxes and any associated fees. If you chose to work with an advisor or counsellor, work on the basis of knowledge and trust. Understand how and why your account is being structured and run the way it is. If you are unclear about any aspect, don't dismiss it. Complexity is a warning sign you should take seriously. A well-run portfolio should give you solid returns consistent with the market and be perfectly comprehensible. With all the choice around you, you should demand nothing less.

Notes

1. Brad Barber and Terrance Odean, "Boys Will Be Boys: Gender, Overconfidence, and Common Stock Investment," *Quarterly Journal of Economics* 116 no. 1 (February 2001) 261–92. The returns cited are annual, risk-adjusted net returns.
2. The survey was reported by James Langton, in "Women Investors Smarter, More Confident," *Investment Executive*, 14 May 2002, and was based on a telephone survey by Harris Interactive of 1,285 respondents between March 26 and April 9, 2002. Margin of error for female sample is +/− 3.3%, for male sample +/− 4.9%. Also see **www.openheimerfunds.comJhtml/Women_tenYearsLater.jhtml**.
3. The qualities of optimists from Daniel Kahneman and Mark W. Riepe, "Aspects of Investor Psychology: Beliefs, Preferences, and Biases Investment Professionals Should Know About," *The Journal of Portfolio Management* 24 no. 4 (Summer 1998).
4. From a Dalbar Inc. press release 21 June 2001, "Dalbar Issues 2001 Update to 'Quantitative Analysis of Investor Behavior' Report: More Proof that Market Timing Doesn't Work for the Majority of Investors," available at **www.dalbarinc.com**.

5. This hypothetical example was based on each investor putting $2,000 a year into the S&P 500 Index without taxes or transaction costs. Anita and Anna, the timers, temporarily placed their money in 30-day U.S. Treasury bills waiting for their investment moment. Catherine invested in 30-day T-bills, also. The time period was from December 31, 1981, to December 31, 2001. The idea came from the Schwab Centre for Investment Research and the example was provided by TD Wealth Management, Media Relations and Investor Communications.

6. Gary P. Brinson, Brian D. Singer and Gilbert L. Beebower, "Determinants of Portfolio Performance II: An Update." *Financial Analysts Journal*, May/June 1991. Based on information from 82 pension funds from 1977 to 1987.

7. The correlations for U.S. equity REITS vs. well-known U.S. indices can be found in "Investing in Real Estate Investment Trusts," by the National Association of Real Estate Investment Trusts. *American Association of Individual Investors Journal*, November 2000.

8. The specific indices were Lehman Brothers Aggregate Bond Index, Morgan Stanley Capital International (MSCI) EAFE Index, the Russell 2000 Index, the Russell Midcap Index and the S&P 500 Index.

9. Professor Moshe A. Milevsky's argument can be found in M.A. Milevsky, *Essays in Wealth: A Fresh Look at Risk and Return*, Captus Press, 2002.

For Further Reading

Atkinson, Howard J., with Donna Green. *The New Investment Frontier: A Guide to Exchange Traded Funds for Canadians* (Toronto: Insomniac Press, 2001). Explains indexing, index products and indexing investment strategies.

Mladjenovic, Paul. *Stock Investing for Dummies* (Toronto: Hungry Minds, 2002).

Moynes, Riley, Nick Fallon and Chris Moynes. *Top Funds 2002: Building Your Mutual Fund Portfolio* (Toronto: Prentice Hall, 2001).

Pape, Gordon, and Eric Kirzner. *Secrets of Successful Investing*. (Toronto: Prentice Hall, 2001).

Rosentreter, Kurt. *50 Tax-Smart Investment Strategies: And Other
Financial Tips to Maximize Your After-Tax Returns and Net Worth*
(Toronto: Stoddart, 2002).

For more information on investor behaviour, see Professor Terrance
Odean's Web site, **www.faculty.haas.berkeley.edu/odean.**

7 To Leave a Legacy: Estate Planning

"To live, to love, to learn, to leave a legacy."
STEPHEN R. COVEY, SELF-IMPROVEMENT CONSULTANT

At the end of the day, our financial and personal strivings come to one thing; the desire for a fulfilling life. We each have to decide what that fulfillment means and, for many of us it takes no small amount of self-knowledge and experience in the world to help us figure it out, but these are mere specifics: job, partners and children. In the big picture, we're really all the same. American self-improvement consultant and author Stephen Covey says there are four things fundamental to human fulfillment. He poetically summarizes them as "To live, to love, to learn, to leave a legacy."

By "legacy" he doesn't mean an estate or bequest. He means a lasting contribution: "...[T]he need to leave a legacy is our *spiritual* need to have a sense of meaning, purpose, personal congruence, and contribution."[1]

Fortunately it's a whole lot easier to leave money.

We can make a final contribution to our children's lives, a charity or a good cause by leaving something behind. There's also the perfectly understandable desire to give to the government only what is required of a lawful and dutiful citizen and not a nickel more. Estate planning allows you to realize both of those goals. Having your affairs in good order when you pass on enables you to direct your money as you see fit while rendering unto Caesar no more than necessary.

Sadly, poor estate planning has more serious consequences than wasted money. Years of family strife can begin when the will is read, sometimes never to heal. That's a legacy few would be happy to leave. A survey by Royal LePage Real Estate Services found that 81% of owners intend to give their vacation property to a family member. Of those,

21% said they expected a family feud to result.[2] The family cottage is a singularly emotional asset, and the fact is that even the best planning can't prevent all conflicts, but some serious thought to the issues can go a long way.

In this chapter, we'll look at the fundamentals of estate planning: wills, powers of attorney, tax considerations, trusts, insurance, charitable giving and the complications of U.S. property ownership in an estate. We'll examine ways to protect your estate and reduce taxes so you can direct at least the financial part of your legacy to those you want to have it.

Death and taxes

Death waits for no one, but CCRA somehow manages to cut to the head of the line anyway. Unless you roll everything over to your spouse or common-law partner (and a few others we'll talk about later), property in your estate is treated for tax purposes as though it had been sold immediately before your death. This means your capital gains must be reckoned and all your registered assets without a tax-free beneficiary must be taken into income. When your RRSP is taken into income, for instance, its entire fair market value is added to your income in the year of your death. You will pay tax on that RRSP money at your marginal tax rate, which will probably be the highest marginal rate because of the increase in your income due to the RRSP money itself. Any costs for settling the estate come on top of that, and probate fees, executor fees and legal costs can easily subtract another 5%.

Take a look at the costs for a sample estate.

Estimate of Taxes and Charges to Estate[3]

ASSET	VALUE	COST	CAP. GAIN
Principal residence	$300,000	NA	NA
Cottage/condo, rec. property	$250,000	$100,000	$150,000
Rental or other real estate	$200,000	$100,000	$100,000
Business/farm interest(s)	0	0	0
U.S. stocks (C$)	0	0	0
Stocks/bonds/mutual funds	$300,000	$200,000	$100,000
GICs, term deposits (non-RRSP)	$50,000	NA	NA
RRSPs, RRIFs (2)	$800,000	NA	NA
LESS: Mortgages, other debt (4)		NA	NA
Total	(1) $1,900,000	(3)	$350,000

1. ADMINISTRATION FEES—PROBATE, LEGAL, EXECUTOR

TOTAL ASSETS	(1): $1,900,000 x 3% =	$57,000
Net of mortgages and other debts	Rates 4%–8%	

2. INCOME TAX ON REGISTERED SAVINGS

TOTAL RRSPs/RRIFs	(2): $800,000 x 45% =	$360,000
Total value of registered funds are taxable	Marginal tax rate at death	

3. INCOME TAX ON CAPITAL GAINS

TOTAL CAPITAL GAIN	(3): $175,000 x 45% =	$78,750
Capital gain (3) less exemptions x 50%	Marginal tax rate at death	

4. ADD: MORTGAGES AND OTHER DEBT (4) NOT LIFE-INSURED:

5. LESS: ANY PERMANENT LIFE INSURANCE PAYABLE TO ESTATE:

Total Expenses against Estate	$495,750

You can easily insert your own numbers in this example and come up with a hair-raising sum for your own estate's tax liabilities and costs.

For many, the first impulse is to do everything possible to reduce probate fees. Because of this, I want to go through the ways frequently advocated to reduce probate and in so doing point out a few reasons why trying to avoid such fees is not always a good idea.

Probate fees

Probate is the process of certifying the legitimacy of the will and confirming your executor's authority to carry out its instructions. If one asset in your estate requires letters probate to be issued, the entire estate covered by your will is subject to the probate fee. Provinces and territories impose a probate fee (though it's not always called that) that varies widely and is tiered so it grows proportionally larger as the size of the estate increases, except for two provinces that currently have maximum fees. (Quebec's maximum charge is a modest $65 and Alberta's cap is $400.) In Ontario, the province with the highest fees, a $1 million estate will pay $14,500 in what is now called an "estate administration tax."

PROBATE FEES IN CANADA*
Alberta
- $25 for estates up to $10,000
- $100 for estates from $10,001 to $25,000
- $200 for estates from $25,001 to $125,000
- $300 for estates from $125,001 to $250,000
- $400 for estates greater than $250,000

British Columbia
- $200 flat rate on the first $25,000
- $6 per $1,000 for estates from $25,001 to $50,000
- $14 per $1,000 on the balance exceeding $50,000

Manitoba
- $25 on the first $50,000
- $6 per $1,000 on the balance exceeding $50,000

New Brunswick
- Up to $100 on the first $20,000
- $5 per $1,000 on the balance exceeding $20,000

Newfoundland
- $60 on the first $1,000
- $5 per $1,000 on the balance exceeding $1,000

Nova Scotia
- $75 on the first $10,000
- $150 for estates from $10,001 to $25,000
- $250 for estates from $25,001 to $50,000
- $500 for estates from $50,001 to $100,000
- $600 for estates from $100,001 to $150,000
- $800 for estates from $150,001 to $200,000
- $5 per $1,000 on the balance exceeding $200,000

Ontario
- $5 per $1,000 up to $50,000
- $15 per $1,000 on the balance exceeding $50,000

Prince Edward Island
- $50 on the first $10,000
- $100 for estates from $10,001 to $25,000
- $200 for estates from $25,001 to $50,000
- $400 for estates from $50,001 to $100,000
- $4 per $1,000 on the balance exceeding $100,000

Quebec
- $65 for non-notarial wills
- $0 for notarial wills—they do not need to be probated

Saskatchewan
- $7 per $1,000 of estate's value

*As of June 2002

One popular planning strategy is to keep as many of your assets as possible out of your estate so the deemed disposition and probate fees apply to only the bare minimum of assets. That's not all that difficult, but you have to be careful that in avoiding probate fees you don't trigger more costly problems later on. Caution is especially necessary if a testamentary trust might be appropriate for you or your beneficiaries. We'll talk in detail about trusts a little later, and when we get there, you'll see why a trust might be a better option than paring down your estate to reduce probate.

Beneficiary designations

RRSPs, RRIFs, LIFs, ETC.

You can start thinning out your estate by designating beneficiaries on your RRSPs, RRIFs and other registered plans. When you die, these assets will go directly to your designated beneficiary without going through your estate. By staying outside your estate, probate fees on that money are avoided. If your beneficiary is your spouse, common-law partner or a financially dependent child or grandchild with a mental or physical infirmity, the money can be rolled over to their RRSP, RRIF or a lifetime annuity with no immediate tax consequences. (The beneficiary isn't obliged to roll it into his or her own RRSP. He or she can choose to receive the cash and pay the tax.)

Financially dependent children or grandchildren without disabilities can also receive your registered funds undiminished by deducted income tax. Financially dependent (but not handicapped) adults and minors who inherit registered money do, however, have to include that money in their own income in the year they get it. This may sound punitive, but it could actually save tax, since your dependants could be in the position of paying less tax than your estate. Beneficiaries who are minors have one tax break available to them. They can place your formerly registered money in an annuity that pays to the age of 18. In this way, they pay tax only on the taxable income received from the annuity each year and not in one fell swoop.

With a RRIF, you can name your spouse or common-law partner as a successor annuitant, which allows him or her to simply take over your plan and continue receiving the income. If you don't name beneficiaries on the registered plan, the legal representative of the deceased plan holder can in some cases roll over the assets to a surviving spouse or common-law partner. If this doesn't happen, the assets are paid into the estate, taxed, subject to probate and then distributed, diminished by taxes and probate fee, to the estate's beneficiaries.

Remember that registered accounts are paid out to your beneficiaries at full value. The estate is responsible for paying tax on that money, which can amount to nearly 50% of the total value of the account. This can easily lead to a strikingly unfair situation when one child gets the RRIF and another gets the remaining estate assets, both of equal value before tax. After tax, the finally tally will be very different.

There's another caution about assigning beneficiaries to your registered accounts. Those planning to fund a testamentary trust will probably want the registered money to go into the trust rather than directly to the beneficiary, but registered assets cannot be transferred directly into a trust. They must first go through your estate and then be moved into a testamentary trust net of probate costs, administration costs and income taxes. (More on that later.)

LIFE INSURANCE POLICIES

The death benefit of a life insurance policy is paid to Canadian beneficiaries tax-free. Sometimes the estate is named as the beneficiary. This is useful when the proceeds are intended to offset taxes on the estate or to fund a testamentary trust. In most other cases, it is usually better to name a person(s) as beneficiary so the benefit does not have to be probated and creditors of the estate cannot lay a claim. It's possible to name multiple beneficiaries, and even alternatives in the event your beneficiary should die before you do.

SEGREGATED FUNDS

Segregated funds are like mutual funds with an insurance element that guarantees the principal (partially or fully) at death and at maturity. These funds used to be sold exclusively by insurance companies but are now more broadly available. Unlike conventional mutual funds, segregated funds allow you to designate a beneficiary so they do not go through your estate or need to be probated when you die.

Joint ownership

Some forms of joint ownership allow assets to pass directly to the surviving owner without going through the deceased's estate. Real estate owned in joint tenancy or investment accounts opened as "joint tenants with right of survivorship" are common examples, as are joint bank accounts.

Joint ownership has its dangers in the sense that you give up exclusive control of your assets. A joint bank or investment account is accessible by either owner and could be depleted by either owner without the knowledge of the other. You also will not be able to sell jointly owned real estate without the approval of the other owner(s). And there may be tax implications in switching from sole to joint ownership (unless your joint owner is your spouse or common-law partner).

Adding someone to your savings and chequing accounts is without tax consequences to you. There is no deemed disposition because the assets are cash, and there is no change in income attribution. If the money was yours in the first place, so is the tax liability on the interest income.

The same isn't necessarily true with an investment account at a brokerage. In that case, adding another person (who is not a spouse or partner) as joint owner of the account could be treated for tax purposes as though you'd sold half an interest in the account. If the new joint owner gives you money for beneficial interest in the account and/or you declare a deemed disposition on part of the account, capital gains tax could be owing. Seniors have to be especially careful, because capital gains can affect means-tested government benefits for seniors. Joint ownership of an investment account also requires you to decide how the ongoing tax liability on the account is to be shared among the joint owners, if it is shared at all. CCRA will generally tax the income of joint accounts in proportion to the owners' contributions to the account.

Want to leave your house to one of your children without having to pay probate fees on it? Reregistering the house in joint tenancy will accomplish this, but caution is required. If your child lives in a house of her own, she may have to pay capital gains tax on her half of your house when it is eventually sold because she will not be able to claim the principal residence exemption if she already claims it on her own home. Her capital gain will be calculated based on the property's value on the date ownership was transferred to her. Land transfer tax could also be due upon reregistering the property unless the transfer was done for "natural love and affection" and no money changed hands.

You could be jeopardizing your security by having a child who is also married and living with her spouse in your home own half of your house. Her half of your home could be considered the "matrimonial home" should she and her husband split up. In many provinces, this means her spouse could well have a claim to her interest in your house.

Giving joint tenancy to anyone other than your spouse or common-law partner will trigger a deemed disposition. When that property is your principal residence, there are no tax consequences to you because of the principal residence tax exemption. But if the property is not your principal residence, you are responsible for paying any capital gains tax owing on the "sale" of that half of the property whether or not you received any money for the title transfer. Keep in mind, too, that your joint owner's creditors could lay claim to your now jointly held assets.

Avoiding probate by arranging joint ownership can be adding a level of complication to your life that may not be worth the savings. It may complicate the affairs of your joint owner, as well, so consider it carefully beforehand.

Gifting

Gifting is the easiest way to get assets out of your estate for the most obvious reason: You no longer own them. The biggest danger with being generous is that you might miscalculate your own needs and run out of money in your retirement. It's hard to get money back from children who have sunk it into their mortgage.

You also have to be vigilant about transgressing the attribution rules. Gifting cash to anyone is completely unproblematic from a tax perspective. Giving away other real or financial assets is more involved, as, again, it triggers a deemed disposition.

Gifting stocks to your adult child (or any other adult) is seen by CCRA as a sale even if no money changes hands. You are required to pay the capital gains tax on the fair market value of those shares on the day they changed hands. This fair market value becomes your child's cost base, and she'll be required to pay tax on all subsequent gains, interest and dividends from that day forward.

Unlike gifts to adults, giving financial assets to minor children or grandchildren does not also give away your tax obligations on those assets because of the attribution rules. Not only must you pay tax on a deemed disposition, but you are also responsible for the tax on interest and dividend income generated by those investments (until the minor turns 18), even though you no longer receive them. Capital gains, however, get taxed in the minor child's hands. Attribution rules are in place to prevent some types of income splitting in families, and you can be subject to them without proper tax planning.

One useful gifting technique involves buying a universal life insurance policy on the life of your minor child. By making generous deposits to the policy, you can take advantage of the policy's tax-sheltered investment growth. When your child is grown, you can transfer ownership of the policy to her with no disposition—or tax—attributed to you. Your adult child (or grandchild) can then either withdraw some or all of the money within the policy or borrow against the policy. Withdrawals will be taxable, but if your child has little or no income, the strategy ultimately should save taxes.

Multiple wills

Estate lawyers should consider the suitability of multiple wills for their clients, says Margaret Rintoul, a lawyer with the Toronto law firm of Aylesworth, Thompson, Phelan, O'Brien LLP, whose practice is concentrated in estate planning and litigation. She says it's a good idea to look at making up separate wills for assets that require probate and those that do not. This way, only those assets requiring probate will be subject to probate fees, and not the entire estate. Of course, you have to ensure that the cost of making up separate wills is not greater than the probate fees you would otherwise pay. And it's important to note that this dual-will strategy has been tested and held up in court in Ontario, but to date it has not been tested in other provinces. Even if it were overruled, however, an estate would pay no more probate tax than with only one will.

Property held in different countries might best be dealt with in a separate will, though not necessarily for probate purposes. An estate lawyer is the best guide about this.

Trusts

Trusts play a big role in reducing probate fees because what is put into a trust is no longer part of your estate even though you may retain control over the assets and even receive income from them. A trust is a legal entity that holds assets for someone's benefit. Using trusts wisely can reduce probate fees but that is not usually the primary reason for establishing one. Trusts can significantly reduce overall taxes and protect assets for your beneficiaries, so let's look at these useful structures in a broader context than probate.

Trusts and what they do

Trusts have a cachet to them that is probably undeserved and certainly less than helpful, because trusts are remarkably useful for many people—not just the ultra wealthy. Trusts can provide for those whose financial interests you want to have protected in some way, keep property out of your estate to help minimize probate fees, and may have significant tax advantages, as well. You do not need a lot of money to justify establishing a trust if it can accomplish your objectives. A rough figure of $300,000 is sometimes used as a minimum but this depends on a number of different factors that need to be worked out with your lawyer and/or accountant.

Trusts come in two varieties. A testamentary trust is set up after your death through instructions in your will. A trust you establish during your lifetime is called an "inter vivos trust," also known as a "living trust." The distinction between the two is important because they are taxed differently. Trusts have three parties: the settlor, the trustee and the beneficiary. The settlor is the person who contributes assets to the trust, while the trustee is the person who has legal title to the assets in trust for the benefit of the third party, the beneficiary.

Almost any kind of asset can be put in a trust—financial instruments, real estate, valuable personal property, even a business—and trusts can be revocable or irrevocable. Assets contributed to a revocable trust can be removed by the settlor and the trust dissolved, while an

The Structure of Trusts

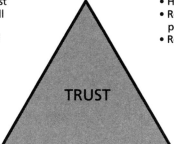

Settlor
- Transfers assets to trust
- Establishes trust in will or while still alive
- Transfers legal title of assets to trustee

Beneficiary
- Has ownership of assets
- Receives assets or property
- Receives income

Trustee
- Manages the assets according to trust agreement
- Makes payments to beneficiary
- Takes legal title to assets

Source: TD Wealth Management, Media Relations and Investor Communications

- If the settlor is alive when the trust is established, it is an inter vivos trust.
- If the trust is established as a consequence of the death of an individual, it is a testamentary trust.

irrevocable trust permanently transfers legal title to the trustee who holds and manages the assets for the beneficiaries.

Every 21 years, most trusts must calculate capital gains tax on the deemed disposition of their assets. (Qualified spousal trusts, alter ego and joint partner trusts are excepted from this rule.) This limits the time capital gains can be sheltered and left unrealized, but this is just a tax reckoning—the investments within the trust don't actually have to be sold unless some cash is needed to pay the tax bill.

Testamentary trusts
You can establish one or a number of trusts for your beneficiaries through your will. The most common of these are spousal trusts and trusts for your children/grandchildren.

SPOUSAL TRUSTS

Suppose you want to leave money for your children in your will, but you're worried that your spouse might run short of money if you do. Or perhaps you're afraid that your spouse won't manage your assets effectively after you're gone. There are any number of reasons for setting up a spousal trust. By putting assets into a trust exclusively for your spouse's benefit, you can be assured that money will be available for your spouse's needs. Once your spouse dies, then and only then will the remaining money be passed on to the children or other beneficiaries.

When you're establishing the trust, you direct the trustee as to how the money is to be invested and paid out. Some settlors give the trustee a great deal of discretion; others grant very little. Some trusts are designed to pay out only the income from the trust investments, while others can pay out principal under certain conditions—usually at the discretion of the trustee. The income beneficiary and the capital beneficiary need not be the same; however, a spousal trust can become "tainted" if someone other than the spouse receives a benefit from the trust while that spouse is still living. Tainted trusts lose their tax advantages.

Apart from probate fees, no taxes are paid when assets are placed in a qualifying testamentary spousal trust. It is considered a tax-free spousal rollover. The income and capital gains earned within a testamentary trust that are not distributed to a beneficiary are taxed at graduated rates just as an individual would be taxed (though the personal tax credits don't apply). This is especially useful for spouses who have an income of their own and don't particularly need the distributions from a spousal trust, which would be taxed at a high personal marginal rate. Money within a spousal trust can compound and be taxed at graduated rates, leaving more money for the spouse later on or ultimately for those who will inherit what is left of the trust. It's also possible for the spouse to receive income from the trust but elect to have that income taxed within the trust to take advantage of the graduated tax rates.

The assets in the last surviving spouse's trust do not form part of that spouse's estate and will not be probated. Had they not been put in a trust, those assets would have been probated twice—once upon the death of the first spouse and then again on the death of the remaining spouse.

Spousal trusts can be established for married, common-law or same-sex partners.

OTHER TESTAMENTARY TRUSTS

Because the income that is not distributed within a testamentary trust is taxed at personal graduated tax rates, leaving money to your grown children or grandchildren through a trust can be very tax-effective. Money that isn't needed can stay sheltered within the trust, generating income and attracting less tax than that income would probably attract in your children's hands. You can establish one trust for all your children, with specific instructions to the trustee for each child or set up separate trusts for each child, as long as administrative costs still make it worthwhile. Any income a trust distributes is taxed in the hands of the beneficiaries. For beneficiaries who reside in Canada, the nature of the trust income is retained: Capital gains, dividends and interest income all keep their tax identity. Trust income distributed to non-resident beneficiaries, however, does not retain its tax character, and withholding tax is levied on it as trust income.

MINOR BENEFICIARIES

Minor children can't inherit assets outright; they must be held in trust for the children during their legal minority. This doesn't necessarily mean establishing a formal trust, however, since investment and savings accounts can be opened "in trust" for minors. These are not formal trusts, but it is understood that the assets in these accounts are in the possession of an adult for the benefit of a minor who is legally entitled to claim those assets when the child reaches the age of majority.

Formal trusts are frequently created to set significant assets aside for minor children. Testamentary trusts preserve and protect the assets and permit them to continue to grow in a fairly favourable tax environment. The trust's settlor can stipulate at what age income and/or principal payments should be made and how much these should be. A settlor may even impose other conditions, the likes of which have given rise to any number of imaginative movie plots. Alternatively, the settlor can leave these matters to the judgment and discretion of the trustee(s) who is required to use that discretion for the beneficiary's interest.

DISABLED BENEFICIARIES

Mentally or physically disabled beneficiaries may already be receiving government assistance that income from a trust could affect. A "Henson" trust, named after an Ontario court decision, may help address this concern (though it isn't available in all provinces). With a "Henson" trust, both the income and the principal are paid to a disabled beneficiary only at the absolute discretion of the trustee. By giving a trustee this absolute discretion, the beneficiary is deemed to have no "beneficial interest" in the trust. This means that the income and capital payments from the trust shouldn't affect the disabled beneficiary's entitlement to government benefits.

In Ontario, you can arrange a very specific type of trust that won't reduce benefit allowances for a disabled beneficiary. *Ontario Disability Support Program Act* trusts have restrictive rules: The trust's capital must be inherited and cannot exceed $100,000. Income and capital from this trust will not affect the benefit allowance so long as it is used for approved disability-related expenses that aren't otherwise reimbursed.

Inter vivos trusts

Trusts that are established while the contributor to the trust, the settlor, is still alive are called inter vivos trusts, which in Latin means literally "from one living person to another living person." [4] Whereas everything in a will, including the terms of a testamentary trust, becomes public after probate, inter vivos trust documents are private. They are also taxed differently from testamentary trusts. Any income that's retained in the trust is taxed at the highest marginal rate, not at the personal graduated tax rates that testamentary trusts enjoy. With some notable exceptions (e.g., cash), putting assets into any trust is considered a deemed disposition, which means that capital gains on assets put into a trust must be recognized for tax purposes. This deemed disposition does not apply to spousal trusts (testamentary or inter vivos) or to two kinds of inter vivos trusts, alter ego and joint partner trusts, that are newcomers on the Canadian scene. In other words, no tax is triggered when assets are transferred into these trusts.

The big advantage with these new inter vivos trusts is that they help you exclude assets from your future estate with no immediate tax consequences. This reduces probate fees when your estate is settled; however, the assets cannot then be transferred into a testamentary trust. In exchange for saving some probate charges, your inheritors receive the trust assets directly and pay tax on the income generated by those assets at their marginal tax rate. Unless your heirs have low incomes (or the amount inherited is very small), they'd probably prefer to be the beneficiary of a testamentary trust, because the one-time savings on probate fees is generally less than the annual tax savings a testamentary trust offers. Sometimes the drive to avoid probate fees has costly tax consequences for your heirs down the road and you should consider this when contemplating these trusts.

It's been suggested that these relatively new trusts can be used to reduce a taxpayer's overall tax liability upon death by exploiting lower tax rates in certain provinces, such as Alberta. Someone facing a very large tax bill on the final disposition of assets could transfer these assets to an alter ego or joint partner trust established in Alberta, for instance. When the trust is finally wound up and the assets taxed, the low personal tax rates in that province could give some significant tax savings. As with all strategies involving trusts, this one requires the careful advice of tax professionals.

ALTER EGO TRUSTS

Those 65 or older can establish an alter ego trust—a trust in which you alone are the beneficiary during your lifetime. At your death, the assets within the trust are subject to capital gains tax and are then distributed to your chosen beneficiaries. Remember, there is no capital gains liability to placing assets in this trust initially unless you elect to declare a taxable disposition at that time. In keeping with other inter vivos trusts, however, income retained by the trust is taxed at the highest marginal tax rate.

You lose the use of the spousal rollover for any assets in this trust, but it is an effective way to avoid probate fees. Anything in an inter vivos trust is not part of your estate and therefore not subject to probate. Not being part of your estate may also make these assets beyond the reach of those who might contest your will, though this has not yet been tested in court.

This type of trust is also useful as a practical will and/or substitute power of attorney. Upon your death, assets are distributed from this trust in keeping with your instructions to the trustee, just as would be done with a will. In setting up the trust, you can also instruct the trustee to look after your assets, pay your bills, etc., once you become incapacitated or mentally infirm, just as a continuing power of attorney for personal property would facilitate.

JOINT PARTNER TRUSTS

This is the same as an alter ego trust except that the settlor of the trust and his or her spouse or common-law partner (of either sex) have entitlement to the income and principal interests of the trust during their lifetimes. The trust stays intact until the last spouse dies, at which time the assets are subject to capital gains tax and distributed to beneficiaries.

The advantages here are identical to an alter ego trust. Assets are kept out of the estate and thereby avoid probate and may afford protection should someone challenge your will. The drawback is that your assets cannot be placed in a testamentary trust after the last spouse dies, so your beneficiaries may end up paying more income tax than might have been the case with a testamentary trust, if such a trust would have been appropriate.

CHARITABLE REMAINDER TRUSTS

Putting money in trust for a charity while you are still alive has some advantages. You can get a charitable donation receipt upon contributing to the trust, and the trust assets will not ultimately be subject to probate fees. On the other hand, this trust is irrevocable. Once you've placed assets in it, you cannot touch the principal: It will be the charity's property. And, being an inter vivos trust, assets put into a charitable remainder trust are deemed disposed for tax purposes, so a capital gains liability may ensue.

This tax liability should be more than offset by the resulting tax credit, however, and the credit could possibly offset other tax liabilities you may have incurred. The amount of your charitable contribution receipt is based on an actuarial calculation of the present value of the assets. (The older you are, the greater the present value of the assets will be.) You can claim a charitable donation tax credit of up to 75% of your net income in the year of your donation and carry forward any unused portion of that credit for five years.

As long as you are alive, you can receive income from the trust, but you cannot encroach on the capital. When you die, the principal is given to the charity. This kind of trust can be set up jointly with your spouse or partner so the assets will go to the charity once both of you have passed away. Major charities have advisors who can help you sort out the tax and legal issues involved in establishing this kind of trust.

A charitable trust can also be set up through your will as a testamentary trust.

COTTAGE TRUSTS

Just about anything can be placed in a trust and the family cottage is no exception. Putting a family cottage in a trust will not give you any tax advantages, but it could prevent some family disputes. By either adding it to a trust with other assets or placing it alone in its own trust, you take the potentially fractious issues of ownership, maintenance and use out of family members' hands and put it in your trustee's.

When you put a cottage in a trust, a deemed disposition is triggered that may result in capital gains tax. Furthermore, the 21-year rule that applies to trusts requires the trust to pay capital gains tax on the growth of the trust assets every 21 years. Both these tax rules usually mean the family has to come up with cash to pay the taxes. For this reason, some families prefer to include the cottage in an estate freeze, which postpones the tax liabilities until the death of the cottage owner.

Calculating the tax liability on a cottage that has been owned for a long time is not entirely straightforward. Prior to 1972, there was no capital gains tax in Canada, and before 1982, a family unit could have two principal residences and two principal residence exemptions. Also, don't forget to check if part of the capital gain has already been recognized. In 1994, many people crystallized capital gains in preparation for the elimination of the $100,000 capital gains exemption. Your tax calculation should take those historical changes in tax law into account.

Estate freezes

You "freeze" your estate when you capture the value of your assets for tax purposes and transfer the future growth and associated tax liability to someone else. Why might you want to do this? It's a way of limiting the final tax liabilities of your estate while still having control of the assets and their income. This can be accomplished in a few ways, but here we'll look at freezes using an inter vivos trust.

You take your tax lumps in the tax year you place your "estate" in a trust, but then all future growth on those assets becomes the tax liability of the trust's beneficiaries, usually your children. The income from the trust assets can be distributed to you, and if you are a trustee of the trust, you retain control of your assets, too.

Small-business owners in particular find estate freezes useful, but do not always employ a trust structure for the freeze. Freezes can be done by placing company shares in a holding company or by simply reorganizing the company's share structure. (See "Running Your Own Show" for details.) This method avoids a deemed disposition when the freeze is implemented. Family cottages can be put into a holding company in exchange for a mix of preferred and common shares, but those using the cottage could be required to pay rent or declare a taxable shareholder benefit.[5]

Large personal investment portfolios or other assets expected to grow in value are also possible candidates for freezes.

A Tax Planning Note

It is tempting to arrange to have much of your property in joint name with your spouse, and to have assets transferred at their adjusted cost base. In fact, those arrangements may not lead to the maximum tax savings. If you have losses that can be carried forward, you will probably want to trigger some capital gains to take advantage of those losses. Shares in a qualified small business corporation may be entitled to enhanced capital gains exemptions (see "Running Your Own Show"). If so, it may be worthwhile to trigger some capital gains on those shares before transferring them.

Tax planning is complicated, and although the information in this chapter will give you good guidelines, it is advisable to get professional tax advice when dealing with estate planning matters of consequence.

Owning foreign property

A villa in the south of France, a desert-view ranch in Arizona or a condo in Florida...

Who hasn't whiled away a slow drive through a Canadian snowstorm thinking of that? It's great when the dream comes true, but owning property outside Canada considerably complicates your estate. You may have to consider making up a separate will for the foreign property, and you certainly have to be cognizant of property transfer laws in different jurisdictions. Some countries have forced-heirship rules that could require you, for instance, to leave assets to your oldest son or your spouse regardless of your wishes. And civil law jurisdictions like Quebec, Louisiana, California, Florida and France also have different rules about property transfer than do common-law jurisdictions.

Owning foreign property when you die could also give rise to tax liabilities that otherwise wouldn't exist. This is a very complicated area that requires the advice of tax experts in this field, but here's a brief rundown of some of the salient issues for U.S. property.

Property that's defined as "situated in the United States" is subject to U.S. estate tax when you die. This sounds deceptively simple. You may think this applies only to real estate and tangible personal property that's in the U.S. with some permanence, but that's not so. Shares of U.S. corporations, regardless of where they are held or traded, are considered "situated in the United States," for U.S. estate tax purposes.

Fortunately, a U.S. tax credit on a US$1 million estate value is available to Canadian citizens and residents, prorated for the value of the decedent's U.S. estate over that of his/her worldwide estate value. (In 2009, that threshold rises to US$3.5 million.) If the worldwide estate is under US$1.2 million, the only U.S. assets that are taxed, as KPMG's tax guide explains, are "the gain on the sale of which would have been subject to U.S. income tax under the [Canada-U.S. tax] treaty."[6] This means that a Canadian decedent's estate under US$1.2 million in worldwide value escapes U.S. estate tax if there is no U.S. real estate. Estates larger than US$1.2 million will likely be burdened with some hefty federal estate taxes on U.S. assets, and possibly some state taxes, as well. U.S. estate tax is charged on asset value, not on accrued gains.

Even if you fall within these thresholds, your estate must file a U.S. estate tax return for U.S. property over US$60,000 in value.

There are a few ways to maneuver around the U.S. estate taxes, all of which require considered professional advice. Holding real estate and U.S. stocks in a Canadian corporation is one possibility. Another approach is to keep the ownership of your worldwide assets down by buying property jointly so you don't exceed the US$1.2 million threshold.

A few points about wills

Dying without a will is called in the rather clinical language of law, "dying intestate"—a small calamity compared to what brought it on, but the legal repercussions might surprise you. Each province has statutory rules for the distribution of assets when someone dies intestate. Most provinces give the first set value of assets to the spouse and then split the remaining assets among children and/or the spouse. If this doesn't seem so alarming, the spouse's preferential share can be very modest. In Alberta, it is only $40,000, compared to Ontario's $200,000. In the absence of a remaining spouse, children or parents, the estate is split equally among the deceased's siblings. The rules vary a little between provinces and with different family circumstances.

These intestate rules are inflexible and do not take into account common-law relationships and blended-marriage situations. In most provinces, common-law partners have no right to inherit property from a spouse who dies intestate, and stepchildren and biological children will not be treated equally, either. Dying without a will could bring hardship to your loved ones, so if only as a courtesy to them, get a will. With some planning, it can actually be a good tax planning tool, as well.

"Don't delay and don't use a kit," is Alan Walker's advice. "Wills aren't expensive and the decisions you make are among the most important in your life. It is always worth getting good advice." Walker is Associate Vice President, Estates and Trusts with TD Private Client Group. He says wills must be properly witnessed and their instructions must be absolutely unambiguous. A lawyer can be very useful in helping you clarify your wishes and expressing them in a way that won't result in years in court or frustrate your intentions. A lawyer will also be able to advise you on how to structure your will so it is less likely to be successfully challenged in court after you die.

Before seeing a lawyer, though, you should think about what you want to accomplish in your will and what the tax ramifications of those objectives might be. If you are leaving everything to your spouse, perhaps you want to consider a spousal trust that will pay your spouse the income from assets that are held in the trust for the eventual benefit of your children. If you want to leave money directly to your children, it might be preferable to establish a trust for each child. That could save taxes and preserve the value of the inheritance.

You should have all your assets organized and a strong idea of how you want them distributed after your death. You may alter your plans in light of some advice from your lawyer, but it's good to know in detail what you are aiming to accomplish in your will before seeing a lawyer.

Anyone with young children or disabled dependants has the added responsibility of naming a guardian in the will. It's a good idea to discuss financial arrangements with your elected guardian so, if necessary, you can include those arrangements in the will. Your guardian might feel most comfortable having your dependants' money placed in a trust or having a trust company manage the assets.

You must also decide who will take charge of your affairs after you die and wind up your estate as directed in your will. Few people realize how demanding being an executor can be, which is why you should first get the agreement of the person you would like to be your executor.

Your executor should be reliable, fair and without bias to your beneficiaries, knowledgeable about financial matters, familiar with your family situation, and able and willing to take on what might become a lot of extra work. Your executor should live fairly close to you so visits to your financial institutions and other professionals won't be a major undertaking. Your executor should also outlive you, and since most people appoint their spouse as executor, it's a good idea to designate a contingent executor in case your primary executor dies before you do.

It's also possible to appoint multiple executors—your children, perhaps. That's not always a recipe for harmony, and the wisdom of this decision will depend how well the children get along and their general agreement with your final wishes. If you do decide to appoint multiple executors, consider applying a "majority rules" clause or some other direction to help ensure a quick resolution to disagreements.

What an executor does

Find the will and arrange the funeral
An executor is responsible for arranging your funeral, so make sure your executor knows your wishes in that respect. A letter to your executor outlining the arrangements you would like is a good idea, and so is pre-arranging your funeral. Including instructions in your will is less than ideal because a will sometimes isn't located until well after the funeral has taken place. It's always a good idea to give a copy of your will to your executor.

Arrange probate
If one of your assets requires letters probate to be released, your executor will have to have your will probated through the court.

Locate and secure the assets
The next thing your executor has to do is locate all your assets and ensure that their value remains intact. Leave a list of all your investment and bank accounts with account numbers, the phone number and address of the financial institution and a contact person. Leave written instructions to find your insurance policies, mortgage and loan papers, and all other similarly important documents.

An executor is personally liable to the beneficiaries for the value of your estate. The executor can be held personally and legally responsible for any errors made while settling the estate.

Pay all the bills and file the taxes

Your executor must pay all your debts from the money in your estate. Tax returns must be completed and taxes paid. Sometimes this involves filing more than one tax return, as it may be advantageous to file multiple returns for the year of death. Once CCRA is assured that all the taxes on the estate have been paid, it issues a clearance certificate. This certificate is CCRA's confirmation to the executor that all outstanding tax issues have been settled. The executor can then distribute the estate to the beneficiaries without any personal risk. An executor who pays out assets before the clearance certificate is issued risks being personally accountable should CCRA find tax still owing in the future.

Distribute the assets

With a clearance certificate in hand, an executor can distribute the assets to your beneficiaries with little worry about overlooked taxes. Your executor is obliged to distribute your assets in accordance with your will. It's not hard to imagine how torn an executor could feel having to oversee what he or she sees as an unfair distribution to people your executor might know and love. If you are contemplating what could be a controversial bequest, consider this when you choose your executor.

Finally, your executor should prepare a summary of the estate and its disposition for the beneficiaries. (See appendix 7 for a detailed list of the executor's duties.)

Compensating your executor

Acting as an executor is a lot of work and you should make it clear that you don't expect your executor to do it all without professional help. Executors can be tempted to be penny-wise but pound foolish in trying to save professional fees while missing out on services that will save the estate money in the long run.

Unless the executor is also a beneficiary, all provinces but Quebec permit an executor to withdraw some compensation from the estate, somewhere in the range of 3% to 5% of the estate's value.[7] It's quite possible your executor will feel uncomfortable about receiving compensation from your estate, especially if you suggest this while arranging for the executor's consent and most likely before he or she knows how demanding the job will be. Out of consideration for your executor, stipulate in your will that the executor is entitled to fair and reasonable compensation.

What a trust company can do

Trust companies charge a fee for their service based on the size of assets under administration, but they can bring some impressive experience and tenacity to the table: They have been known to fight legal battles in court on behalf of minor or incapacitated beneficiaries and to safeguard the welfare of orphans by wresting control of businesses out of the hands of opportunists.

Trust companies look after the financial affairs of individuals, estates and businesses. You might appoint a trust company to take charge of your financial assets some time in the future if you expect to be incapacitated and don't want to place that burden on family or friends. Or you could appoint a trust company as the executor of your will if it is particularly complicated, if you are concerned about the unbiased execution of your wishes or just to spare someone close to you the responsibility of being your executor. A business that suddenly loses its owner-manager might also elect to have a trust company run it temporarily. If you chose to establish a trust, either through your will or in your lifetime, appointing a trust company as trustee will guarantee the trustee will outlive your beneficiaries. Some trusts last for generations so continuity is important.

Trust services can include tax return filings, estate planning, bill payments, legal advocacy on behalf of clients or estate beneficiaries and, of course, the administration and management of financial assets.

Fees for trust services usually start at a minimum and then are tiered on asset value and the level of service you require. When you consider you may be paying the fees of many professionals to deal with your estate, professional trustee services may not look expensive for the value they could deliver.

Powers of attorney

As the saying goes, it's something we hope we'll never need but should never be without.

In Quebec it's called a "mandate" and in the rest of the country a "power of attorney." Basically, it is a document that authorizes someone else to act on your behalf. "Attorney" here does not necessarily mean a lawyer, just someone who will act on your behalf. The powers of your attorney can be as expansive or as restrictive as you specify, but it becomes void when you die. (Your will and your executor take over at that point.) There are two kinds of powers of attorney: one for your property and one for your personal care.

Power of attorney for property

This document authorizes the named person to act on your behalf with respect to your property. You might give a power of attorney to a trusted friend who will manage your affairs while you are on an extended trip or in hospital, but most likely it is prepared so your affairs will not come to a grinding halt should you become mentally incompetent. (In order for your power of attorney to be valid when you become mentally incompetent, the document must stipulate that power of attorney is continuing or enduring.)

The power to act on your behalf can be as sweeping or as circumscribed as you decide. You can give a power of attorney for just one investment account or for every asset you own. You can name alternative attorneys or joint attorneys who can act either jointly or separately, as you decide. You can also instruct them to take some payment for their services or require them to do it free of charge (though the law entitles them to some compensation). Understand that there is always the possibility that your financial well-being could suffer through your attorney's lack of skill or outright dishonesty, so select your attorney with care.

The document becomes valid when it is signed and properly witnessed. It can be exercised on the discretion of your attorney or be given to your attorney only when it is required, perhaps by being held by your lawyer until your doctor confirms your mental incompetence.

If you have a power of attorney for someone else, you should carefully document the circumstances surrounding your decision to exercise that power. A letter from one or two doctors supporting your assessment of the mental competency of your charge would be a good idea. You must perform your duties with care, or you could be sued by relatives or other beneficiaries of the future estate.

Power of attorney for personal care

This is a legal document that gives someone the legal power to act on your behalf in matters of personal health care. You may chose to include written instructions about your future care, perhaps in respect to resuscitation, heroic measures and pain management, or you can leave no specific instructions and rely on the judgment and compassion of your attorney.

The document becomes valid once it is signed and properly witnessed. Your attorney may use it when he or she judges you incapable of making your own personal care decisions. You may wish to require your attorney to get a doctor's opinion on your capacity before being able to exercise the power of attorney, and your attorney would probably wish to do this anyway for her own protection.

You can revoke this power of attorney so long as you are mentally competent by making out a new one or saying in writing that you revoke it and having it witnessed in keeping with the requirements of the original document. To be properly witnessed, there must be two adult witnesses who are not your attorney or his or her spouse, your partner, your child or someone with property under guardianship. Once you are mentally incompetent, you cannot revoke this power of attorney.

A power of attorney for personal care is a grim reminder of our physical vulnerability, but it is a critical part of estate planning. If you neglect to draw one up and become unable to make decisions about your own care, you will become a ward of the state. A close relative can petition the court to become your guardian—which could easily cost more than $1,000—and by then you would have no say over who is entrusted with your care.

Powers of attorney are very inexpensive to draw up with a lawyer. You can expect something in the neighbourhood of $200, and if you get your power of attorneys done in conjunction with a will, they cost even less.

A single, uncomplicated will with a continuing power of attorney for property and a power of attorney for personal care can be as little as $375 in small centres. That's a modest investment for the flexibility and peace of mind it will give you.

Charitable giving

Leaving money to charity when you die will certainly be appreciated by the charity, but it may not ultimately be the best way to do it. You could be denying yourself the gratification of furthering a cause you believe in while you can enjoy it and missing out on some hefty tax savings, too. My point is just that you shouldn't think about charitable giving exclusively in terms of your will. Donations over a few years while you are still alive to see your money put to good use should also be considered.

While you are alive, you are allowed a charitable tax credit of up to 75% of your net income in any one year. Unused credits can be carried forward five years. In the year of your death, that limit increases to 100% of your net income and excess credits can be carried back to the previous year, to a 100% net income maximum.

Large charities can usually accommodate just about anything you care to give them: cash, real estate, securities, valuable objects, insurance policies, royalties, even residual interests. Gift consultants employed by charities or tax accountants can help you sort out the tax implications of your gifts and advise you on different gifting strategies, many of which we'll cover here.

Gifts of property

Gifts of property will trigger a deemed disposition at fair market value that may result in a capital gains tax liability. (In the case of depreciable property, you may also have to deal with recaptured capital cost allowances.) The good news is that credit for capital property donations takes these tax liabilities into account. The 75% credit limit is increased by 25% of the taxable capital gains or recaptured depreciation resulting from gifted properties. Donations of ecologically sensitive lands and certified cultural property may also get the same treatment under certain conditions. You must be mindful of triggering alternative minimum tax with such a large tax credit. (Alternative minimum tax is a federal tax designed to ensure that taxpayers cannot reduce their taxable income below $40,000 by using tax shelters and other write-offs. Minimum tax does not apply in the year of death.)[8]

Think your house or cottage might make a nice venue for a charity? You can gift your property to a charity but continue to live there until you and your spouse pass away. You receive a tax receipt for your donation (at fair market value) when you sign over the ownership, but you get to continue to enjoy your property for as long as you like. You do, however, have to continue to maintain the property at your expense.

Gifts of securities

Special tax treatment for gifts of publicly traded securities (including mutual funds) has made it advantageous to donate the securities on which you have a capital gain, rather than donating the cash from the sale of those securities, because the capital gains inclusion rate for donated securities is only 25% instead of the regular 50%. (In-kind donations to private foundations do not get this tax break.)

Donate Cash or Shares?

Susan has $10,000 worth of Publico shares, on which she has a $5,000 capital gain.

If she sells the shares, she will have to pay ($5,000 × 50%) × 46% = $1,150 in tax.

After she pays the tax, the charity receives $8,850.

Adding in her charitable donation tax credit of $4,071 ($8,850 × 46%), Susan saves $2,921 in taxes from her donation ($4,071 − $1,150).

If she donates the shares instead, the charity gets the full $10,000 and Susan has to pay only $575 in tax [($5,000 × 25%) × 46%].

After the tax credit on a $10,000 donation, Susan's tax savings from her donation are $4,025 ($4,600 − $575).

Gifting the shares in kind has gained Susan $1,104 ($4,025 − $2,921).

This example assumes Susan has already made $200 in charitable donations in the year.

Gifting registered assets

RRSPs, RRIFs and other registered assets that aren't rolled over tax-free to another person are taxed very heavily. All the money in these accounts is taken into income in the year of your death, which likely means you'll be pushed into the highest marginal tax rate if you weren't there already. As a result, this "income" will be taxed at the highest marginal tax rate in your province and you could easily lose just shy of half your registered assets to taxes.

You can avoid this tax bite by designating a charity as the beneficiary of your registered money. When the charity receives the money after your death, it will issue a charitable tax receipt that will offset the tax on those registered assets. The charity gets the full value of your RRSP or RRIF and your estate avoids income tax and probate fees on that money. This is an extremely tax-efficient way to give to a charity.

Perhaps giving away all your registered money is more than you would like to give to any one cause. In that case, you can name more than one beneficiary on your registered accounts and each will receive an equal share.

Gifting insurance

There are a few ways to give your insurance proceeds to a charity. Designating a charity the beneficiary of your life insurance will give you a charitable donation for the death benefit, which can be claimed either in the year you die or the year before your death.[9] The charity gets the money promptly and, because the money never goes through your estate, you pay no probate fees on the insurance proceeds.

It's also possible to make a charity the owner of your insurance policy, as well as the beneficiary. In that case, the value of your donation will be the cash surrender value of the policy along with any accumulated dividends and less any policy loans. If, however, that value exceeds the tax cost of the policy, you will be taxed on that excess as though you had received it as income. Once the policy is no longer yours, you can get ongoing charitable donation tax credits by continuing to pay the premiums.

Robert Aggio, Vice President, Estate Planning Solutions with TD Private Client Group, says gifting securities is more advantageous from a tax perspective than gifting insurance, so if you have the choice, he advises that you gift securities. Then, he says, you can replace the value of those donated securities with insurance that can pay your beneficiaries. That way, you've gotten the maximum tax benefit from a charitable donation and still have the same amount of money to give your beneficiaries, tax- and probate-free, for no more than the cost of the insurance.

Setting up a charitable foundation

This may sound like the domain of Lord Conrad Black, but setting up your own charitable foundation is not only for the rich and famous. Minimums can be as low as $250,000.

The advantage of a private foundation is that you, or a board of directors you select, can control exactly how your money is spent and on what. The disadvantage is that you have to administer the foundation, organize and maintain a board of directors, and pay ongoing costs for tax filings and accounting services.

With a little searching, you might find a foundation already in existence with a mandate in line with your own goals. Foundations provide charitable donation receipts and welcome donations. Don't overlook community foundations, either. You can find out about them by contacting Community Foundations of Canada, a membership organization, at **www.community-fdn.ca**.

Charitable remainder trust

This is an irrevocable trust set up for the benefit of a charity when you die. It can be established while you are alive or through your will. You get a charitable donation receipt when you contribute to the trust, but the assets within the trust belong to the charity and cannot be encroached upon. You, or the trust's beneficiary, can receive the investment income from the trust, but not the capital. (For more details, see the section on trusts earlier in this chapter.)

Charitable annuity

Many large charities sell annuities, so if you are thinking of buying an annuity as part of your retirement income strategy and you want to direct some money to a charity, this is an option to look at. Although the cost of an annuity sold through a charity might be a little higher than one sold directly through an insurance company, you do get some tax benefits.

Payments from a conventional annuity are a combination of interest and return of capital. The capital portion is tax-free, but the interest portion is taxed. Charitable annuities can be arranged to generate completely tax-free payments, as long as the money you give to set up the annuity exceeds the payments the annuity is expected to give you, based on CCRA's actuarial tables. You can also get a charitable donation tax credit for this actuarially calculated excess since the charity receives this money when you die. If, however, your payments are expected to exceed what you paid for the annuity, some portion of your payments will be taxed.

As with all annuities, you must be careful about the terms of the contract. Does it have a guarantee period? Will it pay your spouse after you die? Is the interest rate reasonable, and are the payments adequate for your needs?

Insurance

We've already seen that taxes can take a big bite out of your estate. Unless you can roll your assets over to a spouse or partner, you're likely to lose about half your registered assets to taxes along with any capital gains tax liability you might have. Add to that the cost of probate, legal fees and executor costs and your estate can be diminished pretty quickly. But something can be done about this. Insurance can be used to replace the money lost to taxes and estate settlement costs, or it can form the very foundation of your estate.

Taking our chart on page 210 as a sample, plug in your own numbers to get a rough idea of your estate's tax liabilities and costs (if you are not able to take advantage of a tax-free rollover on any of your assets and you haven't made other provisions for putting your assets outside your estate). Now, with a ballpark idea of the insurance coverage you might want to obtain, you can decide what kind of insurance is most appropriate for you. And don't forget that insurance death benefits are tax-free.

Estimate of Taxes and Charges to Estate[3]

ASSET	VALUE	COST	CAP. GAIN
Principal residence			
Cottage/condo, rec. property			
Rental or other real estate			
Business/farm interest(s)			
U.S. stocks (C$)			
Stocks/bonds/mutual funds			
GICs, term deposits (non-RRSP)			
RRSPs, RRIFs (2)			
LESS: Mortgages, other debt (4)			
Total (1)		(3)	

1. ADMINISTRATION FEES—PROBATE, LEGAL, EXECUTOR

TOTAL ASSETS (1):	×	=
Net of mortgages and other debts	Rates 4%–8%	

2. INCOME TAX ON REGISTERED SAVINGS

TOTAL RRSPs/RRIFs (2):	×	=
Total value of registered funds are taxable	Marginal tax rate at death	

3. INCOME TAX ON CAPITAL GAINS

TOTAL CAPITAL GAIN (3):	×	=
Capital gain (3) less exemptions × 50%	Marginal tax rate at death	

4. ADD: MORTGAGES AND OTHER DEBT (4) NOT LIFE-INSURED:

5. LESS: ANY PERMANENT LIFE INSURANCE PAYABLE TO ESTATE:

Total Expenses against Estate $

Term to 100 and universal life are the two forms of insurance most often suggested in estate planning situations.

Term to 100 insurance is designed to cover you for your entire lifetime. In most cases, the premiums are constant, and must be paid until you die or reach 100. If you stop paying the premiums, your coverage ends. (After age 100, the coverage continues without your needing to pay the premiums.) The premiums are higher than those charged for 10-year term insurance, and as with all term insurance, no cash surrender value is built up and there is no investment element.

Universal life combines term insurance with an investment element. It is permanent insurance because it covers you for life so long as your premiums are paid, either by you or the investment income generated within the policy.

Whichever type of insurance you select, if you have a partner, consider making it "joint and last to die." This means the policy pays when the last surviving spouse dies. For those who are able to use the tax-free rollover provisions, joint and last to die policies are usually suggested. Since a couple's biggest tax hit most often comes when the last spouse dies, this arrangement works well. Joint and last to die policies are also generally less expensive than single policies.

This strategy may not be as expensive as you might think. A couple, both 70 years old and non-smokers, would pay only $7,000 a year in premiums on a term to 100 joint and last to die policy that would pay out $300,000 based on current rates.

A universal life policy would be more expensive because the investment element must be funded, but that can be paid for up front and the subsequent investment growth used to pay for the insurance premiums. Universal life would be recommended for someone with more than adequate resources who is looking for ways to shelter income, move assets out of the estate or deal with the estate's tax liability. Aggio says moving GIC money, for example, into a universal life policy would shelter the interest income from tax while simultaneously removing that money from the future estate. Money that would have been subject to probate fees can now be paid out to the beneficiaries free of tax and probate. Of course, if the purpose of the insurance is to pay taxes on the estate, the policy would most likely be made out to the estate, in which case you've simply set assets aside through the policy to pay the taxes but allowed them to grow in a tax-sheltered environment and given them an added boost with the insurance element.

Insurance in estate freezes

Those who have executed an estate freeze know their estate's exact tax liability because they've frozen it in time. Insurance can pay that liability. It can also be used to equalize your children's inheritance. Frequently, when business owners freeze their estate, new common shares in the family company are given to all of the children and any future growth will accrue to the children's common shares. (The parents retain preferred shares that are fixed, or "frozen," in value.) Seldom do all the children want an active role in the company, and this can force the ones who want the company to buy back the shares from their siblings at a cost they can rarely afford without going into debt. Not many parents are in the position of being able to give the family business to one child and assets of equal value to the other children. Insurance can make this situation easier by making money available for the other children. Then the new business operator doesn't have the pressure of an unwanted debt and the other siblings have something closer to a fair solution.

All these insurance solutions hinge, of course, on your insurability. By the time you turn your mind to estate planning, you may no longer be insurable or a physical condition may make insurance too expensive. Even if you can't come close to estimating how much insurance your estate will ultimately need, you should seriously consider buying a small universal life policy for estate planning purposes while you are insurable. Many policies let you increase your coverage at any time without proof of insurability, so you can fine-tune your insurance coverage later on.

Considerations for common-law couples

In most provinces, common-law partners have no automatic right to inherit property upon the death of their partner. A will is vital to protecting the interests of your common-law partner and in making sure your assets will go to whom you wish. Without a valid will, your property will be distributed according to the laws of your province. In most cases, that means a common-law partner gets nothing, in favour of your children and your legal spouse, if you have one.[10] A marriage revokes a will (unless it was made in contemplation of the marriage), but a separation or divorce does not. Common-law couples should revisit their wills and all their beneficiary designations to make sure they are consistent with their current wishes.

In Ontario, spouses can claim an equalization payment if they're not content with what was allotted to them in their spouse's will. This, too, is a right not accorded to a common-law partner.

Tax laws are more evenhanded with respect to common-law and same-sex couples. As long as your relationship qualifies by CCRA's definition (see page 103), you are entitled to tax-free spousal rollovers of property while you are both alive or when one partner dies. It's the property rights you have to watch out for.

> "We pay for the mistakes of our ancestors, and it seems only fair that they should leave us the money to pay with."
>
> Don Marquis,[11] American columnist (1878–1937)

After a lifetime of working, saving and investing, you should have the final say over where your money goes when you're no longer around to enjoy it. Spend some time making or updating your will, recording all the things your executor will need to know, drawing up powers of attorney and thinking about the beneficiary designations on your insurance, registered accounts and segregated funds, if you have them.

Understanding the tax and legal considerations of estate planning, the use of trusts and the advantages of some charitable gifting strategies could open up possibilities that might not otherwise have occurred to you. It may also give you the sober realization that these matters must not be put off indefinitely or those you love and the good causes you may wish to support could suffer.

A little time invested now could save your family and friends no little inconvenience later on. Your legacy to them, whatever it might be, should not be soured by an estate fraught with difficulties.

Notes

1. Stephen R. Covey, A. Roger Merrill and Rebecca R. Merrill, *First Things First: To Live, To Love, To Learn, To Leave a Legacy* (New York: Simon & Schuster, 1994), 45. Emphasis by the authors.
2. As reported by Garry Marr in the *National Post*, "Family Feud Expected over Cottage Inheritance: Study," 16 May 2002.
3. Chart courtesy of Robert Aggio, Vice President, Estate Planning Solutions, TD Private Client Group. The example provided is for informational purposes only.
4. Lloyd Duhaime, *Duhaime's Law Dictionary*, 30 July 2002, **www.duhaime.org/diction.htm**.
5. This point was made by Michael Berton, in "Life as a Cottage," *Advisor's Edge* volume 5, #6 (June 2002), an excellent article on a number of ways to pass a family cottage on to children.
6. *KPMG Tax Planning for You and Your Family 2002*, 273.
7. Sandra E. Foster, *You Can't Take It With You: The Common-Sense Guide to Estate Planning for Canadians*, 4th ed. (Toronto: John Wiley & Sons, 2002), 63.
8. Alternative minimum tax can be triggered when you have a high proportion of tax deductions or credits in proportion to your income. If you do have to pay minimum tax, you can carry the excess of your minimum tax over your regular tax in that year to any of the next seven years to offset the excess of your regular tax over the minimum tax.
9. KPMG, 316.
10. British Columbia and Nova Scotia have legislation trying to rectify the legal entitlement to property for common-law partners but Nova Scotia's legislation is currently being challenged in the court. The outcome of that case could affect British Columbia's legislation.
11. Quotations on inheritance, **www.quotemeonit.com/marquis.html**, 30 July 2002.

For Further Reading

Foster, Sandra E. *You Can't Take It With You: The Common-Sense Guide to Estate Planning for Canadians*, 4th ed. (Toronto: John Wiley & Sons, 2002).

Gray, Douglas, and John Budd. *The Canadian Guide to Will & Estate Planning: Everything You Need to Know Today to Protect Your Wealth and Your Family Tomorrow*, 2nd ed. (Toronto: McGraw-Hill Ryerson, 2002).

The law firm of Byck & Leckie has a good Web site on powers of attorney to which I am indebted: **www.temlaw.com/poa.html**.

APPENDIX 1

Net Worth Worksheet

Assets		Current Value
A. Liquid Assets		
Chequing account		
Savings account		
GICs and T-bills		
Cash value of life insurance		
Money market funds		
Other (e.g., money owed to you)		
Total Liquid Assets	(A)	_____
B. Long-Term Assets		
Mutual funds (excluding money market)		
Stocks		
Bonds		
RRSPs/RRIFs		
RESPs		
Company pension plan		
Other		
Total Long-Term Assets	(B)	_____
C. Property Assets		
Residence		
Vacation property		
Vehicles		
Jewellery/art/collectibles		
Other (e.g., furniture)		
Total Property Assets	(C)	_____
Total Personal Assets (A+B+C)		_____
Liabilities		
Credit card(s)		
Auto loan(s)		
Education loans		
Investment loans		
Other loans		
Mortgage(s)		
Other		
Total Personal Liabilities		_____
Personal Net Worth		
Total Personal Assets		
Less: Total Personal Liabilities		
Equals: Your Personal Net Worth		

APPENDIX 2

Budget Worksheet

	Monthly	Annually
Cash Inflows		
Net salary (Gross salary—income taxes)		
Bonuses		
Interest income		
Dividends		
Capital gains		
Rental income		
Other income		
(e.g., RRSP, RRIF or pension income, government benefits, a tax refund)		
Total Cash Inflows		
Cash Outflows		
A. Living Expenses		
Mortgage/rent		
Property tax		
Condominium/maintenance fees		
Utilities		
Cable TV		
Internet		
Telephone (land line and cellular)		
Home/condominium/tenant insurance		
Other		
Auto maintenance		
Auto insurance		
Gas		
Parking		
Other transit		
Groceries		
Clothing		
Health and dental care		
Pet care		
Other		
Total Living Expenses (A)		
B. Debt Payments		
Auto loan(s)		
Credit card(s)		
Line of credit		
Other		
Total Debt Payments (B)		

	Monthly	Annually
C. *Investment Programs*		
Life and disability insurance		
RRSP contributions		
Emergency fund		
Other investment savings		
(e.g., education savings)		
Total Investment Programs (C) _____		_____
D. *Discretionary Expenses*		
Entertainment		
Dining out		
Vacations		
Subscriptions		
Membership fees		
Gifts		
Charitable donations		
Household purchases		
Tuition		
Hobbies		
Other		
Total Discretionary Expenses (D) _____		_____
Total Cash Outflows	_____	_____
(A+B+C+D)		
Surplus/(Deficit)	_____	_____
(Total Cash Inflow − Total		
Cash Outflow)		

Notes: *A good way to determine how much you spend on each category is to look at your credit card and bank statements, if you tend to use your credit and debit cards for most purchases.*

We recommend that you use this worksheet as a guide only. Consider setting up your own categories and eliminating those that don't apply to you. Don't make the categories so narrowly defined that you get bogged down in details, but do make them specific enough that you can see where your money is going each month.

APPENDIX 3

Wealth Allocation Model

This is a proprietary investor profile/asset allocation model designed by TD Asset Management Inc. and has been included for reference only. It has been adapted from a longer worksheet that includes specific TD Mutual Fund recommendations. Because the investor profiles and allocations are revised periodically, (the ones set out here expire October 31, 2002) investors should call 1-800-281-8029 or visit EasyWeb at **www.tdcanadatrust.com/mutualfunds** or speak with a Mutual Funds Representative at a TD Canada Trust branch before investing in any of these allocation models.

STEP 1 WHAT IS YOUR INVESTOR PROFILE?
Determine your investment needs and objectives.
The following questions will help determine an asset allocation strategy appropriate for your personal goals. If you have more than one goal—such as retirement, your children's education or a new home—complete a separate questionnaire for each goal.

1. Are you willing to tolerate any risk to earn a potentially higher return?
   - ☐ Yes
   - ☐ No (Mutual funds may not be a suitable investment.)

2. What is the purpose of this investment?
   - ☐ RRSP/RIO*
   - ☐ Non-Registered/RESP

3. How much money do you want to invest today?
   - ☐ Lump sum $_____
   - ☐ Pre-authorized purchase plan (PPP) $_____

4. Which one of the following statements best describes you?
   - ☐ While I want suggestions and guidance in selecting a portfolio that is best for me, I still want the ability to customize my own portfolio.
   - ☐ I want someone to manage my portfolio and fund selection in keeping with my investment objectives.

5. The statement that most clearly defines my investment objective(s) is:

• I want to ensure my capital is safe and I do not need income at this time.	**0 Points**
• I require a steady stream of income from my investments.	**1 Point**
• I have some need of income, but am also interested in capital growth.	**2 Points**
• I would like long-term growth and I am less concerned about income at this time.	**5 Points**
• I'm interested only in growth over the long term.	**6 Points**

6. I plan to start withdrawing money from my investments in:

• Under 2 years (short term)	**1 Point**
• 2–5 years (mid term)	**2 Points**
• 6–10 years (mid to long term)	**5 Points**
• Over 10 years (long term)	**9 Points**

7. My current investments are best described as follows:

• Little or no investment experience.	**0 Points**
• Mostly T-bills, GICs or term deposits.	**0 Points**
• Mostly bonds, strips or income mutual funds.	**2 Points**

*RIO stands for "Retirement Income Option"

- A mix of money market, bond and stock investments
and/or mutual funds.   **3 Points**
- Mostly stock or stock mutual funds.   **4 Points**

8. Investments with higher returns typically involve greater risk. This question presents four hypothetical $10,000 investments with widely varying potential risks/rewards. Which outcome would you be most comfortable with?

Potential value ranges of investment after 5 years

9. I respond to fluctuations in my investments in the following manner:
- I will sell quickly any time my investment loses value or money.   **1 Point**
- Day-to-day market movements make me uncomfortable. If an investment loses value over a 3- to 6-month period, I am likely to sell it and look for a better alternative.   **2 Points**
- I realize that markets may rise and fall randomly. I usually watch my investment for at least a year before making changes.   **4 Points**
- I believe that a long-term investment strategy will maximize potential returns. Even if poor market conditions resulted in sizable losses in a given year, I stay invested.   **6 Points**

Although the following questions are more personal in nature, they are an essential part of determining the best mix of investments for you.

10. The current value of my RRSP and non-registered investment portfolio, including investments held at other institutions (i.e., mutual funds, stocks, bonds, GICs, money market investments, savings/chequing accounts), but excluding real estate is:
- Under $25,000   **1 Point**
- $25,000–$49,999   **2 Points**
- $50,000–$99,999   **3 Points**
- $100,000–$250,000   **4 Points**
- Over $250,000   **5 Points**

11. My current age is:
- Under 30 years   **4 Points**
- 30–45 years   **5 Points**
- 46–55 years   **3 Points**
- 56–65 years   **1 Point**
- Over 65 years   **1 Point**

12. My personal income is in the following range:
- Under $25,000   **1 Point**
- $25,000–$49,999   **2 Points**
- $50,000–$74,999   **3 Points**
- $75,000–$125,000   **4 Points**
- Over $125,000   **5 Points**

Total Point Score (Add scores for questions 5 to 12)
Please proceed to step 2

STEP 2 WHAT IS YOUR OPTIMAL ASSET ALLOCATION?
Match your point score to the chart to determine your Investor Profile and the asset mix that's appropriate for you.

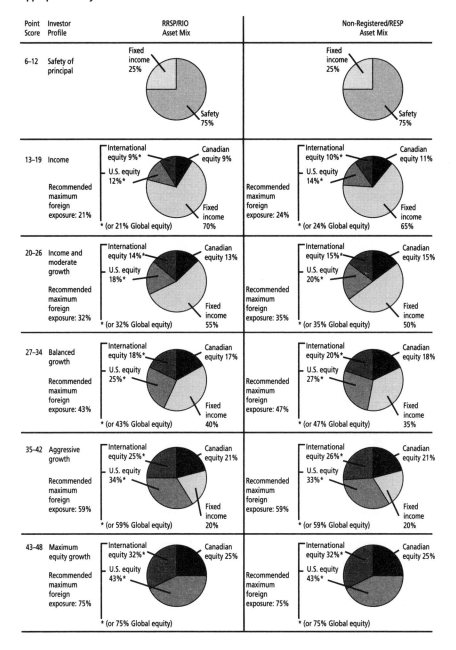

Point Score	Investor Profile	RRSP/RIO Asset Mix	Non-Registered/RESP Asset Mix
6–12	Safety of principal	Fixed income 25% / Safety 75%	Fixed income 25% / Safety 75%
13–19	Income. Recommended maximum foreign exposure: 21%	International equity 9%* / Canadian equity 9% / U.S. equity 12%* / Fixed income 70% * (or 21% Global equity)	Recommended maximum foreign exposure: 24%. International equity 10%* / Canadian equity 11% / U.S. equity 14%* / Fixed income 65% * (or 24% Global equity)
20–26	Income and moderate growth. Recommended maximum foreign exposure: 32%	International equity 14%* / Canadian equity 13% / U.S. equity 18%* / Fixed income 55% * (or 32% Global equity)	Recommended maximum foreign exposure: 35%. International equity 15%* / Canadian equity 15% / U.S. equity 20%* / Fixed income 50% * (or 35% Global equity)
27–34	Balanced growth. Recommended maximum foreign exposure: 43%	International equity 18%* / Canadian equity 17% / U.S. equity 25%* / Fixed income 40% * (or 43% Global equity)	Recommended maximum foreign exposure: 47%. International equity 20%* / Canadian equity 18% / U.S. equity 27%* / Fixed income 35% * (or 47% Global equity)
35–42	Aggressive growth. Recommended maximum foreign exposure: 59%	International equity 25%* / Canadian equity 21% / U.S. equity 34%* / Fixed income 20% * (or 59% Global equity)	Recommended maximum foreign exposure: 59%. International equity 26%* / Canadian equity 21% / U.S. equity 33%* / Fixed income 20% * (or 59% Global equity)
43–48	Maximum equity growth. Recommended maximum foreign exposure: 75%	International equity 32%* / Canadian equity 25% / U.S. equity 43%* * (or 75% Global equity)	Recommended maximum foreign exposure: 75%. International equity 32%* / Canadian equity 25% / U.S. equity 43%* * (or 75% Global equity)

Source: TD Asset Management Inc. Expires October 31, 2002

APPENDIX 4

Choosing a Financial Advisor

A great many considerations go into choosing a financial advisor. Most people look for someone personable and experienced, but many more aspects need to be factored in before you decide to entrust your money and your financial future to someone. Both the advisor and the company that employs that advisor will need to be carefully considered. Here are some points to ponder, followed by a checklist to bring along for a first meeting.

Get referrals

Gather references from people you know who have had a long-term association and are still happy with their advisor. If you feel uncomfortable doing that, you can go to the Canadian Association of Financial Planners' Web site for a list of certified financial planners in your area. The site, **www.cafp.org**, allows you to search by name, area, specialization or compensation arrangement. The Financial Planners' Standards Council, the body that administers the certified financial planner designation, also has a search option on its site that allows you to check if someone using the CFP designation is authorized to do so. (**www.cfp-ca.org**). For an advisor with an insurance background, see the Canadian Association of Insurance and Financial Advisors' Web site at **www.caifa.com**. You can search by your postal code for an advisor near you. Many financial institutions can also refer you to an accredited financial planner or advisor.

Look for credentials

Educational qualifications for financial advisors culminate in certain professional designations, such as certified financial planner (CFP), registered financial planner (RFP), personal financial planner (PFP) or CIM/FCSI (Canadian Investment Management course/Fellow of the Canadian Securities Institute). If you're looking for a discretionary manager, seek out a holder of the chartered financial analyst (CFA) designation. A chartered life underwriter (CLU) designation indicates an experienced insurance advisor. A registered health underwriter (RHU) specializes in disability insurance. Find out what licences the advisor holds: a mutual fund licence, a securities licence and/or an insurance licence. This tells you what they can sell. Someone with only a securities licence can sell mutual funds and stocks and bonds, but can't sell insurance.

Interview a few advisors

Ask about a prospective advisor's experience, his or her kind of clients and specialty (if he or she has one). Is the advisor a good listener and easy to talk to? Does he or she understand your needs? Does he or she have the experience, qualifications and licensing in the areas you require? How long has he or she been an advisor and how many clients

222

does he or she have? Who is an average client? Has the advisor ever had any regulatory action taken against him or her or had any clients take him or her to court? How long has the advisor been with the company? Some advisors change companies frequently, which can be both disruptive and expensive for a devoted client. Transfer-out fees charged to you to move your account can be significant in many cases.

How does the advisor practise?

Ask to see a sample investment policy statement and a sample account statement. The account statement should be easy to understand and generated by the company, not the advisor. Does the investment policy statement have both short- and long-term goals? What is the advisor's investment philosophy?

Ask how your advisor will measure success. Will your returns be compared to a benchmark? How are you to judge the productivity of the relationship?

How is the advisor compensated? If paid by commission, find out how much he or she would stand to make on your account initially and throughout the year. Are there any additional charges, such as Registered Retirement Savings Plan administration fees, rebalancing charges, brokerage fees, transfer-out fees, mutual fund switch fees, deregistration charges, etc?

How often will your advisor meet with you and/or review your portfolio? Can this schedule be adjusted to your needs? Will your advisor be personally overseeing your account or will someone else administer it most of the time?

Will most of the products recommended be proprietary or will you have a full choice of all available products? Would the advisor have a conflict of interest with any investment recommendations? Does the advisor belong to a professional organization with a code of ethics?

Does this advisor regularly work with other professionals? Can he or she draw on the expertise of an insurance advisor, for instance, if he or she doesn't have an insurance license? What about accountants and lawyers?

What about the company?

Can the company the advisor is with provide all the products and services you need at a reasonable cost? Is the company known for supervising its advisors? Is the company itself well respected and well established? Does it have the depth of professional resources your situation requires? Can they help with estate planning, business succession or trust services, if required?

These are the key things to keep in mind when you're looking for a financial advisor. Now here's a checklist to help you prepare to interview potential advisors.

Advisor Question Checklist

Advisor's credentials and experience
- [ ] What is your educational background?
- [ ] What are your professional designations?
  - [ ] Certified financial planner (CFP)
  - [ ] Registered financial planner (RFP)
  - [ ] Personal financial planner (PFP)
  - [ ] Chartered financial analyst (CFA)
  - [ ] Chartered life underwriter (CLU)
  - [ ] Canadian Investment Management course/Fellow of the Canadian Securities Institute (CIM/FCSI)
- [ ] What professional organizations do you belong to? Do they have a code of ethics?
- [ ] What are you licensed to sell?
- [ ] How long have you been a financial advisor?
- [ ] How many clients do you have?
- [ ] May I speak with some of your clients as references?
- [ ] Do you have a specialty?
- [ ] Describe your average client.
- [ ] Have you ever been sued by a client or had disciplinary action taken against you?

How the advisor practises
- [ ] What is your investment philosophy and approach?
- [ ] May I see a sample investment policy statement and a sample account statement?
- [ ] What benchmarks do you use to measure performance results?
- [ ] How are you compensated?
- [ ] How much money would you earn on a portfolio my size initially and over the course of a year? How am I paying for that?
- [ ] How often will we meet?
- [ ] Will you be personally overseeing my account?
- [ ] What investments do you most often recommend? Are they proprietary?

About the company
- [ ] Please describe the services your firm offers.
- [ ] Please outline all the associated fees and charges I could encounter, including any transfer-out costs. Are these fees competitive, given my needs?
- [ ] How long has the company been in business?
- [ ] Is your company a member of any self-regulating organization or professional association?

APPENDIX 5

Choosing Other Professionals

The best way to find a good professional is by word of mouth, but those who are doing the recommending might have very different needs from your own. In most cases, you want to look for a professional who has experience and expertise in the areas you need. Small-business owners, for instance, should look for an accountant who specializes in small business, and those thinking about separating should see a lawyer who does extensive work in family law. All else being equal, a real estate agent who does a lot of work in your area and price range would be preferable to one who usually sells homes in a neighbouring town. Specialization is key, but you still need to do your homework and be sure to make your expectations known up front. Here are some things to keep in mind.

Lawyers

Lawyers themselves feel the best referrals are from other lawyers. If a lawyer is respected enough by peers to garner referrals, that is quite an endorsement.

Given that insight, you can almost approach your search backwards. Try calling a well-known firm specializing in something completely different from what you need. Let's say you need family law advice. Call a corporate law office and ask them if they could recommend a family law lawyer.

Provincial law societies may have referral services, but these, of course, are not implicit endorsements.

Many lawyers offer a free half-hour consultation, so you should be able to interview a few lawyers with no cost. Ask about their relevant experience and case outcomes. How would they suggest you approach your situation? How much do they anticipate it might cost and what is the likely outcome?

Accountants

Professional accountants can be chartered accountants (CAs), certified management accountants (CMAs) or certified general accountants (CGAs). According to the Canadian Institute of Chartered Accountants, "The three professional accounting bodies are quite separate and distinct from each other. Each body has different education requirements and operates under its own bylaws and rules of conduct.... CAs are the only professional accountants who are authorized everywhere in Canada to practise all aspects of public accounting, including performing audits of public companies." CGAs provide tax and financial advice to individuals and businesses of all sizes. CMAs are financial professionals who work within organizations like business and government, and don't take individuals on as clients.

As with other professionals, the best way to find an accountant is to get a referral from someone whose requirements are similar to yours. A financial planner or advisor might also be able to suggest an accountant. If you are a small-business owner, local board of trade members might be a good place to start. CAs and CGAs both have provincial associations you can contact, as well.

When you interview prospective accountants, ask them to describe their typical client and what services they provide for those clients. It's not uncommon to find accountants doing bookkeeping and tax returns but failing to provide higher-level tax planning and estate planning advice for clients. Is your accountant willing and able to provide that for you? How will you be charged, and what can you expect in fees? Will your accountant be doing your tax returns him- or herself or will an assistant be doing them? How would the accountant characterize his or her interpretation of tax law on behalf of clients? How many clients have been audited by Canada Customs and Revenue Agency? What was the outcome?

Real estate agents

You want an agent who is knowledgeable about your location, experienced in your price range and type of building, and a good negotiator. Call a few lawyers who do a lot of real estate work and ask them for the names of some good agents. Ask what kind of properties the agent generally sells and in what price range. Ask how long the agent has been working as an agent and how many properties he or she has sold in your area in the last six months. Be absolutely frank about the commission arrangement. Is the agent prepared to negotiate the commission at all?

Can the agent give you references, especially repeat clients? Ask how much of the agent's business comes from referrals. Ask the agent about his or her personal negotiating triumphs in the past.

Keep in mind that agents can sometimes work for both the vendor and the purchaser. In these cases it is hard to know whose best interests the agent has in mind. Ask your agent if he or she intends to show you his or her own listings and how he or she generally deals with conflict-of-interest situations. A real estate agent wants to make a commission as much as you want to buy or sell a house. Do everything you can in the business relationship to make sure your agent's interests are as fully aligned with yours as possible.

Much real estate negotiating seems to take place late at night, with offers that expire in a few hours. If this prospect troubles you, tell your agent you won't accept offers or counteroffers with less than a certain reasonable minimum deadline, perhaps 24 hours. Your agent is likely able to set negotiating rules that you can feel comfortable with.

Insurance agents vs. brokers

An insurance agent is someone who works directly for an insurance company and sells only that company's products. An insurance broker sells the products of a number of insurance companies with which the broker has a contract. Agents and brokers can specialize in such areas as estate planning, disability insurance, life insurance for business owners and so on. Insurance can be very complicated, so make sure you have an advisor who is experienced with clients whose needs are similar to yours.

Before buying insurance from any company, check the credit rating of the insurance company itself. It's even better if you can find out its ability to pay claims. Your broker or agent should have insurance company ratings, or go on-line to any number of rating agencies, such as A.M. Best Canada's site at **www3.ambest.com/ambca/default.asp**.

APPENDIX 6

Estate Planning Checklist

This was adapted from a longer worksheet designed by TD Private Client Group, Estates and Trusts.

Personal data

Your full name: _____

Full name of your spouse (or other): _____

Date of birth: _____

Social insurance number: _____

Address and postal code: _____

Home phone: _____

Secondary address and postal code: _____

Marital status: _____

Place of marriage: _____

Do you have a marriage contract? _____

Name of previous spouse (if applicable): _____

Is there a separation agreement? _____

Date and place of divorce/death: _____

Occupation/Employer: _____ ; _____

(If retired, previous occupation/employer)

Employment address and postal code: _____

Nature of business: _____

Business phone: _____ ; fax: _____ ; Email address: ___

Citizenship/Country of birth: _____ ; _____

Lawyer's name: _____

Lawyer's address: _____

Lawyer's postal code _____ phone: _____ and fax: _____

Accountant's name: _____

Accountant's address: _____

Accountant's postal code: _____ phone: _____ and fax: _____

Investment advisor's name: _____

Investment advisor's company: _____

Investment advisor's address: _____

Investment advisor's postal code: _____ phone: _____ and fax: ___

Power of Attorneys

Power of Attorney for property given to:

Address:

Relationship: Age: Phone:

Is it valid should you become mentally incapacitated?*

Power of Attorney for personal care given to:

Address:

Relationship: Age: Phone:

*Power of Attorney valid through mental incapacity is variously described, in different provinces, as a continuing, enduring, durable Power of Attorney, or Mandate given in anticipation of the mandator's incapacity in the Province of Quebec.

Beneficiaries

Children

Full name	Address, postal code and phone	Date of birth	Marital status	Children (Yes/No)

Grandchildren

Parents' name(s)	Grandchild's full name	Address, postal code and phone	Date of birth

Other people who are to be beneficiaries of your will

Full name	Relationship	Address, postal code and phone	Date of birth

Charities that are to be beneficiaries of your will

Full name	Address, postal code and phone

Your assets and liabilities

A thorough review of your assets will enable you to fully understand the extent of your estate. While the information you provide today is likely to change over time, it is needed for planning purposes and will assist in identifying some planning options.

Real estate and investments

Real estate: description and location (your home, vacation home, rental property, other)

Owned solely by you: $ Owned solely by your spouse (or other): $
Owned jointly (with whom): $
Investments: description and location
Owned solely by you: $ Owned solely by your spouse (or other): $
Owned jointly (with whom): $
Bank accounts:
Bank accounts: type, account number, institution and branch address
Owned solely by you: $ Owned solely by your spouse (or other): $
Owned jointly (with whom): $
Location of safety deposit box:
Name held in:
Location of the key:
People who have access to the box:
Location of important papers:

Personal property

Household goods and furnishings:

Owned solely by you: $ Owned solely by your spouse (or other): $
Owned jointly (with whom): $
Personal effects (jewellery, clothing):
Owned solely by you: $ Owned solely by your spouse (or other): $
Owned jointly (with whom): $
Vehicles (cars, boats, R.V.s, etc.)
Owned solely by you: $ Owned solely by your spouse (or other): $
Owned jointly (with whom): $
Other items:
Owned solely by you: $ Owned solely by your spouse (or other): $
Owned jointly (with whom): $

Business interests

Type of business:

Sole proprietorship _____ Partnership _____ Corporation _____

Name of the business: _____

Are there any business agreements in place?   Yes _____ No _____

Is there a business succession plan in effect?   Yes _____ No _____

Is there insurance in place to pay tax due on the sale or wind-up of your

business, or to fund a business succession plan?   Yes _____ No _____

Savings plans and insurance

For you:

RRSP/RRIF/LIF/LIRA: type: _____

Institution and address: _____

Locked in? Yes/No _____

Who is the designated beneficiary? _____

Value: $ _____

Life insurance/annuity: type: _____

Institution and address: _____

Paid up? Yes/No _____

Value: $ _____

Who is the designated beneficiary? _____

For your spouse (or other):

RRSP/RRIF/LIF/LIRA: type: _____

Institution and address: _____

Locked in? Yes/No _____

Who is the designated beneficiary? _____

Value: $ _____

Life insurance/annuity: type: _____

Institution and address: _____

Paid up? Yes/No _____

Value: $ _____

Who is the designated beneficiary? _____

Loans made to family members, friends, or others

Name of borrower Documented Yes/No   Made by you or spouse?   Value

_____

_____

_____

Which are to be repaid or forgiven at death? _____

You and your spouse (or other) owned jointly _____

TOTAL ASSETS $ _____

Mortgages and loans
Outstanding mortgages:
Property:
Institution and address: _____

Maturity date:	Life insured: Yes/No	Amount owing: $

Percent of this debt that is yours: _____

Personal loans: _____

Loans: outstanding:$	Is this a joint loan?
Credit cards: outstanding: $	Is this a joint account?

Loan guarantees: type:
Institution and address: _____

Loans on life insurance:
Institution and address: _____

You: $	Your spouse (or other): $

Business debts: type:
Institution and address: _____

Personal guarantee: Yes/No	You: $	Your spouse (or other):$

TOTAL LIABILITIES $ _____

NET WORTH (assets − liabilities) $ _____

Disposition of Your Estate

Personal effects, household goods, and chattels, including vehicles

You should list how you'd like your personal effects such as furniture, jewellery, clothing, boats and vehicles to be distributed. Consider whether any items such as antiques, works of art, or collections require special attention.

1. If your spouse survives, he/she receives all personal effects. Yes. (If no, go to question 3.)
2. If your spouse predeceases you, all personal effects go to your children as they agree. Yes. (If no, go to question 3.) Note: Provision can be made in your will to hold articles for minors or to sell, at the discretion of your executor(s).
3. Personal effects go to the following:

Name:	Relationship:	Articles:
Name:	Relationship:	Articles:
Name:	Relationship:	Articles:
Name:	Relationship:	Articles:
Name:	Relationship:	Articles:

Cash bequests

Cash bequests are a convenient way to remember friends and relatives, who may not be principal beneficiaries, as well as charities.

Cash bequests must be paid before the residue is distributed. The amount you wish each beneficiary to receive should be planned. Keep in mind the cash that will be readily available at your death, as the size of your estate could change substantially over time.

Cash bequests to individuals

Full name: _____

Address: _____

To be paid upon your death: $_____To be paid only if your spouse (or other) has died before you: $_____

Full name: _____

Address: _____

To be paid upon your death: $_____To be paid only if your spouse (or other) has died before you: $_____

If an individual is not living at the time of your death or the death of your spouse/other, do you want the bequest to: be paid to the individual's children or issue? Not be paid but be included in the residue of your estate? _____

Other? _____

Cash bequests to charities

Full name: _____

To be paid upon your death: $_____To be paid only if your spouse (or other) has died before you: $_____

If a specific charity is not in existence at the time of your death, do you want the bequest to: go to a similar charity? _____

Not be paid and be included in the residue of your estate? _____

Residue of your estate

The residue of your estate is made up of all your assets that have not been specifically disposed of after all liabilities and expenses have been paid. Two of the most common ways of distributing the residue are:

1. By an outright distribution to one or more persons (or charities) in such proportions or shares as you may see fit.

OR

2. By directing that the residue or a part be held in trust. The income earned by the trust can be paid to any individual you choose for his or her lifetime, and upon that person's death the capital can be distributed to your other beneficiaries. You may also direct the residue to be held in trust for a stated period of time or until the beneficiary(s) reach a certain age. To protect against inflation or other

circumstances, it is common to empower your executor to make payments from the trust capital for the income beneficiary, if needed.

Disposition of residue considerations

1. Outright to:

Spouse: _____

Children (if spouse predeceased): _____

Others (if spouse predeceased): _____

What share is each beneficiary to receive? Shares need not be equal. If named beneficiary predeceases you, who receives their share?

Full name(s): _____

2. In trust for:

Is the trust to be for life, or a stated period of time? _____

Any special circumstances/disabilities of the beneficiary that should be considered?

Full name(s): _____

May the trustees use the capital from time to time for the care and benefit of your income beneficiary? Yes/No

Is the payment of income to be left to the discretion of the trustees? Yes/No

If no, do you want the income to accumulate? Yes/No

On the death of the income beneficiary, are your children to receive the capital of the residue, and if so, in equal shares? _____

If not your children, to whom do you wish to leave the capital? _____

Full name(s): _____

If a beneficiary dies before receiving his or her share, is the share to pass to the beneficiary's own children or issue? Yes/No

While a beneficiary's share is held, may the trustee use the capital for his or her care, education and benefit? Yes/No

Considerations

You may wish to consider the financial background of your beneficiaries in deciding on shares and the timing of their receipt.

If your beneficiary leaves no children, your will can provide that the share passes to other designated beneficiaries. Making such a provision is usually prudent since it will give the trustee wide latitude in using your assets to the best advantage of your beneficiaries.

Other Estate Planning Considerations

Funeral arrangements

It is the responsibility of your executor to make funeral arrangements. Do you have special instructions you would like followed, or have you prearranged your funeral?
Prearranged with: _____

Is it prepaid?   Yes/No

Guardian

In the event that you and your spouse die before your children reach the age of majority, who do you want to name as the guardian of your minor children? Naming a guardian in your will is not legally binding and the appointment must be confirmed by the courts. However, it does give the court an understanding of your wishes.

Full name: _____

Address and postal code: _____

Relationship: _____ Phone: _____

Legal obligations

Your current legal obligations can remain obligations after your death and can affect your freedom to distribute assets through your will. Are there any marriage contracts, separation agreements, other dependants or children, business buy/sell agreements, debts, or outstanding taxes that should be considered? _____

Safe custody of your will

Your will should be held in safekeeping either in a safety deposit box, with your lawyer or with a trust company if you have appointed a trust company as your executor.

Location: _____

Will review

It is important that your will be kept up to date. Generally your will should be reviewed every three to five years, or whenever there are significant changes in your personal or financial circumstances, or those of your beneficiaries. In addition, changes in law may affect your estate plan.

Source: TD Private Client Group, Estates and Trusts (with adaptations)

APPENDIX 7

An Executor's Duties

Preliminary steps
- [ ] Locate the will and review it to determine whether there are any special funeral directions.
- [ ] Assist in making funeral arrangements, if necessary.
- [ ] Ascertain the whereabouts of beneficiaries.
- [ ] Determine the immediate cash requirements of beneficiaries.
- [ ] Obtain funeral director's statement of death or apply for provincial death certificate.
- [ ] List the contents of any safety deposit boxes.
- [ ] Arrange for the safe custody of valuables.
- [ ] If the deceased lived in a rental property, terminate the lease or arrange a sublet.
- [ ] Determine entitlement to and apply for Canada Pension Plan death, survivor's and orphans' benefits.
- [ ] Notify Human Resources Development Canada to cancel Old Age Security and Canada Pension Plan cheques.
- [ ] Notify the previous employer(s) and determine any survivor pension benefits or insurance proceeds.
- [ ] Cancel driver's licence, magazine and newspaper subscriptions, cable television, telephone, and club memberships and request refunds, if applicable.
- [ ] Cancel health insurance coverage.
- [ ] Confirm outstanding balances and cancel credit cards.
- [ ] Request Canada Post to reroute the deceased's mail, if necessary.
- [ ] Complete or cancel any outstanding securities trade orders.
- [ ] Ascertain assets and liabilities by writing to financial institutions, insurance companies, brokers, employers and RRSP/RRIF trustees.
- [ ] Obtain the prior years' tax returns. Prepare and file any T1 returns for previous years.
- [ ] Locate and obtain title documents for real property mortgages, share certificates, bonds, debentures and guaranteed investment certificates.
- [ ] Arrange valuations of real estate, securities, personal property and automobiles.
- [ ] Review the adequacy of insurance coverage and alter, if necessary.
- [ ] Arrange for a review of the investment portfolio.
- [ ] Send a copy of the will to each beneficiary.
- [ ] Open an estate bank account.
- [ ] Notify dividend- and bond-disbursing agents to change the address of record.
- [ ] Prepare an inventory of assets and liabilities.
- [ ] Consult with an estates specialist regarding probate procedures, notice to beneficiaries, and all other preliminary administrative matters.

Administration and distribution

☐ With professional assistance, apply for grant of probate or administration.

☐ When probate is granted, obtain enough notarial copies to transfer assets.

☐ Report to the beneficiaries on the progress of administration and provide each residuary beneficiary with a copy of the summary of the estate's assets and liabilities.

☐ Arrange for publication of an advertisement for creditors prior to the distribution of estate assets.

☐ Ask an estates specialist to register probate on title to real estate, if necessary.

☐ Settle all claims and debts.

☐ Close any safety deposit boxes and take possession of contents.

☐ Complete all documentation required to transfer securities.

☐ Close bank accounts and transfer the balance to the estate bank account. If there are joint accounts with right of survivorship, provide the financial institution with a death certificate and request transfer to the surviving joint tenant.

☐ Invest surplus cash in accordance with the terms of the will.

☐ Review the will and determine the division of estate assets. Consult with the beneficiaries on the form of distribution (in cash or in kind) where appropriate.

☐ Review with an estates specialist any time periods or restrictions imposed on the distribution of the estate, e.g., family law considerations or claims/litigation.

☐ Initiate the reregistration and transfer of securities or arrange for the sale of securities, if converting to cash.

☐ Prepare cheques for payment of debts, legacies and interim distributions.

☐ Deliver personal effects to beneficiaries and obtain receipts.

☐ Deliver securities to beneficiaries, if distributing in kind, and obtain receipts.

☐ Deliver legacies to beneficiaries and obtain receipts.

☐ Arrange rollover or transfer of RRSP/RRIF proceeds.

☐ Prepare and file necessary estate tax returns for foreign assets, if any.

☐ Prepare and file a terminal T1 tax return and other returns with Canada Customs and Revenue Agency and request a tax clearance certificate.

☐ If the will provides for outright distribution, obtain a release for distribution and transfer assets or funds to the beneficiaries. Retain sufficient funds as a reserve for income taxes and any outstanding accounts.

☐ If the will provides for trusts, set up testamentary trusts and arrange for ongoing review of the investments and ongoing compliance with the rest of the terms of the trust, e.g., payment of income.

☐ Prepare and file a T3 trust information return.

☐ Obtain Goods and Services Tax clearance.

☐ Prepare accounts for passing or approval by the beneficiaries. Prepare releases and obtain approval.

☐ If the beneficiaries approve accounts, confirm that all releases have been received.

☐ Calculate executor's compensation.

☐ If accounts are to be audited by the court, ask an estates specialist to prepare the application and all necessary notices and to arrange an appointment.

☐ After obtaining approval from the beneficiaries or the court, charge executor's compensation, maintain a holdback/reserve pending receipt of necessary tax clearance certificates and distribute any remaining funds or deliver assets.

☐ Ensure tax clearance certificate has been received.

☐ Arrange for closing of the estate bank account after confirming all cheques have cleared.

☐ Write to the beneficiaries with a final report on all aspects of administration.

Note: Estate administration practice and requirements may vary by province or territory. The information in this checklist is for informational purposes and intended only as a guide to assist you in administering an estate and should not be considered as income tax or legal advice.

Source: TD Private Client Group, Estates and Trusts

Index